D0872348

Face to Face with Orchestra and Chorus

DON V MOSES

ROBERT W. DEMAREE, JR.

ALLEN F. OHMES

Face to Face with Orchestra and Chorus

A Handbook for Choral Conductors

SECOND, EXPANDED EDITION

INDIANA UNIVERSITY PRESS
Bloomington and Indianapolis

Music autography by Branden J. Meuller
Graphics by Joan Addison

This book is a publication of

Indiana University Press
601 North Morton Street
Bloomington, Indiana 47404-3797 USA

http://iupress.indiana.edu

Telephone orders 800-842-6796
Fax orders 812-855-7931
Orders by e-mail iuporder@indiana.edu

First edition published by Prestige Publications 1987
Second, expanded edition © 2004 by Indiana University Press
All rights reserved

The paper used in this publication meets the minimum requirements of American National Standard for Information Sciences—Permanence of Paper for Printed Library Materials, ANSI Z39.48-1984.

Manufactured in the United States of America

Library of Congress Cataloging-in-Publication Data

Moses, Don V, date
    Face to face with orchestra and chorus : a handbook for choral conductors / Don V Moses, Robert W. Demaree, Jr., and Allen F. Ohmes. — 2nd, expanded ed.
        p. cm.
Includes bibliographical references (p.) and index.
    ISBN 0-253-34437-9 (cloth : alk. paper) — ISBN 0-253-21699-0 (pbk. : alk. paper)
    1. Conducting. 2. Choral music—Interpretation (Phrasing, dynamics, etc.) 3. Orchestral music—Interpretation (Phrasing, dynamics, etc.) I. Demaree, Jr., Robert W. II. Ohmes, Allen F. III. Title.
    MT85.M68 2004
    782.5′145—dc22

                                                                                2003027307

1 2 3 4 5   09 08 07 06 05 04

To those who,

having been educated as choral conductors,

experience now both the anxieties and the joy

of bringing a major choral and orchestral work

to full fruition

and

To Anne, Lynn, and Dawn

for encouragement, patience,

good humor, and faith

Contents

Illustrations

Foreword to the First Edition

Demaree, Moses, and Ohmes
Wrote together from separate homes.
Demaree was a musicological wizard,
While Ohmes knew the fiddle from Alpha to Izzard,
And Tricky-Stick Moses was quick as a lizard —
Which only enhanced the remarkable tomes
Of Demaree, Moses
Of Demaree, Moses
Of Demaree, Moses, and Ohmes.

Messrs. Moses, Demaree, and Ohmes have done a very good thing indeed for choral music and choral musicians.

It may be that the most striking development on the American musical scene of the past fifty years has been the emergence of the choral art as a worthy technical and stylistic companion of the instrumental and orchestral arts. With few exceptions, choral performance a half-century ago was either a social and recreational venture with emphasis upon post-rehearsal partying, or a Sunday potpourri of singing greeting-cards and responses with a "message."

No more. The degrees in choral conducting offered by our leading schools of music are as rigorous in their demands upon musical scholarship and practical know-how as their matching degrees in the orchestral field.

There is not a choral conductor in a responsible college or university, a church which aspires to serve a discriminating congregation or a community arts program, who does not today come "face to face" with the great historical choral/orchestral literature—and "face to face" with instrumentalists and orchestras. And this book goes a long way towards making that confrontation a pleasurable and productive one.

Two things strike me as being very special about the book: first, it is remarkably efficient and practical. No flying off into feathered ethereality. (The information it offers concerning the three detailed works is so precise and thoughtful that even those who have performed these works scores of times should find it profitable to check these pages as they prepare their orchestral materials for their next performance.)

Second, in spite of its expertise and good counsel, it somehow manages to escape "authoritarianism." It invites, even "inspires," the reader's (conductor's) further study, exploration and individual creativity as regards performance practices and stylistic detail.

It's a good book—and, probably, the only way you'll get Moses, Demaree, and Ohmes in the same classroom.

Robert Shaw

Preface to the Second, Expanded Edition

When the authors began drafting in 1985 a text for choral conductors who needed experience facing instrumentalists, no handbook of that sort existed. We wondered if enough professors and young conductors would be interested to make publication worthwhile.

The late, great Robert Shaw himself reassured us. Herewith we thank him again for his enthusiastic embrace of that original edition, and for his considerable contribution as a poet (!) in the foreword.

Professional response to the first edition has given the authors much pride and pleasure. Many colleagues and students have written or spoken to tell us that this book fills a real need in their working lives through its general description of the conducting tactics and personal attitudes needed in dealing with instrumental ensembles, because of its detailed discussions of specific works of music, or both. At the same time, some have suggested other works about which they would like this sort of advice. After a time we have decided to accept that counsel, and so we have added three works from the Viennese Classical world to the three Baroque masterpieces with which we began this project almost twenty years ago.

There are others besides Bob Shaw to whom we want to acknowledge debts and express our gratitude: to Dr. Ray Robinson of Prestige Publications for his confidence in the book at its first imprinting, to pianist and Professor Robert Hamilton of Arizona State University for his experienced performance judgments regarding the Beethoven Choral Fantasia, to violinist and Professor Shi-Hwa Wang of Weber State for providing us the point of view of a concertmaster, to Dr. Robert K. Demaree of the University of Wisconsin–Platteville for editorial assistance and good counsel, to the Schurz Library staff at Indiana University South Bend—especially Kathy Plodowski and Adrian Esselstrom—for much patience and assistance, to Branden Mueller for his work with the musical examples, and to Joan Addison for reproducing the line drawings.

There is one more to thank: we have had the particularly happy if somewhat unusual experience of having an editor who is a distinguished scholar in her own right, one who honors and understands that frame of reference as thoroughly as she manages matters of editing and publishing. It has been a pleasure to work with Gayle Sherwood of Indiana University Press on this newest version of *Face to Face.* . . .

The Authors
February 2004

Part One: Working with an Orchestra

1 The Nature of the Orchestra

A substantial share of the greatest music of the Western World is intended for performance by chorus and orchestra in combination. Handel's *Messiah*, Bach's *Passions*, and the *Requiems* of Mozart, Verdi, and Brahms are among the works that require these forces. To list the repertoire for voices and instruments combined is to call the roll of the masters: Monteverdi, Vivaldi, Haydn, Beethoven, Schubert, Mendelssohn, Mahler, Britten, Stravinsky, and their contemporaries. Each year millions in America and around the world rejoice in one of these major works.

That means choral conductors lead thousands of such performances every year in churches large and small, in colleges and universities, and in auditoriums both renowned and little-known. Some of their choirs are huge and others modest; some orchestras are world-famous, while others are improvised aggregations of amateurs and students. Sometimes the entire work is presented; often, on the other hand (especially in the case of Christmas performances of *Messiah*), only portions of the masterpiece are attempted.

Choral conductors generally have only limited experience rehearsing and performing with orchestras. Accustomed to the nature and the special techniques of choral work, we may find it strange to deal instead with the expectations and needs of instrumentalists. As a result, many of us prepare ourselves badly for rehearsals and concerts. Working with amateur players, we may not be able to help them enough; working in turn with professionals, we may feel intimidated. In either case, we find ourselves unable to achieve our best intentions.

The problem is not with the players. Most of it can be eliminated by preparation, precise language, and experience. To confront an orchestra with confidence, one first must understand as much as possible about the instruments, the musicians, and their standard ways of communicating with each other.

Fundamental Matters

Orchestral players are trained in a tradition different from that known by choral musicians. Accustomed to that tradition and its routines, they may find the language, conducting style, and rehearsal procedures of a good choral conductor peculiar—perhaps even confusing. Among the differences between singers and players:

1. Orchestras generally have fewer hours of rehearsal per concert, and have to cover more music more quickly. They expect to do so.
2. Orchestral musicians are likely to have had more years of individual training than the choral singers performing with them.

3. They do not memorize the music they play; it follows, then, that direct eye contact between players and a conductor is sporadic and difficult. As a consequence, they depend very heavily on the baton.
4. Players more commonly are paid for their work. Thus they are less likely than volunteer singers to establish a "personality cult" around their conductor. For the same reason they tend not to respond to "pep talks," as some choirs do.
5. Although string players, like choral singers, work in sections, the wind and percussion players are soloists. In that sense, every note these people perform is "exposed."
6. In an orchestra there is no expert pianist present to lead the ensemble through the difficult spots of a rehearsal (as accompanists often do for choral ensembles). The conductor and the players must find and solve all the problems.

Recognizing that orchestras differ from choirs in these (and other) respects, we can begin to see why special conducting procedures must be used. As a choral conductor rehearsing an orchestra you must expect to *cover the music more quickly* (stopping fewer times than you might in a choral session), *depend more on the players* than you usually do on your singers, *refine your conducting gestures and signals* (remembering that these instrumentalists are less familiar with you and your intentions than are your singers), and *work in a very direct, objective way.*

Review your conducting technique. This may be a fine opportunity for you to practice and enlarge your craft. You need not be afraid that any adjustments you make will prove detrimental to your work as a choral conductor; many of the distinctions between so-called "choral" and "instrumental" conducting are more habitual and artificial than substantial. (Europeans, for example, generally acknowledge no difference; the dichotomy is primarily an American one.)

Neither need you fear that orchestra players will be somehow prejudiced against you because you are a choral conductor by training. It is unlikely they will wonder much about your background, or care very much how you were taught. They will be concerned only with working quickly and effectively in rehearsals to solve their own uncertainties and learn how their own parts fit into the whole fabric of the music. *If you are well prepared to rehearse them,* and if you treat them in a professional manner, they will respond positively to you and your ideas.

Some choral conductors prepare a chorus, hire an orchestra, and then proceed to rehearse these forces as if only the chorus were present, remaining all the while detached from the special considerations which arise when one works with instrumentalists. There are many important decisions which should be made with the players: bowings, handling of *divisi* passages, articulation options in the winds, and the like. Someone must make choices. If the conductor does not, the concertmaster and the players will—and will do so, perhaps, without knowing clearly the conductor's interpretive wishes; worse yet, they may make haphazard, inconsistent choices, with the result that conflicts of bowing, articulation, and the like continue right into the performance.

The Basic Needs of the Conductor

One of the purposes of this handbook, then, is to *let you, as chief interpreter, join in on performance decisions* that relate to instrumental matters. These should be part of your basic concept of the work at hand.

A second goal is to put you at ease with the orchestra, and to *get rid of all the barriers of experience, training, and terminology that can block clear communication.* You must learn to express yourself clearly both with the voice and the baton, so you and the players can get on to music-making.

A third aim is to help you *prepare yourself to use a very limited amount of orchestra rehearsal time effectively.* You need to deal directly with the unhappy reality that choral conductors usually get better results in an oratorio from the choir than from the orchestra.

Fourth, you can *learn technical approaches that*—applied here to particular works—*will prove useful later in a wide range of repertoire.*

Finally, this handbook deals specifically and in detail with three of the greatest choral/orchestral masterpieces (*Messiah,* the Bach *Magnificat in D Major,* and the Vivaldi *Gloria*—of all oratorio literature perhaps the works most commonly chosen by novice orchestra conductors), showing you danger spots, discussing applicable style and performance practices, and offering interpretive choices. Once you combine this measure-by-measure study with the chapters of general instruction about instrumental characteristics, score preparation, baton technique, and rehearsal procedures, you should be ready to stand face to face with your orchestra.

2 The Orchestral Instruments

If we are to communicate clearly with the members of an orchestra, we must understand something of the characteristics of their instruments, and of the variety of ways they can produce sounds. Above all, we need to have some idea of what is difficult for each instrument, and what is easy.[1]

The Strings

We begin with the string family because the violins, violas, violoncellos (or 'cellos), and contrabasses (or bass viols, double basses, string basses, etc.) are the core of the orchestra, both in numbers and in terms of the demands traditionally placed on them by composers.

Already in the Baroque period composers were dividing the strings into four orchestral sections: first violins, second violins, violas, and the *basso continuo*. From the eighteenth into the nineteenth centuries a gradual process separated the contrabasses—which originally had played in the same octave as the 'cellos—from the latter, first assigning them a separate staff on the score and a separate octave in the texture, and later allowing them (initially only for special effects) to undertake discrete melodic lines. In this way we came eventually to the standard format of five string sections.

Parallel to this historical evolution of the orchestral ensemble ran experimentation with seating arrangements for the players.[2] In the pattern that has become traditional, all the strings except the basses are seated two-to-a-stand, so the lower-ranking one (the "inside" player, generally upstage of his partner) can turn pages, as necessary, while the other plays. By an early stage in this evolutionary process, as orchestras became continuing organizations (rather than *ad hoc* aggregations) the first player in each of these sections was given the title "principal," and his partner on the first "desk" (or stand) was called the "assistant principal." By a further convention, the principal first violinist was called the "concertmaster" and his cohort the "assistant concertmaster." All the principals have some responsibility for the unity and discipline of their sections.

There has been much experimentation with the placement of the string sections within the orchestra. Perhaps the most common practice (shown in figure 1) is to put the first violins on the conductor's left, with the 'cellos on his

---

1. You may wish more detailed information with respect to these matters. The following could be of help: Ivan Galamian, *The Principles of Violin Playing and Teaching;* Elizabeth Green, *Orchestral Bowing;* and Walter Piston, *Orchestration.*
2. There is quite a thorough summary of this evolution, complete with seating charts, in the *New Grove Dictionary of Music and Musicians, 6th Edition,* pp. 679–691.

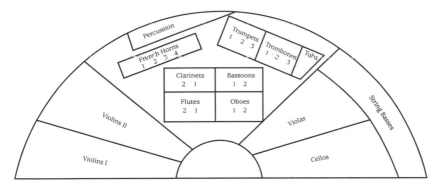

Figure 1. A standard arrangement of the string sections of the orchestra.

right, and the contrabasses behind them. This arrangement has the advantage of facing all the violins "toward the audience" (for a significant increase in the carrying-power of a violin is gained by aiming its "F-holes"—the openings in the top of the violin—at the listener); the second violins are "hidden" behind the firsts in this placement, however, so that any sense of the antiphonal playing which sometimes occurs between the two violin sections is reduced.

A common alternative (seen in figure 2) provides for that antiphonal effect by placing the second violins across from the firsts, on the conductor's right. This arrangement has the added advantage of moving both the violas and the 'cellos to positions from which they speak more directly to the audience; it turns the F-holes of the seconds toward the back of the stage, on the other hand, further weakening what may already be the less confident of the two violin sections.

The Violins

You already know much about these instruments from your experience and observation. To review concisely a few fundamental considerations:

1. The four strings of the violin are tuned (with very rare exceptions called *scordatura*) to the G-natural just below "middle C," and— ascending by perfect fifths—to D-natural, A-natural, and E-natural. (The player begins by adjusting the A-natural until it is pitched as he wishes, and then tunes the other strings to it.) The upward range of the violin is quite large, and depends primarily on the skill of the player.
2. The strings are stopped with the fingers of the left hand. The right hand is used to produce sound either (a) by drawing the bow across the strings, or (b) by plucking them (the technique called *pizzicato*). On very rare occasions the composer may instruct the player to use the

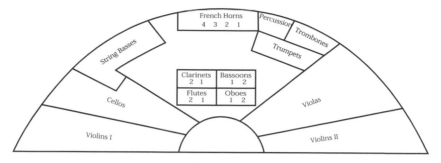

Figure 2. A common alternative to the arrangement in figure 1.

wooden part of the bow against the string (the *col legno* process) or to pluck the string with the left hand. Violinists tend to avoid playing the four strings "open" (that is, unfingered, or "unstopped") because they prefer to use the warmer, richer sound created by *vibrato* (the slight variations in pitch caused by rapid back-and-forth motion of the finger stopping the string that is in use at that moment).

3. If the composer has planned carefully, it is rather easy for string players to produce two notes simultaneously ("double stops"). This is feasible whenever two notes can be played on adjacent strings (within the reach of the fingers of the left hand). Even triple- and quadruple-stops are possible, and are frequently used, but—since the modern bow cannot actually bend enough to contact all four strings at the same moment— these chords must be produced by a quick, rolling, arpeggiated effect. Only the last one or two notes of the arpeggio will be sustainable. Much of the time in orchestral playing, *written* double stops actually are performed *divisi*—that is, with half the section playing one note and the other half producing the other.

4. Violinists play melodic skips either (a) by moving up or down a single string, stopping that string with the left hand at the proper acoustical points, or (b) by taking the two notes on separate strings, which may minimize the amount of left hand movement needed. (The former is called "shifting positions.") Normally the fingering of a particular passage is the responsibility of the individual player, and colleagues on the same desk may simultaneously and properly use differing fingerings; on occasion, the concertmaster (in order to have shifts of position occur in unison) may stipulate fingerings.

5. Because modern violin strings vary both in thickness and in the materials of which they are made (the lowest string is usually of gut, wound with metal wire, while the E-string is made of steel), the sounds they produce vary from string to string. Although the choice of the string

on which a given note is to be played is generally left to the individual player, the composer, the conductor, or the concertmaster can designate a particular string to be used for *any passage within its practical range* whenever a specific timbre is desired. Thus the marking *sul G* ("on the G-string") indicates a wish for the dark, powerful sound which the violins produce from that string.

6. The nature of the sound produced by a violinist derives from (a) the manner in which contact is maintained between the bow-hair and the string, (b) the speed at which the bow moves across the string, (c) the speed, width, and consistency of the *vibrato*, (d) the quality of the violin used, and (e) the quality and condition of the bow and bow-hair. The first three of these considerations are factors which can vary considerably from player to player and moment to moment within a rehearsal or a performance.

Within the orchestra, the first violins sometimes overbalance the seconds, and generally the firsts are faced with the more difficult passages (although this is not always the case). The seconds may double the firsts at the unison or the octave, may play a counter-melody of their own, or may engage (with or without the violas and lower strings) in an accompanimental pattern of some sort. *It is a fundamental error for a conductor to discount the second violins in rehearsal,* giving always his best attention to the firsts, for there will come a time when trust and confidence between the conductor and the seconds is of real importance.

The Violas

These are not simply "bigger violins"; the tone of the viola is distinct in timbre from that of the violin because the proportions of the two instruments—relative to the tunings of their strings—are substantially different. Both the bow and the strings of the viola are larger than those used for the violin, of course.

Playing technique for the viola is, nevertheless, much like that of the smaller instrument. Among the important distinctions are the following:

1. The open strings of the viola all four sound a perfect fifth lower than their violin equivalents; they range upward from the C-natural an octave below "middle C" to the A-natural, the highest string.

2. Although melodic passages often carry the viola up into the treble clef, the standard notation for this instrument is in the alto clef. (If you are not experienced with the so-called "C clefs"—especially alto and tenor clefs—it will be well for you to practice reading in them. As you may realize, some older scores use alto, tenor, and even soprano C-clefs in the choral block itself. With a little familiarity, you can deal effectively with this notation in study and in rehearsal.)

3. As with the violin, there are differences in timbre between the strings of the viola. The lowest one is quite dark—even portentous—in charac-

ter, while the top string has, in comparison to the A-string of the violins, a very strong, penetrating quality.

For generations composers depended on the violas primarily for the filling-out of basic harmonies, leaving melodic dominance to the violins, woodwinds, or voices; even as late as the mature scores of Haydn, one finds the viola committed to a supporting role; one sees more melodic equality among the strings in the nineteenth and twentieth centuries, but a large share of viola playing is still accompanimental. This activity may take the form of repeated notes, arpeggios, double-stop or *divisi* patterns, or other figures. On other occasions (one thinks of Haydn and Beethoven passages) the viola section may play a bass line (without the 'cellos or contrabasses) under the violins.

The Violoncellos

The most obvious distinctions between the 'cello and the upper strings derive from the size of the instrument and from the circumstance that it is played in a seated position, with the bow held horizontally. Playing the 'cello—the largest and lowest-sounding of the violin family—is quite unlike playing the violin or viola, although many of the underlying concepts remain the same:

1. Since the instrument is supported by the floor and the player's body, the left hand is free; it need not hold up the 'cello, as it must the violin and viola. In high passages, then, the cellist's left hand can move around in front of the fingerboard, avoiding the body of the instrument.
2. Since the 'cello bow is held level, there is—in a physical sense—no "up-bow" for the 'cello. The customary terminology still is used, nevertheless; the stroke which moves the player's bow hand (normally the right hand) to the right and away from the instrument still is called the "downbow," just as with the violin.
3. The strings of the violoncello are tuned an octave lower than their viola counterparts. The lowest (and the nearest to the bow hand, unlike the violin design) is the C-natural two octaves below "middle C." Above it, tuned in fifths, are the G-natural, D-natural, and A-natural. In spite of the size of these strings, every part of the 'cello range is capable of producing vibrant, singing quality, from the rich, dark C-string to the highest reaches of the A-string.
4. While the 'cello normally is notated in the bass clef, higher passages are written in the tenor and treble clefs, as necessary.
5. In arranging seating for the orchestra, remember to allow enough room for all the players. Be particularly careful to gauge the space needed for each desk of 'cellos. The length of that horizontal bow must be unobstructed in both directions.

Violoncellos served the orchestra first on the bass line, and they still do so. Often lines have been written for them which combine bass notes, on the strong beats, with arpeggiated or chordal figures; thus the 'cello can serve as the bass instrument in an ensemble and—at the same time—fill out the harmonies higher in the texture. Their technique developed rapidly, however, and Haydn (for example) began in his quartets to call on 'cellos for important melodic activity before he experimented with assigning such passages to the viola.

The Contrabasses

This actually is the lowest of the viols: it is not a member of the violin family. (You will notice that the sloping shoulders of the body of the contrabass are quite unlike the more rounded ones of the violin.) Contrabasses themselves come in various sizes; the variety most commonly used by orchestra players is the so-called "three-quarter bass," which stands generally a bit over six feet high.

These are unique instruments in many respects:

1. The open strings are tuned in fourths, not fifths—the lowest one to the E-natural almost three octaves below "middle C." Above that are the A-natural, D-natural, and G-natural strings. Many professional players, moreover, have a device known as the "C attachment," an extension on the low E-string which permits the bassist to perform (below the open E-string) the half-steps down to low C-natural, a full three octaves below "middle C."

2. Contrabass parts are transposed; unlike the other strings, they sound an octave lower. This permits bass lines to be written within the bass clef, without extreme use of confusing leger lines or other cumbersome notational devices. (Occasionally higher clefs are employed.) When you are studying a score, be careful not to forget this bass transposition; if you read the score at the piano, be sure to play octaves when they occur between the 'cellos and the contrabasses, or you will gain no real idea of the sound of the whole orchestral fabric.

3. The bow used for contrabass playing (whether "German" or "French") is *much* shorter than one might expect, and heavier too. It is held in a horizontal position, of course. Because the bow is not long, contrabass players expect to change bow direction more frequently on long notes than do their violin, viola, and 'cello peers.

4. Contrabass strings are quite thick. (They must be in order to sound the low pitches demanded of the instrument.) This is the source of what may be the greatest problem young or inexperienced bass players can bring to an orchestra: such thick strings are slow to speak. The player must be very careful to attack the string at the exact moment, and in precisely the right way, to match up cleanly with the rest of the ensemble. Like the bass drummer, with his large beater, the bassist must *anticipate the beat*, if his instrument is to speak on time.

5. *Pizzicato* occurs frequently in contrabass parts, perhaps more often

than in the upper strings. Be certain that your bassists, when they are playing "pizz," are conscious of tone quality.

The obvious function of the contrabass is to provide the foundation of the harmonies. It does not follow, however, that these instruments have no melodic purpose; recent composers have given melodic lines to the basses (without doubling them in the 'cellos), and there are many other instances—including early ones—of *lyric* lines in which the contrabasses and 'cellos are doubled. In such cases, it is important that the bass players perform deftly and with much grace.

Bowing: Central Concepts

String playing is a process of alternating downbow (⊓) and upbow (V) strokes. In theory, the amount of downbow used in a given spot should equal the amount of upbow used in the same passage; this keeps the player from "running out of bow" on one stroke or another. (Of course, two short consecutive downbows can equal one longer upbow, and *vice versa*.) In practice, however, you can count on the players to make quick, experienced judgments which balance out the amounts of down- and upbow used. They do this all the time.

The end of the bow held by the player is called the "frog," and the opposite end is the "tip." A downbow stroke is begun with the hand of the player over or near the string. In theory, since it is relatively easy to apply pressure through the bow to the string in this position, and since that pressure tends to ease as the downbow moves the hand away from the string, the overall dynamic effect of a downbow should be a decrescendo; conversely, an upbow should imply a crescendo, since it starts with the tip near the string, and gradually brings the weight of the player's hand more and more to bear on the string. In practice, of course, good performers succeed in minimizing the impact of this factor, or string playing would produce an irritating "sing-song" effect. Nevertheless, it is from this physical circumstance of the weight of the hand at the frog that the most basic rule of bowing arises: *since in every downbeat there is an implied metric accent, it is traditional that the downbow occur on the downbeat and the upbow on the upbeat.* (Of course, we will observe that there are appropriate exceptions.)

Related to this is a second important concept: that *phrasing and articulation in the string instruments are managed through the type and direction of bowing chosen.* Rhythmic and metric clarity, the shaping of the phrase, and dynamic expression all are affected by bowing choices.

Further, since bowing relates to the efficient use of the instrument, and since players learn to make good bowing choices as a part of their development of good technic, it follows that *a good bowing makes a difficult passage easier, and a poor one makes even an easy passage unclear.*

Bowing is more sophisticated, of course, than simply playing alternating up- and down-strokes. There are various kinds of attacks and releases of the string. There is the whole technique of connecting or separating consecutive strokes. There is the relationship of bowing and *vibrato* to the quality of sound. Beyond

12 *Working with an Orchestra*

all these considerations, there are certain kinds of special effects and techniques obtainable. Finally, there are individual judgments to be made with respect to the bowing of a given passage: in particular, remember—in choosing bowings for an orchestra—that you must consider the overall level of technical development of the ensemble you are to conduct.

The Basic Strokes

All bow-strokes fall into one of two general categories: on- and off-string playing. An *on-the-string stroke* is one which begins with the bow-hair physically touching the string. (Players speak, in such cases, of "setting" the bow; they mean that they rest the bow on the string a moment before commencing the horizontal motion of the stroke itself. If they did not do so, you might get as many separate attacks as you have players.) An *off-the-string stroke* is one which approaches the string from above.[3] (Players use this terminology comfortably, by the way. One frequently gets the question put simply in these terms: "Do you want this on- or off-the-string?") *Most orchestral playing—no matter how skilled the players—is done on-the-string,* using one of these techniques:

Legato implies up- and down-strokes with smooth, virtually inaudible connections between them. When you ask the players for *legato,* or a "singing quality," they seek to minimize the turn-around time at the end of each stroke. *Slurs* are played within what essentially is a *legato* bow, and this stroke is useful also for hiding string crossings.

Detaché, used for passages which require only one note per bow, is the most common stroke. Properly played, it can be very even in dynamic level from frog to tip, in both directions. By definition, *detaché* implies some separation between notes; if you ask for "more space," the players will tend to change direction in the middle of the bow; if you prefer briefer separations, they will probably change in the upper third, nearer the tip.

They can lighten the release of each note, too, if you ask them to "lift." (In this procedure, they ease pressure on the string just at the end of each stroke.) This process of "lifting" (*almost* off the string) is a variant of *detaché* sometimes called the *brush stroke,* and you will find it especially useful for accompanimental passages and for bass lines which demand lightness and finesse. In some passages, this sort of separation is indicated by dashes marked above or below the notes.

Similar to this is the *portato,* notated ♩ ♩ ♩ ♩, in which more than one note occurs within each stroke. The player eases pressure between notes, so that new weight makes the beginning of the next note audible. This technique is particularly useful in repeated-note passages, especially those in the 'cellos and contrabasses. There always is a danger, however, that the gaps between notes will grow too long.

Martelé (derived from the French word for "hammered") is a fast, angular, dramatic stroke, usually played in the upper half of the bow. The stroke begins with the bow more firmly planted into the string than is the case with *detaché,* and continues with a quick, energetic motion either up- or downbow. (The player must

---

3. Note, however, that for clean orchestral playing the initial note of an off-the-string passage should begin on-the-string.

be careful at the end of the stroke; if he is careless, he will produce a rough, ugly release.) *Martelé* bowings accent each attack, of course; they also provide space—a sharply-defined separation—between notes.

There are other on-the-string variants, but these are the primary ones. Turning to the more virtuostic *off-the-string* category:

Spiccato is played with a motion which "drops" the middle of the bow onto the string. One note occurs per stroke. This bowing can be very useful for light accompanimental passages, for it produces quite a short, "dry" (as players sometimes say) sound. You can ask for it by name, or by saying "middle of the bow, and off-the-string, please." (With a youthful orchestra, be careful the players do not use too high a bounce, or you will not get clean ensemble.)
   Note that by asking for "spiccato" or for "detaché with lots of separation," you get spaces between notes much like the effect singers call "staccato"; be careful, nevertheless, not to use that term! For string players, the word *staccato* does not imply a note with a dot under it; it refers, instead, specifically to another type of bow-stroke— one in which several short notes are played per bow. This is a very difficult bowing, and is used almost exclusively for solo playing. *If you direct the word "staccato" to a string section, you risk confusing them and wasting valuable time.*

There are a number of other off-the-string strokes: the *richochet*, for example, the *flying spiccato*, and others. In general, however, these are reserved to solo work. Since they are of little use in orchestral playing, they are of little interest to our present discussion.

Attacks and Connections

Just as you concern yourself with "the legato line," with consonants, elisions, releases, and similar features of the singing of your choir, you must give thought to the kinds of attacks and connections you want between bow-strokes. Listen to the strings just as carefully as you do to your singers.

The "full bow" is basic to good technique for string instruments, just as the "legato line" is the central concept of vocal production. When string players produce even, full-length bows, they find it easy to give attention to producing richness and consistency of tone, and to making smooth, efficient direction-changes. (In a sense, it is "easier" for them to create space—that is, separation— between notes.) *When you are unhappy with the tone quality of a section, make certain that they are using as much bow as possible.* Ask them for "full bows." This makes them think about good, basic tone production, and *it can remind them to listen closely to themselves again.*

Accented attacks require some subtlety; the difficulty with an accent, a *marcato*, a *sforzando*, or a *fortepiano*, is not the *forte*, but the *piano* that follows the initial attack. (The player must keep bow-speed the same, but ease the pressure— just enough, and quickly!—to produce the result desired.) *Be certain that you know exactly what effect you want.* You have several choices, each applicable to certain circumstances:

1. Remember that *separation* and *accent* are two different effects: the former is a *rhythmic* matter, and depends on timing the *release* of a note; the latter is a matter of *dynamics,* involving an *attack.* Both procedures lend an element of emphasis—either to the note accented, or to the one after the separation.
2. You may not want a *powerful* dynamic effect. Be careful about applying the word "accent" too casually; speak instead, for example, of wanting "more articulation" or "a little more 'bite.'" In accompanimental passages, it may help to define what part of the bow you wish used (once you have some experience in these matters): a stroke begun near the frog, downbow, tends to produce more "bite," while a stroke begun near the tip, upbow, tends to result in less definition. *Marcato* attacks on the lower strings will be especially emphatic, or even gruff.
3. If you do want a dynamic accent, then listen carefully to make sure you get exactly the amount of emphasis you need—and not too much. Inexperienced players, when *asked* for an accent, may overdo it in an effort to be cooperative. The result may be harsh, uneven, and unclear. A sharp, clean accent at a *forte* level will have more real impact on your audience than a rough, uneven one at *fortissimo* (as you already know from your choral work).

Vibrato

This technique is as important to good tone and fine playing as the bow-stroke itself. *Vibrato* is central to our aural concept of good string sound; with it, the tone has a singing quality; without it, the instrument can sound lifeless and dull. The left-hand motion that produces *vibrato* is routine for any experienced player, but—like firm breath support—it may be the first thing to deteriorate when (near the end of a long rehearsal, for example) a less-disciplined player loses concentration. Keep an eye on the string sections. Even on short notes the players should be using *vibrato* (save in very rare spots where they have been instructed to avoid it). You can remind them of their responsibility, if necessary, simply by saying "Vibrate!"

For more left-hand clarity, the phrase "Use hard fingers!" is sometimes employed, but it can lead to harsh results. "Keep the left hand clean!" may serve better.

Pizzicato Playing

Many string players fail to practice *pizzicato* technique enough, yet this is no trivial matter, for the very greatest of our composers have tended to use this effect—not casually—but in very special musical passages.

Worry about the *quality* of *pizzicato* sound, and ask the players to concentrate on it. (There is an exact spot—for every individual pitch—at which one gets the best response from the plucked string; often it is about an octave above the fingering, where this is feasible. Closer to the bridge the tone becomes more metallic.)

Remember that *vibrato* is needed for "pizz" notes, too. You may have to remind inexperienced players to use it. (And if you are dealing with very young players, that "twanging" sound you may hear comes from fingernails that need trimming.)

Special Effects

There is also the possibility of *nonvibrato* playing: you will find passages in which—for dramatic effect, or an especially subdued *pianissimo*—you may wish to ask the musicians to play without *vibrato*. (Composers specify this effect at times.) The amount of *vibrato* employed is related also to the stylistic period, to some extent; you may want rather more of it in Tschaikowsky than in Mozart, for example.

With respect to tone quality, there is a standard point for bow contact with the string. This varies somewhat with the particular string itself, occurring further from the bridge for the G-string of the violin, and closer to it for the E-string, for example. (This same principle applies to the corresponding strings on the viola, 'cello, and contrabass.) The composer may deliberately seek another sound, however; thus when he wants the more transparent quality one gets by bowing on the bridge, he marks that spot *sul ponticello;* conversely, when he wishes the rather hollow sound obtained by bowing near the fingerboard, he marks the part *sul tasto* (for which a somewhat faster bow may be needed).

Harmonics are clearly audible overtones produced when only a segment (mathematically half, a third, a quarter, etc.) of the string is permitted to vibrate. (This phenomenon is produced by one's touching the string at the desired dividing point without pressing it down against the fingerboard; the technique, as you may realize, goes back to the Pythagoreans.) The result is generally a very high pitch with a clear quality. Notation of harmonics is complicated: there is the point (a pitch) at which the string is to be touched, there is the "fundamental" of the overtone series involved, and there is the actual pitch desired. Some contemporary composers—because of this potential confusion—superimpose all three on the music page, one on top of the others. It may be best, depending on the style period of the work you are performing, to discuss such a passage with your concertmaster.

When you particularly want the unique tone quality produced by a certain string, you can ask for it (*sul G, sul C, sul E,* etc.) as composers sometimes do. Otherwise, remember that fingering—unlike bowing—is a matter of individual preference for string players, as it is for the winds.

Occasionally one may wish two or more long notes (perhaps with *fermatas* over them) attacked in the same way, avoiding any difference in emphasis; consecutive downbows, for example, occur frequently. If you need this effect to be managed without the rather wide separation that occurs when the player must lift the bow, recover its length, and attack again, you can use the marking ⊓ V over *each* of the two notes involved. The players will change bow direction unobtrusively (*legato*) during each long note, timing their upbows to bring them back near the frog for the next attack. To help make the upbows unnoticeable, the players deliberately will change directions at different times—that is, they will "stagger" their bow-changes just as your choir members may "stagger" breaths" in long phrases.

You can ask the players to use this same technique on *very* long notes, of course—the final chord of a movement, for example. Thus the string players can sustain a *fermata* for as long as you wish (which means that the breath control of the wind players may become your prime practical concern). If you do not want this "staggered" effect on a long note, watch the concertmaster's bow, as it approaches the tip; this will help you time your cutoff effectively.

The Woodwinds and the Brasses

As a choral conductor, you may feel more comfortable with the wind players than the strings; like singers, bassoonists breathe! High notes really *are* "higher" for oboes, just as they are for sopranos; a long passage in a high tessitura has the same exhausting effect on a trumpet player as on a tenor, and the term *staccato*—already forbidden for use in conversations with the strings—means about the same thing to a clarinetist as it does to a bass-baritone. You will find it easy to be as sensitive to the breath problems wind players have on long notes and difficult phrases as you are with your singers.

It cannot be our concern in this handbook to detail every feature of all these instruments—every possible or impossible trill, every register change and alternate fingering. That is the domain of orchestration texts, and you have been referred to those already.[4] Our concerns here are those basic characteristics and potential problems which may require decisions from you before or during rehearsals. We will discuss the winds in the order in which they usually appear in the conductor's score.

The *flute*, in brief, is a cylindrical pipe in which sound is produced by causing the column of air within it to vibrate; this is done by blowing across an opening at one end. The lowest possible pitches are obtained when the fingers stop all the fingerholes arranged along the pipe. When one or more of the fingers is raised, opening one or more holes, the acoustical effect is to "shorten" the pipe, and that produces a higher pitch. The player's tongue stops the opening between his lips until he wants an attack; pulled sharply back, it permits air to pass over the mouthpiece; returned to its original position, the tongue stops the air stream and the resulting sound. (This "tonguing" process is more sophisticated than that, however, for subtler patterns of movement called "double- and triple-tonguing" enable the player to attain great agility in fast passages.) Slurs are

---

4. See above, p. 6.

played without tonguing (that is, without stopping the air stream); in general, in all the winds, slurs upward are easier than downward ones. Tongued skips downward are easier than ascending slurs.

The lowest octave of the flute has a warm, gentle sound. Flute tone grows brighter and more penetrating as the pitches ascend, becoming quite brilliant in passages written above the treble clef.

The *piccolo* is a miniature, truncated version of the same instrument, sounding an octave higher than notated. (The formal name is actually *flauto piccolo*.) Because it is relatively short, in comparison to the flute, the lowest part of its range can be disappointing in quality. The higher register is quite bright, however—even piercing. In *tutti* passages the piccolo often doubles the flute at the octave.

Oboes, which have been assigned major solo responsibilities and now sensual, now sprightly melodic lines by every major composer since the seventeenth century, have a mixed reputation. Played skillfully, the instrument has a haunting beauty; it is sometimes jocularly known, nevertheless, as an "ill wind nobody blows good." Conical in shape, not cylindrical, it employs a "double reed"—actually two separate pieces of cane, bound together to vibrate against the tiny opening between them—to initiate motion in the column of air. (The tongue closes the reed opening for articulation.) Much of the difficulty of the instrument rests in reed problems: getting good cane, preparing the reed skillfully, and maintaining the proper moisture level at performance time. Too thick, too thin, too wet, too dry—all these conditions produce unfortunate sounds.

It is quite difficult to play quietly in the lowest register of the oboe, and the top notes (a fourth or so above the treble clef) grow thin. In between these extremes lie the distinctive, rich, somewhat nasal registers for which the instrument is well known. In spite of the demands of the instrument, it can be very agile in use, especially in the heart of its range. It should be noted, however, that while one often can choose to double both flutes on a part marked for only one of them, intonation problems make this riskier for all but very able oboe players.

The so-called *English horn* (no more British than the French horn is Gallic) is actually an alto oboe, larger in size than its higher counterpart, with a bulbous bell instead of a flared one. Like almost all "secondary" instruments, it is transposed; it sounds a perfect fifth below the written notes. Save for this transposition, it has range and registration features very like the oboe. In the orchestra it usually is employed for solo work.

Just as the piccolo normally is covered by the third flutist, the English horn generally is the responsibility of the second or third player in the section. While this may not necessarily imply a less competent musician, it may mean a lower-quality instrument (sometimes borrowed, or poorly maintained by a school, rather than by an individual). If there is an important English horn part in your score, you may want to investigate beforehand both the player and the instrument to be used (unless you have the advantage of conducting a fully-professional orchestra).

The *Oboe-d'amore,* in size lying between the oboe and the English horn, sounds a minor third below the notated pitch. It may be important to you, for

Bach used it frequently. Again, the problem with the oboe d'amore may not be the competence of the player so much as the quality of the instrument available.

The *clarinet* is cylindrical. A "single reed"—a flat piece of cane bound by a metal "ligature" so that it vibrates against the mouthpiece of the instrument—is the means of moving the air column inside it. The tongue acts against the narrow opening at the tip of the reed and the mouthpiece. Clarinets, built in various sizes, sound in corresponding keys: in modern orchestral playing, almost everything written for the instrument is played either on the B-flat or A-natural instruments; the former sounds a whole step, and the latter a minor-third below the notated pitch. On occasion the smaller instrument in E-flat (which sounds a minor third *above* the written note) is used. Players are often instructed in their parts to "change (from B-flat) to A," and *vice versa;* this can be dangerous, for sometimes they miss that instruction.[5]

Registration is a very important feature of the clarinets, for the instrument has a wide range, and the registers vary quite a lot in sound. The standard clarinet quality is probably that heard in the upper half of the treble clef, which is bright and clear. Above that clef the tone becomes increasingly penetrating (at *forte*). In the lowest register (the so-called *chalumeau*), however, the sound can be quite dark and unique.

The clarinet is an extremely agile instrument. Even on the highest and lowest notes, players can be trusted for *pianissimo* attacks. Arpeggios are rather easy for the instrument, perhaps more so than for any other wind; skips, in general, can be quite secure and subtle.

The *alto and bass clarinets and the basset horn* (the latter used by Mozart in his *Requiem,* and by others) are essentially larger versions of the standard B-flat clarinet, each transposing in relation to its size. The larger instruments have a curved tube to hold the mouthpiece, and a bell shaped rather like that of a saxophone. The registers of these instruments generally are consistent with those of the higher clarinets.

The *bassoon* is conical (within what appears to be a cylindrical tube), and the air column inside is activated by a double reed larger than, but similar to that of the oboe. A difficult wind, like its higher cousin, it is not a transposing instrument; parts for it normally are written in the bass and tenor clefs. For its size and range, it can be quite agile, though the length of the instrument makes some fingerings difficult.

It is a mistake to think always of the *staccato,* dancing passages which have given the bassoon its unfortunate nickname, "the clown of the orchestra," as the real sound of the instrument. It is capable of sustained, lyric lines of great beauty. Tonguing which is too emphatic can contribute to this limited image. The registration is surprisingly even, from top to bottom, compared with—for example—the clarinet; only the extreme tones sound significantly different in

---

5. In an almost legendary example, Arnold Schönberg arrived in Berlin to find that the fine players of the Berlin Philharmonic had been preparing his *Pierrot Lunaire* for 20 rehearsals, yet had failed to notice just such a change. William W. Austin, *Music in the 20th Century,* p. 195.

character. (The opening of Stravinsky's *Le Sacre du Printemps*, beginning on a high C-natural, is a famous example.) You may use the instrument in a bassoon section, or—in a Baroque work—it may serve as a member of the *basso continuo* group.

The *contrabassoon* is a larger, more convoluted relative of the bassoon, sounding down an octave from the written pitches. It has a range actually reaching below the C-extension of the contrabass, and (because of the size of its column of air) it demands great breath control; for the same reason, it is not quite as facile as the bassoon. Here again, as with the English horn, the oboe d'amore, and the basset horn, the quality of the instrument available to your player may be a problem in any but a professional orchestra.

The (*French*) *horn* is a bridge between the woodwinds and the brasses; physically a brass instrument, it is used traditionally both in woodwind quintets and in brass ensembles. Partly cylindrical and partly conical, the modern horn is the latest stage of a long evolutionary history; perhaps the most important practical step in that evolution was the substitution of valves for the interchangeable "tuning crooks" of the earlier "natural horn" or "hunting horn." The modern instrument can play any note in any key without inserting a crook; this contemporary facility exists side by side, however, with anachronistic aspects of horn technique: the many transpositions notated in scores, the "stopping" of certain tones with the hand, and the interlocking orchestration of the traditional four horn parts. It is the so-called "double horn" (actually a union of F and B-flat horns, between which the player switches back and forth quickly by means of a special valve) that is in modern use. With rare exceptions, all symphonic horn parts are performed on this instrument.

Horn writing tends to lie higher (in relation to the overtone series' produced by this instrument) than is the case with other brasses. Much of the difficulty of playing the horn derives from this acoustical circumstance, both with respect to facility and intonation. Great subtlety of embouchere (lip placement and manipulation) is required, and modern players still adjust tuning by "stopping" certain tones—by closing part of the bell opening of the horn with the right hand (thus lowering the pitch), as "natural horn" players used to do.

Both treble and bass clefs are used for horn parts. When three or four of these instruments are employed, two staves are used; in keeping with the tradition of "interlocking" them, the two "high horns"—the first and third—are notated one on top of each staff, with the "low horns"—the second and fourth—below them. (Often, of course, the high and low horns double each other at the octave.) Since extended passages can be especially demanding on this instrument, it is a common practice for an "assistant first" (a fifth player) to be assigned to alternate with the first horn, as needed.

In dealing with horns in rehearsal, you should consider that this instrument simply is not as agile as certain others of the winds, and react accordingly. Difficult as it can be to play the horn, added psychological tension is not likely to help the player do his best.

The *trumpet* is mostly cylindrical, becoming conical near its bell. It is a powerful instrument, capable of dominating the entire orchestra. (It has been said, in fact, that "whatever a bad trumpeter plays is the melody.") Two centuries ago trumpets were fitted with crooks which suited them for a wide range of keys; the standard modern instrument, with its piston valves, is built in B-flat, and has a special sliding crook that converts it to an A trumpet. (The B-flat version sounds a step lower, and the A trumpet a minor-third down.) Fine players are ready to shift to C, D, or even E-flat trumpets, however, when the repertoire demands it.

The low register of the trumpet sounds sizable; above that, the quality becomes more and more brilliant. High notes can be wonderfully clear, when played by an expert, but it is difficult to deliver them *pianissimo*. Arpeggios are easier for this instrument than for the horn. Tonguing can be very crisp, and fine players double- and triple-tongue with great facility.

The trumpet mutes deserve mention, for they are much-used by composers for timbral changes and ensemble effects. (Muted trumpet can sound remarkably like the oboe, for example.) There are several types of mutes; of them, the simple "straight mute" is the one most frequently needed for symphonic work.

The *trombone* is cylindrical through most of its length (as it must be, for otherwise its slide could not function), but it becomes conical—as does the trumpet—near the bell. The standard version is the "B-flat tenor," so called in spite of the fact that it is *not* a transposing instrument. It is notated in the bass clef, save for high passages written in the tenor or (on rare occasions) alto clefs.

Pitch is obtained by adjusting the lips to produce the various overtones of seven fundamental slide positions. Tuning is managed simply by making tiny modifications of those positions with either slide or lips. In spite of the length of the arm movements involved, fine players have good agility on the instrument.

The nature of the trombone makes slurs more difficult, however; in practice many slurred notes have to be joined by subtle tonguing (a process much like the *legato* connection of a downbow to an upbow).

The tone of the instrument is often called "noble." When it is desired, tremendous power can be generated by a trombone section, and thus younger players must be careful not to "bark" attacks. Mutes are employed, but less frequently in symphonic work than is the case with trumpets.

The *alto trombone* was much used in the Romantic era, when a trombone section might include two altos and a tenor, or some such combination. It is seldom seen now. The *bass trombone,* on the other hand, is common, especially in the form of a hybrid—a tenor trombone with a larger bore, a bigger bell, and an "F attachment" (a device which enables the player to utilize a section of tubing, otherwise bypassed, to extend the range downward). Some orchestra sections these days are made up exclusively of these flexible, full-voiced instruments.

The *tuba* is the bass of the brass section. Conical, save for its valve tubing, it comes in a complicated range of sizes and keys. Because low-pitched instruments can have increased tuning problems, tubas are built with three, four, five, and even six valves—the extra ones added in attempts to correct faulty intonation in certain combinations of valves. Tuba parts are written as they sound, and the players accustom themselves—unlike contrabass or contrabassoon performers—to reading many leger lines below the bass clef.

It is a mistake to regard the tuba as ponderous, either in agility or in quality of sound. Although the instrument demands vast resources of breath, and in spite of the frequency with which this breath supply must be replenished—for it takes great energy to initiate motion in the huge column of air contained by all its tubing—the tuba is, in the hands of a fine player, a *lyric* instrument. It need not always sound bombastic. It can manage wide melodic leaps effectively, and double- and triple-tonguing are quite possible. Deft *staccato* passages are common in the literature.

The Percussion Section

In this limited catalog we cannot begin to consider the whole range of instruments sometimes included in what is called "the percussion battery." Our attention can be confined to four of the most common ones. (When you conduct literature which employs a more extensive percussion section, it would be well for you to consult the principal of that section in advance, just as you would the concertmaster in matters of bowing.)

Some percussion instruments have pitch. Among these, probably the most regularly employed are the *timpani*. Large, kettle-shaped drums tuned by various kinds of devices (of which the most common today is a pedal system), timpani come in several sizes, and appear in orchestras in combinations of two, three, four, or even more. The standard timpani for the orchestra have diameters from 23 up to 30 inches; with these, pitches both below and above the bass clef can be provided.

Timpani are struck by pairs of mallets, which come in a wide variety of hardnesses. The player chooses mallets which will produce the kind of sonority apparently called for by a given passage. In normal combinations of strokes, the hands alternate; just as with consecutive up- or downbows, however, there are patterns which include consecutive strokes by one hand or the other. Although the tremolo (the so-called "drum roll") is played on one tympanum, more melodic passages are possible, if several instruments are employed.

Three difficulties are common. Over-enthusiastic, yet under-experienced timpanists are a hazard, for the instrument can overpower the rest of the orchestra. Careless players may let the sound ring too long, as well; for clean playing they must be ready to stop the vibrations by touching the drum head with a hand. Finally, timpani often must be re-tuned by the player while the orchestra is playing, and this demands a fine ear; out-of-tune timpani can result.

The *bass drum* is unpitched, but its head must be carefully and evenly tightened to the tension which gives the best resonance. It usually is struck by a "beater"—a mallet—with a large, soft head, and it has great power, providing that the percussionist strikes it in the proper spot (which is *not* the center point). Improper stroking or uneven adjusting of the head can result in a lifeless sound.

A greater danger with the bass drum is rhythmic: because all low-pitched instruments can be slow to speak, the bass drummer must anticipate the conductor's beat, just as the contrabass and tuba players should. If he does not do so, he will drag behind your beat.

The *snare drum* is quite shallow in shape, its lower head vibrating against strips of gut or metal; the latter give it its characteristic timbre—a flat, vibrant sound akin to rattling paper. (The snares can be loosened so that they will not vibrate, and *this must be done when the instrument is not in use*—or it must be dampened in some other way; otherwise, *the playing of other instruments will cause the snares to vibrate against the head quite audibly.*)

The normal sticks are hard wooden ones, but their size and weight varies; brushes are used on occasion, too. In addition to the tremolo (or "roll"), the snare drum plays complex patterns of left- and right-hand sticking. Many of its written notes are ornamented in traditional ways by the players. (If you are uncertain about these matters, consult the principal.)

Cymbals come in a wide variety of diameters and thicknesses. (Orchestral cymbals tend to be larger and thicker than those used by players of jazz and popular music.) Be certain to judge the sounds you hear, and ask to audition different sets of cymbals, if necessary.

Cymbals are *not* struck directly together; instead, they are swung from opposite directions, so that they strike each other in passing. Good ones will sustain tone for a long time, when properly struck. Extra sound may be transmitted into the concert hall if they are held face out toward the conductor after impact. *Staccato* effects and rhythmic releases are gained by the player's pulling the edges of the cymbals back into his chest quickly, stopping their vibrations at the proper moment. When one cymbal is suspended from a fixture of some sort, a tremolo—which can be played with various types of mallets—is possible.

Keyboard Instruments

After the Baroque period the use of keyboard instruments is infrequent in orchestral writing. Rather than discuss Baroque usage of these media at this point, we will consider their application to that repertoire in chapter 6.[6]

Related Matters

Just as with singers, if you are to know what you have a right to expect in terms of tone quality and technique from your players, you must have a clear aural ideal of each instrument, an ideal that reflects its characteristics when it is skillfully played. There is no short cut here: listen as much as you can to fine performances by great instrumentalists.

---

6. See below, pp. 48 ff.

Remember to use your players efficiently. Do not keep them in place through movements or works for which they are not needed.[7]

It is characteristic of parts written for the brasses and the percussion battery (and, to a lesser extent, the woodwinds) that long tacet passages occur. The players are responsible for counting out these measures of rest, and they expect to do so. Recall this, however, when you must stop in mid-movement during a rehearsal; before you begin again, be certain that the starting point you choose is one known to them. (You may be somewhere in the middle of a 125-bar rest for the trombones, for example.) Refer to a rehearsal letter or bar number shared by all.

You cannot know as much—no matter how hard you study—about all these instruments as the players themselves understand. If you do not know exactly what you want, be honest with them. Ask to hear more than one option, and then choose. Above all, be certain you get far enough into scores in your own study to really *know* them. The players will respect that, whether or not you have experience in all the subtleties of instrumental technique.

---

7. Specific instructions touching this point are offered in chapter 5, p. 39.

3 Preparing for Rehearsals

As we approach a performance, we need to take this as our first rule: that *every bit of work which properly can be done in advance* must be completed before the first rehearsal. All the score study, all the planning, all the conferences with concertmaster and principals, all the basic interpretive decisions that need not wait—these should precede your first meeting with the orchestra, if you hope to take maximal advantage of every minute of rehearsal time.

Try to visit and observe the orchestra you are to conduct some weeks before you have to rehearse them. Get acquainted with them. If they have a regular conductor, watch him work with them, and make notes, especially about his terminology. While there should be no difference between what "choral" and "instrumental" conductors do in an artistic situation, there *is* a critical divergence in the language each uses. Listen to what an orchestra conductor says to the strings. He uses words like "vibrate" and "sing"; in a given case, he asks them to "play more at the tip," or "use more bow," or "less bow," and so on. Get both the phrases and the results they produce into your ears. Make this language as much yours as you have the specialized phrases you use to get specific results from your chorus.

The Overriding Concept of the Work

Your first responsibility, of course, is to develop your concept of the work to be performed, and the style in which you want to present it. As you already know from your experiences with choral music, you must study until you know the proportions and momentum of each movement and passage; with these shapes in your mind, you can choose tempos, observe how climaxes are approached and delivered, and determine how movements are related. You can make preliminary decisions, at least, about such matters as articulation, dynamics, *ritards*, and phrasing.

Judgments about style come easier if you study and learn a lot of music by the same composer and his contemporaries. Beware of getting your interpretation from a recording of the work you are to conduct! Avoid imitating someone else. Listen instead to other works from the same historical period. *Get the sounds of that time into your ears, and the shapes of those works into your mind;* then apply what you have heard and learned to the case at hand. (If you do listen to a recording of it, make sure you try out four or five other versions too.)

When you study, use a full score. *The music the orchestra plays should be considered right from the beginning.* Remember that the orchestra is not just a composite accompanist: much of the most important material has been voiced into the orchestra, and there may even be passages in which the choir "accompanies" the players. At the least, the nature of the orchestral material will affect your decisions about tempos, balances, articulation, and other features of your interpretation.

And watch the "seams!" In longer pieces of music, you will find—especially in working with an orchestra—that much of your conducting responsibility will derive from how you control these transition points, the "seams" between tempos, dynamic levels, textures, etc. The way you move from one tempo to another, the way you signal new attacks, the association between one articulation pattern and another: consider all these in terms of the relationships they represent between sections.

Score Preparation

The very appearance of a full score can be intimidating to the choral conductor. All those staves! Can one really follow twenty or more of them at once, transposing clarinets and tracking violas through the alto clef?

Like all skills, reading an orchestra score is largely a matter of practice. The instruments are arranged in families (except in a few recent works): by custom, the woodwinds appear at the top, the brasses next, the percussion below them, and the strings at the bottom. The choir may be notated between the brass and strings or—sometimes—in the middle of the string staves. If there are soloists, they usually are shown just above the chorus. A typical nineteenth century full score could appear as follows, from the top staff to the bottom:

(Piccolo)
Flutes I and II
Oboes I and II
(English Horn)
Clarinets I and II
(Bass Clarinet)
Bassoons I and II
(Contrabassoon)
French Horns I and II
French Horns III and IV
Trumpets I and II
Trombones I and II
Tuba
Timpani
Other Percussion
Soloists (SATB)
Chorus (SATB)
Violins I
Violins II
Violas
Violoncellos
Contrabasses

There can be differences, of course, in the arrangement of the instruments in Baroque, Classical, and later scores. Compare the three layouts shown in examples 1, 2, and 3.

If you have had little experience with full scores, you may want to mark the margin of each page with one or more colored pens to bracket clearly the brass family, the chorus, and so on. That will help your eyes gauge instantly where each family is as you turn each page. Other symbols—arrows, braces, etc.—will help you "find" entrances you need to cue, dynamics you must indicate in your baton, and other developments.

Even in the beginning, when the size of the score seems overwhelming, be certain you have a clear concept—even if you cannot yet follow every line— of the *sound* of the orchestra. How much doubling of parts is going on at a given moment? Is the texture chordal, melody-with-accompaniment, two-voice counterpoint, three-voice writing, or what?

During this period of study, you may want to write in margins and on blank pages relevant quotes from authorities, teachers, and other sources. Historical and analytic material you have found in studying the work can be written in the score, where it will be found quickly on future occasions when you conduct or teach about this work. (Remember, however, that this material is for your own study—not for lectures to the orchestra.)[1]

One *crucial* bit of editing: check the actual orchestra parts, and be certain you *mark into your score every rehearsal-letter or rehearsal-number system* you find in those parts. If your score does not include measure-numbers, add them. (Often the rehearsal letters in the full score do *not* match the notations in the orchestra parts, and sometimes rented parts may combine [or have written in by hand] two or three different systems.) Confusion about rehearsal-letters can cost a great deal of invaluable time, and can keep you from rehearsing passages that need work. Nothing makes tempers flare in rehearsal quicker than the frustration that arises when players are unintentionally starting in different measures because of this problem. Careful work during your preparation period is the answer.

This is the time to begin estimating where the trouble spots are going to be. If you believe you are going to have to stop and drill a particular passage, or return to it after completing the movement, plan where you are going to start, and know what rehearsal-letter or measure-number you are going to use. (Some conductors mark numbers—+14, −12, etc.—into their scores at problem spots as signals that, when trouble occurs in rehearsal, they will instruct the orchestra to count "14 bars after F" or "12 measures before K" to start again. Such a system saves time counting bars while the players wait.)

Although you may choose to mark full scores very heavily, perhaps in several colors, perhaps with a whole system of shorthand symbols, some conductors feel that such a process hinders the imagination. Returning to a work several years after you conducted it for the first time, you may find many of your

---

1. See the cautionary note in chapter 5, pp. 40–41.

Example 1. One page from a typical Baroque period score: Bach, *Magnificat,* first movement, measures 1–4.

ideas changed; some of your earlier markings may seem naïve—or even wrong. (Marking in pencil permits you to change your mind, but pencil smudges badly, of course.) Another possibility: if it is feasible for you to obtain two scores, you might study one of them with penciled notations, and mark it heavily for rehearsals; then edit the second, clean score for the performance(s).

However you decide to prepare your score, *be certain the process helps you keep*

Example 2. One page from a typical Viennese Classical score: Haydn, *Nelsonmesse,* Kyrie, measures 1–5.

your overall aural conception clear in your mind. The whole purpose of a score, after all, is to keep you well oriented throughout the work at hand.

Pre-Rehearsal Conferences

Once you have a clear, overriding concept of the whole work in mind, you will find it useful to pass a Violin I part to your concertmaster and schedule

Example 3. One page from a typical Romantic era score: Brahms, *Ein deutsches Requiem, Op. 45,* second movement, measures 1–9.

a bowing conference. Set up a music stand, give the concertmaster a comfortable chair, and try out your tempos. See what problems arise.

String parts which have been used before (parts from your orchestra's library or from a rental source) will have bowings written in. You may want to change a bowing here and there, or make another choice for an extended passage, but generally you will find these "inherited" markings useful. Try them yourself. (Actually make your right hand "bow" the part!) Then go over them with your concertmaster, and make such changes as seem necessary. (Don't be afraid to mark tentative bowings into your own score, by the way; even if they are impractical, your concertmaster will see what sort of effect you want, and will know better how to get it.)

It may be best to arrange a second such conference—especially if your orchestra is made up of amateurs or students—with all five string principals. Start each movement, giving them an idea of your tempos, and check all the important bowings. The principals now are ready to transfer the agreed-upon bowings into all the string parts.

These conferences may take a couple of hours, but *they will save critical rehearsal time later.* Moreover, they will give your principals a clear idea in advance of the style of the work, as you conceive it. *Plan now to use your concertmaster and those principals in rehearsals.* Trust them to deal with some questions that arise within their sections. They have become your assistants, and—with their knowledge of string techniques—they can be of great help.

Do not forget to talk about ornamentation, if you want embellishments in the work you are performing. *Do not assume that the players will know how to play trills, appoggiaturas, and the like.* They may not know how, nor will they know whether the ornament should come on the beat, or before it. Neither will they know whether to start above or below the note. Even if you are blessed with a professional orchestra, there will be differences of opinion within the section. Know what you want, and talk it over with the principals in advance.[2]

Seating the Strings

Several factors influence the size of the string body of your orchestra, among them: (1) the historical period from which the work comes, (2) the size of your choir, (3) the size of the auditorium, and (4) the acoustical character of the hall. We know, for example, that Bach used about 20 singers, and that would imply a string distribution of perhaps 3-3-2-2-1 (Violins I through bass viols); we have seen the record of employment in Haydn's case, and know that (for his choir of 20 to 25), the strings were about 6-5-4-4-2. With the larger choirs and huge auditoriums we use today, however, these numbers are minimal; for a Bach *Magnificat* with a 60-voice chorus, 6-6-4-4-3 is probably appropriate. For a Haydn *Nelsonmesse* with the same size choir, 8-6-4-4-3 is probably reason-

---

2. Some conductors actually pencil in trills in advance, writing them in margins or on unused staves.

able. For a Brahms *Requiem* in a church—with crowded conditions—6-6-4-4-3 would be an acceptable minimum, but the string section for such a work ordinarily should be larger, for several reasons: (1) in Romantic works, the strings must support a larger wind section, (2) they must play more divisi passages, (and sound credible doing so), (3) the nature of the choral writing changes the balances, and (4) this style implies a warmer, richer string sound than in Bach, Haydn, or Mozart. Much depends on the security of the players, and on their leadership in each section.

If the orchestra you use is an established one, you will find the seating decided for you. Some conductors have tried placing the Violins II on your right, so that the arrangement of sections in front of you, left to right, is Violins I, violas, 'cellos, and Violins II, with the basses behind; this has the advantage of separating the sounds of the violin sections geographically, but the disadvantage of pointing the F-holes of the Violins II upstage, creating a balance problem. The more usual pattern, again left to right, is: Violins I, Violins II, violas, and 'cellos, with the basses behind the 'cellos.

In most professional cases, the concertmaster, having been chosen first, will know the abilities of the other string players. If you are responsible for seating within the sections, the concertmaster and the other principals can advise you. It is likely that the other players will respect the judgment of the principals, and this makes the seating decisions easier. Here are several tips about seating:

1. Get a strong assistant concertmaster.
2. Choosing a principal Violin II is more a matter of finding leadership than of choosing a strong player. (Your assistant concertmaster may play better, in fact, but can be less dominant as a personality.)
3. Some conductors like to put one or two very good players near the back of each section, to "play through" and encourage weaker people.
4. In stronger players, especially at the front desks, you are looking for audacity (for entrances) as well as technical skill.
5. It is normal for the quality to drop off faster, desk by desk, in the Violins II than in the other sections.

If you are seating 14 violins, and if the leadership qualities you need are present in the right individuals, you might arrange the two sections (in terms of technical ability):

Violins I: 1 (concertmaster), 2 (assistant), 3, 5, 8, 9, 6, 7
Violins II: 4 (principal), 10, 11, 12, 13, 14

Similarly, seating violas and 'cellos, you might build some strength into the back of each section:

1 (principal), 2, 4, 5, 3, 6

Arrange the basses in order of ability, working to achieve a blended sound from them. Remember that there is a vast difference in quality between the bass viols played in professional orchestras and the instruments used by student and amateur players. The quality of college-owned basses can be very low.

Some Other Considerations

Plan at least one reading session for the players (getting through the entire work once), but use the choir in orchestra rehearsals as soon as you can. Until the players hear the singers (especially in accompanimental passages) they cannot know how the work really sounds, and can make only limited artistic judgments about their own playing.

Experiment with placement of soloists. (There are at least three problems here: the audience must see these singers, the soloists must be able to carry over the sound of the orchestra and chorus, and they are accustomed to standing in front of the orchestra.) Historically, up to Beethoven or so, soloists were chosen from the choirs used, and stood among their colleagues when they sang. Do not lock yourself into the pattern of always putting the soloists in front of the orchestra; between the orchestra and chorus may be best, providing the sightlines are reasonably good. This arrangement makes it easier for soloists to hear balance, and *much* easier for the orchestra players to hear the soloists. When these singers cluster around the conductor, on the other hand, the principals often have difficulty seeing the conductor, and—unable to hear the soloists well—play too loudly.

Know the score, and make careful plans, but try to avoid becoming rigid about interpretation. Leave some music-making for the rehearsals, for you will find that you learn as much from good players as they do from you. Just be sure you *never* wait to learn the music in rehearsal!

4   Adjusting Your Baton Technique

The physical process of conducting a chorus is more like that of conducting an orchestra than is generally believed. *Good* choral conductors—while they may be using somewhat different gestures—understand and use the same concepts behind those gestures as their instrumental counterparts. This handbook assumes you already are a skillful choral conductor; what we must pursue in this chapter is a sense of the importance of precise physical movements in orchestral conducting, and of the special procedures which are used.

Leadership

As we have said before, choral conductors have, in general, more rehearsal time per measure of music than orchestral conductors. Many of us have excellent accompanists, too, and they assist us routinely in leading the choir through new works, correcting wrong notes, helping to maintain intonation, clarifying and emphasizing meter and rhythm, and influencing phrasing. Many choruses memorize most or all of the music they perform, and, in the process of doing so, they *overlearn* these works.

As a consequence of these and other advantages, many of us become—rather than *conductors,* in the active sense of that word—*coaches,* who work and rework passages until they are refined. Some of us almost stop conducting, spending our time on the podium only starting, stopping, and shaping well-drilled choirs.

When we confront an orchestra, then, we have to really *conduct* again, and we feel ill at ease—perhaps even inadequate. Unlike the singers, the players have not yet heard this work (at least, not lately), and the truth is that they need more help than the singers do. Nevertheless, intimidated a bit by the manner and routine of instrumental rehearsals, and used to coaching our chorus, we may fail to *lead* the orchestra. They wait for us, and we wait for them; tempos get flabby, rhythm becomes ragged, and morale sags. What they need us to do is conduct!

Prepare yourself physically by re-examining your baton technique. Like a good athlete training, go back to basics. Get a videotape of yourself, if possible; be self-critical. Have a colleague watch rehearsals and coach you. Be suspicious that you have developed a bad habit or two in the years since your last formal class in conducting.

Prepare yourself mentally, too. Give the orchestral score all the consideration it deserves; realize that—in a standard oratorio—you will spend perhaps 75 percent of your time conducting the players, and only 25 percent of it directing the singers. Be careful not to conceive the music as a choral work accompanied by an orchestra (for that is not the nature of any of the masterpieces).

Preparation of the Beat

The story is told that the great George Szell once deigned to drink a beer with a group of his Cleveland Orchestra players following a rehearsal. After a happy time at a nearby pub, he rose to go; one of the players called out, "See you on the downbeat. . . ." Szell shot back: "NO! On the preparation!"

Young conductors sometimes give a downbeat, and then wait for the orchestra to play, instead of going on. That will not do. When the orchestra members are playing one beat, you prepare what they are to do next—*signalling to them the speed and manner of the next notes they are to play.* You should not be conducting *with* them, but one beat ahead of them; they should be trying constantly to catch up with you. The most frequent complaint young conductors make about orchestras—that they respond late—is *invariably a failure of the preparation beat.*

The orchestra needs to know—to see—what sort of energy they should use to begin a phrase. They need to be able to see where the peak of that phrase will be, and what sort of cadence they will have to provide at the end. To show them these images, always one beat ahead, *you must have that image in your own ears one beat early,* convey it in the gesture you are making at that moment, and keep going.

One frustrating difference between players and singers: remember that, since orchestras never memorize music, they really have to read it all the time. As a consequence, they seem not to be watching; actually, of course, they are using peripheral vision *to watch the baton. They do not watch the face much* (which tells us that the passionate expressions some famous conductors use have little to do with the orchestra).

Delivering the Beat

The players have been trained to raise their instruments when you first lift your hands. Do not raise your hands, and then begin to talk. The players get tired, and cross, waiting for a downbeat from you. Lift your baton only when you have finished your instructions.

In this respect, note that there is a rhythm to the whole preparation process with an orchestra, just as there is with a choir. You may train your chorus to "all breathe together" during your preparatory beat, in order that they get a sense of the coming pace, and of their rhythmic responsibilities as an ensemble: in the same way you can prepare an orchestra to sense beginnings together. It is a matter of readiness, concentration, and consistency of timing, and it is very important if you are to get clean attacks.

There should be no real difference between a *good* "choral beat" and a good

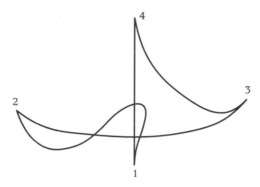

Figure 3. A recommended baton pattern for *legato,* carrying rebounds forward and using the horizontal plane effectively.

"instrumental beat," but to say so assumes that the choral conductor uses a clear, clean motion. Many do not. The beat pattern used should avoid any unnecessary sub-dividing (which some of us develop into a habit from years spent trying to teach rhythm to choirs), and it should shun the ultra-sostenuto motion some conductors use to "pull" a *legato* sound out of a chorus. The "bounce beat" or "stopped beat" is dangerous, too; while it is useful at times, it is limited, for it cannot be used to show an *accelerando* or *decelerando.* It is helpful in syncopated passages, but it should not become a habit.

What the orchestra wants to see is the cleanest, clearest pattern possible. Everything you want must show in the stick, hence the character of the beat changes with the passage being peformed. Practice a variety of motions, each designed to signal a certain character—*legato, marcato,* loud, soft, etc. Many conductors bring their rebounds back to the same spot as the beat itself. Try carrying the rebound in the direction of the next beat; this will keep the pattern clean, while producing a more *legato* sound. And learn to use the horizontal plane more. Most of us overemphasize the vertical plane. (See figure 3.)

You have to get them "on the end of your stick." Make them play *with* you. If they are insecure with you, they may wait, watch the concertmaster, and all attack with him, even though he may not be with you. If this happens, it probably is your fault, and it is likely to stem from inadequate preparatory beats. The players simply are acting defensively, to protect themselves from raggedness.[1]

Conducting *ritards* is one technique many choral conductors really do not have. They coach their choruses into slowing down at certain points, and then

---

1. In a famous example, a renowned twentieth-century composer, appearing as a guest conductor, insisted absent-mindedly on beating *two* in a difficult passage which he himself had written in *three.* The orchestra stood it for as many rehearsals as possible. Then, rebelling, they turned to watch the scroll of the concertmaster's violin, with which the latter beat three as he played. (The aging genius on the podium, nearsighted, never knew what was happening.)

depend on the singers to do it. Orchestras do not work that way. *If you want a ritard, or an accelerando, you will have to conduct it.* Start mentally subdividing about one measure before you are going to change tempo. (The players will see that happen.) Then move the stick gradually slower, and simultaneously increase the size of your beat; at the right moment, begin beating the subdivision. They should follow you. (For an accelerando, just reverse the process.)

Fermatas are quite different with orchestras. Many choral conductors continue to move the beat hand during a *fermata* in order to encourage the choir to maintain breath support and tone quality. This only confuses instrumentalists. With a *fermata,* an orchestra conductor stops until the preparatory beat for the next sound. And remember to watch the orchestra at such moments, as you do the choir, to gauge when the strings are running out of bow, and the winds out of air. (Keep an eye on the concertmaster, and he will let you know.)

Surprisingly, left-hand cutoffs do not work very well with players, because they watch the baton and obey it. *Everything*—again we say it—needs to be shown in the stick.

Watch out for the fringes of the Violins I and the 'cellos. The downstage players see a one-dimensional beat, and there are times when they may not be able to tell your "two" from "three." In dangerous spots, turn the ends of your lateral beats well toward them.

Do not be surprised if you find yourself mirroring the pattern of your stick with the other hand, even though you were taught never to do this. An orchestral environment is different; even if you are right-handed, the Violins I are still on your left, and you may keep a left-hand beat in their faces in touchy spots. In oratorios, too, soloists can get between you and the downstage players. Adjust as necessary to be certain they can see the stick.

Cueing the Players

Singers, who are given scores which display all the vocal parts, do not really count measures of rests. They learn the music, and come to know exactly when they are to attack again. Orchestra players see only their own parts, and *they really do count measures.* Especially is this true of the wind and percussion players, who may have hundreds of measures to count—and count accurately. For this reason, it is very reassuring to them if you cue them for important entrances, particularly after long periods of rest.

Just as left-hand cutoffs are not so effective with players as with singers, left-hand cues are less apt to be seen. Make more cues with your stick hand. In difficult spots, the size and nature of the gesture used can affect the result, but in other cases—to reassure the trumpets when they return after a hundred measures out, for example—a glance at them may be enough. (You probably will find them looking at you, hoping they have counted acccurately, and appreciative of your reassuring nod.) Use nothing less than a big, baton-hand thrust for important, risky entrances, however—especially for crucial cymbal crashes and timpani rolls!

If you raise your left hand to signal a soft passage, be careful not to leave it hanging there in midair. Such gestures tend to make the string players restrict their arms and shorten their bow strokes, which takes richness away from their tone. Be sure you mean what you signal.

In a fugue, it is not necessary to cue every new attack someplace in the orchestra or chorus. Do prepare yourself to designate entrances of the subject and any countersubjects (in order to help make the texture clear), and watch out for dangerous or unusual attacks.

Finally, in every gesture you plan to make, work to be economical. Use just what is both needed and clear. Every unnecessary motion risks a moment of confusion.

5   Rehearsing the Orchestra

Before you walk into the first orchestra rehearsal, be certain you have planned carefully what you hope to accomplish during the session. Time the movements you intend to rehearse, and allow something extra for drilling the difficult passages. Then try to stay on schedule. It may surprise you how much work can be done, even in the last five minutes of the rehearsal, if you know exactly what you want to achieve.

If the members of your orchestra are unionized, be sure you know the local rules about rehearsal duration, length and location of breaks, and related matters. Find out who calls the orchestra back to its seats at the end of each break. Watch the clock closely during the last part of each rehearsal, too; running over schedule with a chorus may not be serious, but it can cost a great deal of money for overtime with a union orchestra.

It is customary, if it does not disrupt the continuity of the work, to release players who are not needed. Chart the use of woodwinds, brasses, and percussion prior to the rehearsal to determine if any of them are tacet in one or more movements. If it is practical to do so, then, begin the rehearsal with the movements or works which require the entire orchestra; continue later to those movements or works which use fewer players, excusing unneeded instrumentalists as you proceed. Nothing is duller than a rehearsal in which you do not participate.

Tuning

Be certain you allow time for the players to tune. There is a protocol here, and—except with the youngest student orchestras—you are excluded from it. The concertmaster is in charge; he calls for an A from the first oboe, and then invites the instrumental families to tune to that A, one body at a time. Usually the woodwinds come first, then the brasses, the strings, and the whole orchestra together.

There are exceptional circumstances, of course. For example, if the work at hand includes no oboe, the first trumpet may give the pitch. If a keyboard instrument is scored—piano, organ, harpsichord—it serves as the source of the A (for its intonation is fixed).

The tuning process is always a compromise. The strings generally want the pitch higher (they usually say "brighter") while the winds want to keep the pitch down. Sometimes real friction results. (European orchestras, by the way, usually tune higher than American ones. Some years back, a famed soprano refused to appear any longer with one of the major Continental orchestras, saying: "If they want me to sing high C-sharps, instead of C-naturals, they must pay me for C-sharps.")

First Reading

Give them an uninterrupted first hearing of each movement, with no stops at all, if possible. (If you know of points at which you fear they might really break down—tempo changes, meter or key shifts, tricky passages, etc.—warn them before you begin.) Let them have a chance to see the whole movement, and to make and recognize their own mistakes. Don't leave anything out —not even the obvious accompanimental passages. Let them try everything.

Then go back and rehearse spots as necessary. Give them a chance—remembering this is just their second opportunity—to correct the mistakes they made the first time. Encourage them to drill the technically difficult passages on their own. Work to help them sightread well, for they need this skill in their profession.

Remember to bring the choir into rehearsal as soon as that is practical. Many things about the work will be clearer to the orchestra once they hear the singers. It is wasteful, in fact, to try to do too much without them.

Talking: What to Say, and What to Avoid

The first rule for working with an orchestra may be this one: *don't talk much!* In the beginning, it is a good idea just to walk up and start into the music. Do not take time to say how happy you are to be there, or what a wonderful piece of music this is. Simply tell them whether you are beating it in 3 or in 1.

"Pep talks" get you nothing in an orchestra rehearsal. Players care little (at the moment) about biography, history, analysis, and such subjects. As Robert Shaw (who knows a lot about both choirs and orchestras) sometimes says: "Orchestra players don't want to know about musicology; they just want you to tell them whether you want the passage faster or slower, or louder or softer."

Orchestras hate to be stopped, especially in the middle of a major section of the movement. (This is a *basic* difference, for many choral conductors make a regular practice of pausing almost phrase-by-phrase for repairs.) Constant stopping messes up the orchestra's basic rehearsal process, interrupting their checking of markings, and causing them to lose any sense of continuity through the movement. Most of the errors you hear will be repaired without your having to stop for them, anyway, and many of the corrections you want to make can be made later, at an appropriate moment. Cultivate the ability to remember these criticisms; collect them, and deliver them all at once.

Do not stop, then, unless you have a very good reason; if you must, explain *quickly* why you have done so, call out a rehearsal letter, and begin again.[1] Be careful not to let the rehearsal lose its momentum.

---

1. At least one well-known conductor manages rehearsals without using rehearsal-letters or measure-numbers. Working with professional players in a first-rank orchestra, he finishes his instructions,

Beware, too, of repeating passages without cause. If you must go over something a second time, give the players a clear reason for doing so. They need to know what you expect them to do differently.

Remember that many of the corrections you want to make, particularly in the strings, can be communicated through the principals. If you hold such matters until a break—changes of bowing, for example—these revisions can be made during the break itself, saving you important rehearsal time.

By the way, while you are striving to avoid unnecessary talk, you will catch the players chattering among themselves—while they are playing, and while you are talking. Don't scold them! They are catching and correcting wrong notes, checking bowings and string crossings, and fixing other details, in keeping with standard orchestra rehearsal tradition. Be glad for this: every item they correct is something that you will not have to fix yourself. (You may come to wish that your chorus worked out details as efficiently as your orchestra does.)

How much should a conductor say to strings about technical matters? Choral conductors routinely talk to their choirs about choice of vowels, emphasis on consonants, amount of vibrato, choices of tone color, breath support, and other technical considerations. Should you instruct your string players about the length and speed of the bow, about the *portamento* (sliding the finger on the string, in order to connect two pitches with a Romantic effect), or about the amount of *vibrato* they use, for example?

If we choral conductors stood in front of an orchestra as often as we stand before choruses, we would feel both competent and confident about discussing every performance detail—*vibrato* and all.[2] The amount of technical instruction you need to offer depends largely on the experience and stature of the players, of course. With younger instrumentalists you must expect to tell them a great deal; at the same time, you may want to grant them more freedom to experiment with these matters, showing them the shape of the piece and the outlines of the style they are learning to express. With older players you may be more explicit.

You can expect all players, however—whatever their age and experience—to suffer lapses of energy during long rehearsals. Call them back to full concentration by making them listen to themselves. When you ask the strings to "sing," for example, you will find they start heeding tonal quality again; they become more careful about their *vibrato*, more aware of bow speed and length, and even more precise about pitch. With experienced players, such subjective criticism may be more productive than detailed technical commentary.

A word about the Violins II: generally they are weaker players, by definition, and their responsibilities often are less demanding than those of the Violins I. They may go through a lot of music without playing alone as a section, and then—suddenly—after all the accompanimental passages, find themselves con-

---

sings a phrase some measures earlier in the movement, and gives a downbeat at a logical moment. They know the music well enough to follow his singing and begin. Few amateur or student orchestras could do this.

2. We already have suggested that you visit orchestra rehearsals before you take up the baton, learning the language they employ.

fronted with a really difficult, important line. *Treat them in every rehearsal as important players*—just as important as the Violins I—by calling attention to the passages they are playing. Build up a relationship with them. Enhance their morale.

There is one circumstance in which confidence and strength in the Violin II section can be crucial to you: composers often begin important fugal passages with them (as in the fast section of the "Et vitam venturi" in Beethoven's *Missa Solemnis* and in the last movement of the Brahms *Piano Concerto No. 1 in D Minor*), saving the first violins for the climactic entrance later. Because the seconds lack confidence, and because they may not produce as big a sound as the Violins I, you may need to ask them to play at least one full dynamic marking louder than what is marked.

Prestige is a factor with the whole orchestra, too. Be certain the players understand that you respect their responsibilities; if you give them the impression that they are only accompanists—that your real interest is in the soloists and the chorus, and that the players are only accessories—they will respond dully, if not sullenly. Let them see that they are important to you. Make them feel they are equal partners with the singers.

Balance Problems

Because they are not accustomed to the sound, and misjudge it, 90 percent of choral conductors facing an orchestra for the first time think the instrumentalists are playing too loud. Balance problems do occur, especially in early rehearsals, but many of them seem to cure themselves before the performance. Consider the following before you either change the dynamic markings, or begin to cut down the number of players:

1. It is healthy for the orchestra to play louder in the beginning, when they are sightreading. (Most choirs do not sightread well at *pianissimo*, either.) Avoid constantly hushing them. They will respond better once they know the work. Go back into the hall, then, about the third time through a danger spot, and listen for balance; by that time, there may be no problem. *First get ensemble, and then strive for dynamics.*
2. Anticipate, however, that the reverse may happen. Growing more confident, and anxious to contribute to the concert, the orchestra may begin to "play out" during the performance itself. *Be alert to balance throughout the concert,* and react to any unexpected changes in dynamics. The players should respond quickly at that point.
3. Remember that *the violin mute is not to be used to solve balance problems* (any more than is the trumpet mute). Mutes are devices for changing timbre, not loudness; they are ancient contrivances, and since they were known to Haydn, Mozart, Beethoven, and the others you can assume their scores would have been marked *con sordino,* had they wanted mutes employed!
4. You may reduce the number of string players in a given passage, if that

proves necessary. If you do so, always take the front desks (not one-on-a-stand), for they are the stronger players. In more drastic cases, cut to either one player per section or three; never take two. Three will blend better, while two will clash. And remember that one-on-a-part changes the timbre, because the individual's vibrato is heard more clearly. One person playing *mezzo forte* is a different sound than four people playing *piano*.

5. Understand that *there are places where the orchestra is intended by the composer to dominate the chorus and soloists,* just as the reverse can be true. Let the players have their climactic tutti, when it occurs.

6. Balance problems may be caused by wrong playing. You may need to correct bowings; players may need to "lift a little"—to shorten notes. They may need to conceive the passage as lighter in articulation than they thought.

7. Consider that not all balance problems are the fault of the orchestra—not by any means. (Your high-priced soprano soloist may be loafing in the Kyrie, saving herself for the demands of the Agnus Dei, and its high B-flats.) *Using immature singers against experienced, mature players can cause imbalances.* (This is often the basic problem when professional players are hired to appear with a student choir.) *Be careful you do not force your orchestra to play softer than it can play beautifully.*

8. With respect to balances within the orchestra, you should know that it is perfectly permissible to double the winds in certain instances. (Many famous conductors have done so.) If you are not hearing enough of the first flute, add the second to it. (This problem occurs often in Beethoven, for example, because we use more strings in modern orchestras than he had available; melodies in the winds can be drowned by a vast string sound.)

9. When you rehearse in a performance hall, *have an assistant check balance for you all the time.*

Preparing the Chorus for Orchestra Rehearsals

Choruses are accustomed to detailed, loving attention. They expect to be shown every nuance *every time* by the conductor. The trouble is that a major oratorio is a more complex work than an Italian madrigal, and the conductor has more performers to coordinate.

You cannot devote full time to your choir in a choral/orchestral performance, as you would in an *a cappella* concert. No conductor can, or should. The choir must take more responsibility for themselves, and you need to prepare them for that circumstance. The following considerations are especially important ones:

1. Train them to total the number of beats in very long notes, and to mark cutoffs in their choral scores. They should deliver releases (and final consonants) together without depending on a signal from you.

2. Drill them on attacks. They should be ready to enter on time, without a cue. (You may be busy stemming some pending disaster in the orchestra right at that moment.)
3. *Double the dynamic level of the consonants.* (They can learn to sing the vowels softly and still articulate the consonants loudly, where necessary.) Move really important consonants off the beat, if possible; orchestral attacks on the beat will obscure the choir's diction.
4. Be certain they understand the dynamics expected of them, and that they take responsibility for maintaining the proper dynamic levels.
5. Point out danger spots throughout the work, and prepare them *defensively* to respond to problems that may arise—and as much on their own initiative as possible.

When you first bring the chorus and orchestra together, you may want to ignore the chorus. (Warn them beforehand that this may happen.) They likely are overtrained anyway. Leaving them to fend for themselves causes them to listen to the orchestra and to realize how important some of the orchestral music is; it also helps them understand that they must be responsible for their own performance, with less help from you than usual. By giving full attention to the orchestra, at the same time, you reassure the players that they are *not* of secondary importance in your mind, and that you will give consideration to their needs during the performance, as well as to those of the choir. This procedure can bring into balance the best energies and attitudes of the entire force in front of you.

Now you are ready to tackle one of the greatest works of music.

Part Two: *Conducting Three Baroque Masterworks*

6   Studying the Scores

Each of the Baroque masterworks we analyze in the chapters which follow is accessible to choirs and orchestras of standard size and instrumentation. Each is introduced in this handbook with a brief recollection of the circumstances of its composition. Details are provided to you about its place in the career of its composer, about its early performances, and about the forces employed on those occasions. Information about editions currently available is included also, along with commentary on performance practice.

Then follows a careful discussion of each movement of the work at hand, with emphasis given particularly to bowing decisions. Moving bar by bar, wherever necessary, we proceed through the work, pausing to examine performance alternatives at important points of decision. Special attention is given to handling the "seams"—the important transition points within (and between) movements.

Use of technical language in these analyses has been held to a practical minimum; some is necessary, of course, and for that reason a glossary has been included.[1] With all this help, you can feel well prepared to face your orchestra.

Elements of Baroque Performance Practice

In the eighteenth century important writings by Johann Joachim Quantz, Carl Phillip Emanuel Bach, Leopold Mozart, and Johann Mattheson, among others, delineated the characteristics of standard performance practice in the Late Baroque and Rococo periods. In recent years there has been a wave of new research on the same topic. If you want to make a detailed study of these matters, you will find good modern translations of the historic sources available, and you might gain especially important insights from books and articles written during the past two decades; among the latter, see the Veilhan, Babitz, Neumann, Monosoff, Donington, and Rothschild writings particularly.[2]

One concept stands out sharply from all this historic and modern literature: *no fine performance of a Baroque masterpiece will or should sound exactly like any other presentation of the same work.* Like good jazz, each Baroque performance is a unique one, for a great many options are conceded to the conductor and the performers; the forces chosen, the kinds of keyboard instruments, the choice of bass instruments, the bowings of the strings, the distribution of solo lines, the division of chorus movements between concertists and full choir, the realization

---

1. The glossary can be found on pp. 189 ff.
2. All these are listed in the bibliography.

of the continuo part, the embellishments added to solo lines, the tempos selected, the use of ritards—all these and more are within the province of the performers. Let us address these variables one by one.

The "Basso Continuo"

One of the unique features of Baroque style is the ubiquitous linkage of a keyboard instrument with one or more string and/or wind instruments; this *basso continuo* unit provides a harmonic and rhythmic foundation under the melodic lines in the upper levels of the texture. In the historic sources, all the notes to be played by these instruments were implied only by a given bass part, supplemented by numerical chord symbols. The process of choosing and shaping this shorthand into interesting and effective musical lines was called "realization," and it meant that the keyboard player, particularly, was responsible for improvising solutions appropriate to the signals given him in the rather limited notation.

For *Messiah*, by way of example, we know that the written bass line would generally be covered by 'celli (probably not more than four), together with one or more contrabasses (or *violone*, as they might have been called in that era). Handel specifically asks for a bassoon, too, which (1) gives the line more of a singing quality, because it obligates the low strings to match their phrasing to the breathing of the bassoon, (2) lends more focus to the continuo line by making its timbre more distinctive, and (3) connects that bass line's timbre to that of the upper winds, in a choir effect.

In such circumstances, unless the specific uses for the bassoon have been marked on the original score, the conductor must decide what combinations of bass instruments to employ at various points in the work. For any given movement or distinct, discrete section, he might conceivable choose to employ (1) bassoon alone, (2) 'celli alone, (3) a single 'cello, (4) bassoon and 'celli, (5) 'celli and contrabass(es), (6) bassoon and contrabass(es), or (7) all these forces together. (In the style, it is unlikely, however, that he would choose to use contrabass alone.) Handel has stipulated some of these choices in *Messiah;* the second movement is marked *senza fagotto,* for example, while the third begins with the indication *con fagotto* (even though *no other woodwind is used for this aria*). In the case of J. S. Bach's recitatives, on the other hand, we find—though we know he also used 'cellos, bassoons, and *violone*—he did not specify what continuo forces he wished employed. In short, the conductor has a reasoned authority over this aspect of orchestration in many Baroque works, and can use that power to reinforce his own structural and expressive concepts.

As to the keyboard component of the *basso continuo,* we have another set of choices to make—especially these days, when the revived interest in antique instruments and in reproductions of famous ones broadens our contemporary alternatives. These options deserve your careful consideration, for the *core* of the orchestral sound in Baroque music is the continuo keyboard. With the exception of measures in which the melody in the upper part(s) stands quite alone, with *no* bass notes indicated below it, there is no point in this music at which the keyboard can be omitted without detriment to balance, timbre, and style. Such an omission would produce a misrepresentation of the composer's harmonic intentions in some cases, and in virtually all passages it would mean loss or distortion of the essential color of the Baroque orchestra.

For many sacred works of the Baroque era, the organ was the only intended keyboard instrument; nevertheless, there is solid historical evidence that many performances employed *both* organ and harpsichord. One scholar has called attention to church ledgers which cite fees for providing and tuning a harpsichord.[3] The great J. S. Bach's own son wrote:

> The organ is indispensable in church music with its fugues, large choruses, and sustained style. It provides splendor and maintains order. However, in all recitatives and arias in this [churchly] style . . . a harpsichord must be used.[4]

Many modern performances do employ harpsichord *and* organ. The conductor with both instruments available has many more good orchestrational choices, for (1) the harpsichord can be used alone—for intimacy—in recitatives and arias, (2) the organ—or both instruments—can be assigned to choral passages, and (3) either can serve for brief, coloristic interpretational effects. The historical use of both instruments can be confirmed in many cases; such a practice offers great possibilities for timbral contrasts, and thus can enhance the sound of your performances.

The Organ

For many Baroque works, then—especially cantatas and oratorios—one may choose to use an organ. Again, however, you must concern yourself with timbre and balance. The giant instruments available in many American and European churches these days have little in common with their Baroque ancestors, and are capable of overpowering your entire ensemble. Where can you turn?

1. There are Baroque instruments available, with lower wind pressure and so-called "tracker action." Beyond the legitimacy of their timbres, these have the advantage of some portability (for which reason their ancestors were called "portatives"), which means you can place them where you want them—inside your ensemble, for example, rather than dealing with the distance factor implicit in the use of most large church organs.

2. Such authentic instruments are not immediately at hand in most cities, however, nor are they inexpensive to obtain. If you cannot get access to one, a more practical solution may be available to you: locate a good, flexible, modern organ in an appropriate church or auditorium; a competent organist can find a successful "registration" (choice of stops) to represent the Baroque timbre you seek.

---

3. Robert Donington, *A Performer's Guide to Baroque Music*, p. 235.
4. W. J. Mitchell, *Essay on the True Art of Playing Keyboard Instruments*, p. 172.

In addition to supervising somewhat the choice of registration, you may need to caution your organist not to forget the *silences* which are important to clean articulation. Finer organists understand this well, and will articulate as cleanly as artful singers or orchestral players; less experienced musicians in *any* medium may tend to sustain sonorities too long, producing "muddy" textures.

The Harpsichord

For recitatives, arias, duets, and the like, the use of a harpsichord will help you obtain the characteristic Baroque timbre, balance, and improvisational ornamentation. Your first consideration will be to find a skilled player. (Remember that not every pianist has adequate experience on the harpsichord.) If you have such a musician at hand, have you alternative instruments available to you? How should you choose the appropriate one? (Not all of them are alike, of course.)

1. Try to determine what would have been used in the same historical period, rather than turning to a harpsichord from another era. (Thinking of *Messiah* again, as an example, we know that Handel's own harpsichord was built by Johannes Rückers, of Antwerp, in 1612; it was willed by the master to J. C. Smith, Sr., and given by his son to George III. Restored about 1885, it is now on loan to the Benton Fletcher Collection in Hampstead, England. While a knowledge of this instrument tells us nothing about the keyboards actually used for early *Messiah* performances, it does make clear what sort of instrument was "in Handel's ear" at the time he composed the work.) Even if the harpsichord you must employ has little in common with the historically-appropriate type, the research you do will give you a clearer idea of how your performance should sound.

2. Many kinds of harpsichords—and many very good ones—are available these days. In general, depending on what you learn of the composer's intentions, models with two keyboards are advantageous, even if only an "eight-foot stop" (a set of strings sounding the *notated* pitches) is provided for each of these "manuals." A "coupler"—a device which causes both sets of strings to sound together when either manual is played—is of great value to you for balance, and so is a "four-foot stop" (which sounds an octave above the notated pitches).[5] Finally, a "lute stop" (which dampens and shortens each of the notes, causing them to sound lute-like) can work well for some recitative work, and for sections for which you need a special timbre.

A *good* harpsichord will have resonance which makes it capable of easily balancing a small orchestra. A poorly-built commercial instrument (or one made

---

5. Also available are "sixteen-foot stops" (sounding an octave *below* the notated pitch), but these are less likely to be stylistic.

badly from one of the kits on the market) may lack carrying power. If you have nothing better available—or in circumstances where you *must* use a larger choir than would have been employed historically—it is possible to utilize more than one harpsichord; be careful about their tuning, however, and be certain the players know which of them is to be responsible for ornamentation.

Harpsichords lack the enormously strong bridge which holds the tuning pins of the piano. As a consequence, the harpsichord does not "hold pitch" as long or as consistently across its range as does its modern cousin. When using a harpsichord, seek a player who can tune it; it is not practical to keep a professional tuner-technician on call to adjust the instrument (between works during the concert, in fact, if need be). The stage lights should be turned on, if possible, before the harpsichord is tuned (to the organ, if one is to be used), and they should be left lit until the performance, for changes in ambient temperature will immediately affect harpsichord strings, just as they do the violins and oboes. The pre-concert tuning should take place at the last discreet moment before the performance, of course. Be certain the instrument is tuned to standard pitch (if you have a choice), for—if it is set low—it will give the strings and winds great difficulties.

The Clavichord

A third (and less likely) possibility for your keyboard choice is this ancient instrument—one which uses brass "tangents" to strike the strings (instead of the felt hammers of the modern piano, or the plectra which pluck the strings of the harpsichord). Even the best clavichord produces such a small tone, however, that you may find it will not balance the modern orchestral instruments with which it must compete.

Realization of the Keyboard Part

As we have said, the written continuo part, as it appeared in a Baroque score, consisted only of a bass line and a scattering of figured-bass numerals and signs. The ability to read these symbols and to translate them into "realized" harmonies was considered one of the primary duties of a keyboard player in that period (and long thereafter). Nor was this process of "filling-out" these harmonies a routine one: the tradition left the player *free to create*—to improvise, in fact—an original part, complete with choices of chord spacing, thickness of texture, rhythmic articulation, and melodic embellishment, *within the limits imposed by the figured-bass symbols and the given bass line.*

Some modern editions (which reflect the fact that few contemporary pianists are required to develop these techniques) print realizations—sometimes in small notes—designed by the editor. Whether your keyboard player has such a printed solution available or not, however, you may be certain that *the Baroque tradition both intends and demands that the music he plays* (so long as it conforms to the limits set by that original continuo part) *should be fresh and original, and should vary somewhat, in fact, at each rehearsal and performance.* Permit us to put it even more bluntly: *to bind the keyboard player to some stipulated realization is to violate the spirit of this music.* As we said early in this chapter, no fine performance of a Baroque masterpiece will or should sound exactly like any other presentation of the work.

There is a somewhat limited number of fine harpsichordists and organists who are skilled in these disciplines, and it may be that you can obtain one; that would be the optimal situation. Any good player, with practice, can develop these abilities, however, as did our ancestors.

Beyond simply filling-out the indicated harmonies, there are a number of considerations:

1. One is voice-leading. Good realizations tend to be contrapuntal in character, displaying good melodic practice in each voice. Simply providing chords in quarter- and half-notes is not musical.
2. Another is registration. The player must decide what harmonic notes are to appear in a given octave—or are to be doubled into more than one octave—at any given moment. How thick is the texture to be? How wide the spacing?
3. A third has to do with wit and imagination. "Madrigalisms"—those musical figures which picture the text (melodic lines which descend, as portrayals of Christ's interment in the tomb, ascending arpeggios which picture His resurrection, and the like)—are legitimately part of the style of the period, and of the responsibility of the continuo player. To create them, the player must know something of the text, of course.
4. And there is embellishment. To play an undecorated line, we are told, is like serving a birthday cake devoid both of candles and icing. Some ornaments are merely decorative, coming in the midst of the music; others are structural: penultimate trills and arpeggios have much to do with the manipulation of tempo and meter as one approaches important cadence points and ends of movements, for example.[6]

Soloists: The Concertino and the Ripieno

Throughout Baroque music, composers call for alternations of a full ensemble with one or more soloists. In the *concerto grosso,* the former is called the *ripieno* or *tutti,* while the latter is the *concertino.* (Both these elements are supported, of course, by the *basso continuo* section we have been discussing.) This same principle—the juxtaposing of small and large forces—penetrates other Baroque forms and textures, as well. Often, however, this alternation was not marked in the score, and we must make our own judgments about it, determining what editing would be stylistic.

---

6. Baroque ornamentation is much too elaborate a topic for further consideration here. The reader should refer to the Bibliography and to other sources for additional information and instruction in this area.

Where the alternation *is* clearly marked, as it is in the second movement of *Messiah* (note the *senza ripieno, con ripieno,* etc., for the orchestra), the conductor must decide how many players—one or more a part—are to constitute the *concertino,* defining thereby a clear contrast against the full ensemble, the *tutti.*

Where this alternation is suspected, but *not* marked, you may choose to edit the parts, knowing that this was an accepted practice in the period. Given ensemble size, the acoustics in the hall, the amount of preparation time available to you, the proficiency of your singers and players, and the apparent value of textural contrast in the work, you can make decisions regarding the points at which these exchanges are to take place. In conceptual terms, one can say that the most virtuosic passages and those written as accompaniment for individual soloists could have been intended for concertists; beyond this broad generality, one must study and deal with specific cases.

As all this implies, Baroque soloists—including singers—were not so distinct from their surrounding ensembles as they became by the time of Liszt, Joachim, and Jenny Lind. This means you have wide latitude with respect to placement of the soloists. In some works, you may wish to stand your "vocal concertists" in the midst of your choir, as would have been done in the choirs of Baroque churches. In other cases, you may want a more standard sort of separation.

Realization by the Concertists

Although Baroque composers did not leave to individual chorus and orchestra members the sort of creative opportunities they gave to their keyboard players, the concertists do have similar responsibilities with respect to ornamentation. Embellishment was a primary feature of solo singing and playing in that period, as it is in jazz today. An *authentic* performance of Baroque repertoire nowadays must include ornamentation which is *improvised,* rather than routine; yet the ease of expression required to freely improvise embellishments, which comes reasonably quickly to some instrumentalists, is not part of the training of most modern singers. Here are some suggestions which may help both singers and players:

1. Encourage them to listen to good performers who employ ornaments.
2. Admire their early efforts, no matter how clumsy or inappropriate they seem, for this will help them conquer their inhibitions.
3. Start asking for ornaments from your concertists at the outset of your rehearsal schedule—not at the final dress rehearsal.
4. Insist that they vary the ornaments they use from day to day, and case to case. For *da capo* arias and similar forms, expect that they *embellish the repeated section differently the second time.*
5. Make certain that your instrumental concertists understand that their embellishments are just as important as those of the singers.
6. Don't give up! This technique, seemingly so foreign to our time, does not seem so difficult when one considers that every "pop" musician

learns to do these things. The rest of us must conquer our intimidation, or we will remain too bound to the notation to perform Baroque music with the imagination and freedom intended for it by the greatest of its composers.

Accompanying the Recitatives

The most obvious passages in Baroque music in which freedom and spontaneity are of critical importance are the recitatives, of course. Ideally, they would not be conducted, but would have the character of chamber music—soloists, keyboard, and bass working together in unity of motion and phrase. (Remember that the conductor would most likely have been at the keyboard himself in that era.) Train your colleagues to manage without you, if you can. If the musicians lack sufficient experience to handle all the recitatives without a conductor (or if there is not enough preparation time available to put the soloists and continuo players at ease with each other), you will have to conduct these passages.

In either circumstance, your principal duty is to pace and balance the accompaniment so that the words of the text are given the clearest and most expressive presentation possible. The singer must be at liberty—within the limits of good taste—to vary speed from phrase to phrase, and note to note.

In a sense, the recitative form combines a simple regularity within the continuo body with an irregularity and flexibility in the singer. Contemporary sources are quite clear on this point:

> . . . in the recitatives of Italians . . . the beat is often not very regular because it is a kind of declamation in which the actor must *follow the movement of the emotion which agitates him, which he wishes to express* more than [he does] an equal and regular measure.[7]

Not all recitatives are the same, but—as Carl Philipp Emanuel Bach notes—sharp concentration is still essential on the parts of the conductor and the continuo players:

> Some recitatives, in which the bass and perhaps other instruments express a definite theme or a continuous motion which does not share in the singer's pauses, must be performed strictly in time for the sake of good order. Others are declaimed now slowly, now rapidly according to the content, regardless of the meter, even though their notation be barred. In both cases, especially the latter, an accompanist must be watchful. He must listen constantly to the principal performer, and when there is action, watch him as well, so that his accompaniment will always be ready; he must never desert the singer.[8]

So flexibility for the sake of the text is fundamental in the recitative, yet, at the same time, the orchestra must know exactly what you and the singer(s)

---

7. Sebastien de Brossard, *Dictionaire de Musique,* under the entry "Largo," p. 44. (Italics added.)
8. W. J. Mitchell, cited earlier, p. 420.

want, on a moment-to-moment basis. Here the preparatory beats discussed in chapter 4[9] are vital. Traditionally, of course, whole measures of rest for the orchestra are "wasted" with a single downbeat. (You even may deliver quickly two or three of these, where several bars of rest occur.) This is done, however, only when the entire orchestra is tacet, including the *basso continuo,* and that rarely happens in Baroque music. Generally, you will find yourself conducting every beat of each measure, using very small beats for moments when the players are sustaining long notes, or resting, and then delivering larger preparatory beats for isolated chords or fresh attacks.

Practice such passages extensively and carefully. If you are well prepared, the players will wait for your cues, no matter what else happens (an early entrance from a soloist, for example). Security and trust between you and the orchestra can save a serious situation at such moments.

By convention, the final chords of recitatives (and sometimes of sections within recitatives) can be delayed—for the sake of clarity—until after the singer has reached the cadence, even though the notation may indicate a simultaneous cadence for singer and orchestra.[10] Be certain that all affected know exactly what to expect in such spots.

A word also about the durations of keyboard chords in recitatives: there is ample evidence that a case like "Behold, a virgin shall conceive" would have been performed with *short* chords in the keyboard part, instead of the half- and whole-notes indicated. We have, for proof of this theory, the testimony of no less an authority than C. P. E. Bach (who must have known his great father's practices):

> In recitatives with sustained accompanying instruments, the organ holds only the bass, *the chords being quitted soon after they are struck.* Organs are seldom purely tuned, with the result that held chords, which are often chromatic in such recitatives, would sound ugly and disagree with the other accompanying instruments. It is often difficult in such a case to make an orchestra . . . sound in pitch.[11]

While C. P. E. Bach is speaking here of *recitativo accompagnato,* we know that the same principle applied to *secco* recitative. Johann Samuel Petri, writing in 1767, advises the same procedure ("the notes must be taken off short"), though the bass may be held, as may some of the chords, since releasing all of them quickly can sound too dry.[12] "Just how long each chord should be sustained," says Arthur Mendel in the introduction to his edition of Bach's *St. John Passion,* "must be left to the individual interpreter." And he continues:

> Such a [sustained-chord] style obscures all the narrative interest of the story— which is what recitative was made for—in favor of that stuffy Sunday atmosphere which an irreligious age thinks of as religious, but which is as far as possible from

---

9. See above, p. 35.
10. See the final bar of the recitative "Behold, a virgin shall conceive"—*Messiah,* no. 8—for an instance of this problem.
11. W. J. Mitchell, p. 422. (Italics added.)
12. Robert Donington, p. 235.

the vividness that the Biblical narratives had for such genuinely religious composers as Schütz and Bach. *Nothing will do more to restore that narrative vividness to their works than to play the chords short, and thus leave the Evangelist singing out into a silent church or auditorium. He will feel lonesome at first, and this will lead him to reach out and make a real contact with his listeners,* as any true narrator must, rather than rob the recitative of all its life and pace by merely going through the motions of piously intoning something that in its unending sostenuto is not complete as pure music.[13]

However you decide to treat note lengths in these Baroque recitatives, remember that careful preparation and quick responses are necessary, if you are to keep these marvelous movements from bogging down. Do not regard them as transitions between arias and choruses—transitions to be gotten over as quickly as possible; they offer much of the expressive beauty you are seeking.

Determining Baroque Tempos

Of all our conductorial decisions, tempo choice may be the most difficult and the most important, for it influences planning of phrasing, breathing, bowing, articulation, accentuation, and dynamics, and it affects technical problems, clarity of text, clarity of texture, handling of dissonances and consonances, drama, pace, and overall musical syntax.

There is much to decide. The familiar tempo words (*Allegro, Adagio, Largo,* etc.) were used in the Baroque era in ways we now find misleading and contradictory. Time signatures were in a state of flux after the Renaissance. *Tempo ordinario* was no longer a reliable benchmark. While some sources suggest that Baroque dance tempi can provide us with sure guidelines, it is likely that they are more applicable to choices of tempo for instrumental suites than as influences on oratorios or other vocal works. Even the contemporary writings of the time suggest that there were no certain standards, but that much was left to the judgment and taste of the performers. Leopold Mozart, writing in 1756, advises that tempo must be deduced "from the piece itself, and *this it is by which the true worth of a musician can be recognized without fail.*"[14] And C. P. E. Bach writes:

> The pace of a composition . . . is based on its general content, as well as on the fastest notes and passages contained in it. Due consideration of these factors will prevent an allegro from being rushed and an adagio from being dragged.[15]

Among the factors which can help you determine the tempos you will use in the works that follow this chapter are: (1) the given tempo markings, (2) the time signatures, (3) the fastest note values, (4) the nature of the hall and its

---

13. Arthur Mendel, ed., in his introduction to J. S. Bach, *The St. John Passion,* p. xix. (Italics added.)
14. Editha Knocker, *A Treatise on the Fundamental Principles of Violin Playing,* p. 33.
15. W. J. Mitchell, p. 151.

acoustics, (5) the size of your chorus and orchestra, (6) their technical skills, (7) the character of the music, and (8) the nature of the text.

There usually is a reasonably wide latitude available to us in "choosing the right tempo." Rarely is there a single valid choice for a given movement of a work. Studying the score may lead you to a particular choice, but the performers with whom you work may force you to make adjustments. Ultimately a good tempo should be a mixture of study, good taste, and compromise.

The tempo you intend to use in performance may not be exactly the same as the one you enjoy in rehearsals. Experienced conductors often rehearse a fast tempo slightly slower—or a slow tempo slightly faster—than their eventual performance goal, depending on the intensity and excitement of the concert to help the players sustain the real intention. This may or may not work in your situation, depending on the forces available to you.

Only experience can make you as certain of tempo choices in works with orchestra as you may be of tempi in the *a cappella* repertoire. Just be certain to give as much thought to orchestral considerations—bowings and other instrumental characteristics—as you give to breathing, tessiturae, and other vocal concerns.

Other Rehearsal Considerations

Many American choral conductors give emphasis in programming to Baroque and Classical repertoire. Their choirs are familiar with this literature, and they adapt quickly to new works from these periods.

This is not necessarily the case with instrumentalists. Many orchestras lean heavily on standard nineteenth-century selections, playing on occasion something from the Viennese Classical composers or the contemporary repertoire; as a consequence, though it is startling to us, some orchestra players know surprisingly little about Baroque style. These may tend to perform everything in lush, Romantic character, with long, *legato* bows and a lot of *vibrato;* often they overplay the *tutti* passages.

The concept of "space" within Baroque lines (about which we will have something to say in coming chapters) could be new to them. If this is the case, you may want to try a special rehearsal approach:

1. You will have to go in with your own ideas. Plan carefully what you are going to do, and what music you will use.
2. Let them play one movement of the work at hand in a Romantic fashion, lush *vibrato* and all.
3. Quickly point out the limited number of articulation marks in use in this score. (For Bach or Handel, slurs, dots, and wedges may be the only ones employed.) Define how much space you want, if any, in each case.
4. Then have all of them play one line in unison, clearing up any uncertainties (and any "muddiness" at the same time).

5. Insist that they maintain these standards as you proceed.

This should give your players a clear aural image of the sort of Baroque sound you favor. From this point on, make certain that a sharp visual image of what you want is coming out of the tip of your baton.

Now to the music.

7 G. F. Handel: *Messiah*

It has become legend that Handel composed *Messiah*[1] in just three weeks in late August and September of 1741, working rapidly through a libretto of scriptural passages chosen and woven together by Charles Jennens. The first performances took place in Dublin in April of 1742 and in London in March of the following year. More-or-less regular presentations of it continued during Handel's lifetime; his last public appearance, we are told, was as conductor and *continuo*-player—blind, at that—for a *Messiah* performance on April 6, 1759, just eight days before his death.

Although the work came to tower over all his other achievements in the minds of audiences, *Messiah* was neither Handel's first oratorio (*Saul* and *Israel in Egypt* both date from 1739), nor was it culminative, for he wrote a dozen more such works over the following decade. Handel had been a professional composer for thirty-five years at the time he created *Messiah,* and—even if his oratorio design was a new one—he had been writing recitatives, arias, choruses, and overtures all that time. It should not surprise us, then, that *Messiah* is a mature work, but that he wrote all of it in only three weeks verges on the astonishing, especially in the light of the consistent greatness of the writing; one can see that his imagination did not flag.

This is not to say that every note in it was brand new. Like other composers of his time, Handel borrowed ideas (and sometimes whole, complex movements) liberally from music of his own and of contemporaries; some of the most famous Handelian passages have prior sources.[2] ("For unto us a child is born," for example, is a revision of a secular Italian duet he had written years earlier, and for other purposes.[3] The technical term for this practice—which had no tinge in that era of the moral burden borne by the modern-day word "plagiarism"—is "parody," as any student of Renaissance masses knows.)

The impact of *Messiah* is not to be doubted. Two hundred years ago, Dr. Burney was already writing:

> This great work has been heard in all parts of the kingdom with increasing reverence and delight; it has fed the hungry, clothed the naked, fostered the orphan and

---

1. The reader should remember that *Messiah* is the full title of the work, not—as one so frequently hears—"The Messiah."
2. For a detailed exposition of Handel's borrowing from himself and from others, see Sedley Taylor, *The Indebtedness of Handel to Works by Other Composers.*
3. The original sources of four great *Messiah* choruses can be found in G. F. Händel *Werke*, vol. 32, pp. 116 and 122, and in Edition #6455, C. F. Peters; nos. 1a and 1b became "His Yoke is Easy and His Burden is Light" and "And He Shall Purify," while nos. 2a and 2b became "For Unto Us a Child is Born" and "All We Like Sheep."

enriched succeeding managers of Oratories more than any single musical production in this or any other country.[4]

In our era Burney would have been able to add the names of Haydn, Mozart, Beethoven, Brahms, and many lesser figures to those whom this masterwork has moved.

Choosing Performance Forces

If it is relatively easy to judge with certainty today that a particular score "*is* the Brahms *Symphony No. 4 in E Minor*," it is not so simple to say the same thing about *Messiah*. We know by existing manuscripts from the 1741–59 era that Handel himself modified movements of the work as he performed it (especially in order to adapt it, one suspects, to the strengths and weaknesses of the individual soloists he employed over that span). Watkins Shaw writes in the introductory pages of his edition that "we depart entirely from the spirit of his performance if, year after year, we follow a rigidly unchanging assignment of numbers to the customary solo quartet."[5] (Thus the demanding melismas of "For He is like a refiner's fire" may legitimately be assigned to a contralto, a counter-tenor, or even a bass.)

We may be rather more arbitrary about the choir and orchestra. Even in Handel's last years a chorus of 50 was a spectacle, and—more typically—he performed *Messiah* with choirs of two dozen or so. Thus when Bernard Shaw attended an 1891 Handel Festival at which a chorus of 3500 and an orchestra of 500 were employed, he was on firm ground in deriding those who were

> . . . listening to the fiercely tumultuous "He trusted in God," with its alternations of sullen mockery with high-pitched derision, and its savage shouts of "Let Him deliver Him, if He delight in Him," jogging along at about half the proper speed, with an expression of the deepest respect and propriety, as if a large body of the leading citizens, headed by the mayor, were presenting a surpassingly dull address to somebody.[6]

There has been a lot of this with Handel—overblown, pretentious efforts to magnify Handel's music without trusting that it will make manifest its inherent power.[7] Whatever one may say about enormous forces for *Messiah*, one cannot say they were part of Handel's own experience.

One must judge in each case, then, how the size of the choir and orchestra,

---

4. Dr. Charles Burney, *A General History of Music*.
5. Watkins Shaw, in the prefatory passage "Allocation of Solo Work" in his edition *Messiah, a Sacred Oratorio*.
6. George Bernard Shaw, in a concert review written on July 1, 1891, found today in *Music in London 1890–1894*, vol. 1, p. 232.
7. Robert Shaw himself, describing his concept of *Messiah* as a chamber work, confesses to having contributed to the ponderous image with reference to "That grandest of 'Hallelujahs' (which—horrors!—I once conducted with five thousand voices in one of our country's leading livestock arenas . . .)" in Klaus George Roy's liner notes for the revolutionary and influential recording by the Robert Shaw Chorale and Orchestra. See *Handel's Messiah*, RCA Victor LSC 6175.

placed in a particular hall, affects the nature of the music. Robert Shaw has written of striving to see

> ... that *Messiah* sheds its ponderous, sanctimonious, morbid musical and religious pomposity and becomes again what Handel certainly intended it to be—a light, bright chamber-oratorio, celebrating with a secular deftness a remote but responsive religious mystery.[8]

Performing Editions

Those considering a performance of *Messiah* will find the following editions of interest:

1. The Watkins Shaw version[9] includes a score, a supplementary volume on performance practice, and two sets of parts. It identifies possibilities for alternating concertists with tutti forces, and presents choices of voices and keys for soloists, all based on Handel's own history of performing the work. The Watkins Shaw orchestral parts may be considered the most authentic among recent editions. The score itself is somewhat more difficult for the eye, perhaps, because it mixes both small and large notes in certain passages as a means of illustrating the various modifications Handel made in his performances.
2. The Alfred Mann edition[10] came first as a score. Excellent for study purposes, it includes a very clear description of the historical background of *Messiah*, and excellent critical notes for every individual number. The doubling choices presented are much easier to read, and the *continuo* part is effective.

Current trends in *Messiah* performance—in the light of these and other recent scholarly efforts—make other editions dated (as of this time of writing). As everyone who has worked with *Messiah* will know, there are some very questionable versions—even a revision of the work done by Mozart himself (and popular in the United States until the 1960s)—which bear little resemblance to Handel's real intentions. There were also editions prepared in the late nineteenth century and the early years of the twentieth, which, working on the basis of editorial practices then acceptable, re-orchestrated and obscured Handel's ideas, as Mozart had done. It is probably best for you—no matter how limited your forces, or how traditional your audience—to study the most modern editions and parts, and to employ choral and instrumental forces appropriate to these concepts. Those who have conducted *Messiah* in recent years, adhering to these ideals, have found audiences genuinely thrilled and moved anew by the fresh,

---

8. See above.
9. Watkins Shaw, editor of *Messiah, a Sacred Oratorio*.
10. Alfred Mann, editor of *G. F. Handel, Messiah, An Oratorio* (in three volumes). Parts have been published recently.

clear, vivacious spirit of the work, once it has been set free from the pompous heaviness of the older practices.

Concertists, the *Basso Continuo,* and Tutti

With respect to the distribution of our forces, Handel's own performance practices encourage us to act intelligently and flexibly to suit the hall, the soloists, the talents of the orchestra, the size of the chorus, and the uniqueness of a given evening. Here, as throughout Baroque music, there is no single perfect solution.

If your full orchestra is a small one—strings 4-4-3-3-1, say—then one concertist on a part (1-1-1-1-1) is probably appropriate. For a substantially larger ensemble, you might assign as concertists a 3-3-2-2-1 group. The principle is to use your best players, of course; avoid pairs of violins or contrabasses, however —designate three or one, but not two.[11]

Chapter 6 included an extended discussion of *basso continuo* instrumentation.[12] An excellent solution for *Messiah* would be to cover the bass line itself with a number of 'cellos matched to the size of the overall string body, plus one bassoon (for Handel's *con fagotto* indications); harpsichord could provide the keyboard for the recitatives, with organ (or organ *and* harpsichord) for the choruses.

The overall impression created by the tutti should be one of equality between the vocal and instrumental forces. If the aural fabric sounds to you like a chorus *accompanied* by orchestra, the choir is probably too large or too loud; this is Baroque music, and a rich, complex mixture of voice, wind, string, and *continuo* timbres—all in balance—is what you are seeking.

PART THE FIRST

No. 1: Sinfonia

Now to the work itself.[13] We suggest you consider a tempo between $\quarternote =$ 48 and $\quarternote = 60$ for the *Grave* opening of this movement—on the high side of that range ($\quarternote = 56$–60), if possible.[14] In making this determination, one of your primary considerations, here as in all music, must be how much *space* (i.e., silence), if any, you wish between certain notes, and to communicate that preference, in practical language, to the concertmaster, the principals, and the rest of the orchestra. This judgment is basic to many of the decisions you make about articu-

---

11. See above, pp. 31–33.
12. See above, pp. 48 ff.
13. From this point on you will find it important to have your full score of *Messiah* at hand. Our discussion is based on the Alfred Mann edition already cited.
14. Remember that the size of your forces, their technical abilities, the nature and acoustics of the hall, and other factors will influence your tempo choices. (See above, chapter 6, pp. 56–57.) The tempos suggested in these discussions are offered only as departure points for your own study and thought.

lation, phrasing, some matters of balance, and other aspects, as well as tempo itself. Think through the section, listen to the bowings on which you and the principals have agreed, and compare all this to the aural image you have; be certain that the bowings and articulations chosen are giving you the space you need for the conception you have formed.

It has been traditional to double-dot the long notes, but there have been recent performances—including recorded ones—using single dots; the decision is an important matter of interpretation, and it is yours.[15]

If you decide to double-dot, it probably will be best to "hook" the short note to the *previous* long note in each instance.[16] Thus the first measure will include, in order, a downbow and an upbow. In bar 2, the sixteenths in the first violins will be taken on separate bows—the first of these a second consecutive downbow.[17] Separate bows for the first two notes in bar 3 would get the first violins back to a hooked pattern on the second F-sharp;[18] thus, in measure 4, the downbow would come on the first beat, in keeping with the traditional principle.[19] From this point, the first violins will "take it as it comes," as they say; that is, they will apply these bowings they have been using throughout the passage at hand—in this case, to the end of the *Grave*.

Pursuing the double-dotting alternative, the second violins, violas, and *continuo* bass would follow the same practices—a bow for each half note (beginning on a downbow, of course), hooking shorter values together as the first violins are doing. Example 4 displays these bowings for measures 1 to 4.

Should you decide, on the other hand, to play the short notes with single dots, as marked, it may prove best to take every note with a separate bow (*detaché*), save perhaps the sixteenths. The result of this choice can be a less lyric, more emphatic sound than the hooked bowings above. The passage will convey a sense of energy either way; the difference is that—with single dots—the energy will seem to come from the separate bows, while—with double dots—that vitality will derive from the shortness of the sixteenths themselves.

With respect to the trills (bars 9 and 11, for example), it will help to remember that *a common reason for incorporating a trill into this music is to highlight a dissonance* within a melodic line. (Young players, and even experienced ones, you will find, often know surprisingly little about ornamentation. It may not even prove productive to seek their advice on this matter.) Frequently players

---

15. For elaboration of this point, see the Alfred Mann edition (cited above), p. 85, and Robert Donington, *A Performer's Guide to Baroque Music*, p. 237.

16. The bowing technique called "hooking" involves playing two notes on the same bow stroke, but does not imply slurring. The forward progress of the bow is interrupted briefly between the two notes, and then resumes. (If a separate stroke is used for a very short note, the player may be left with insufficient bow for the return stroke.)

17. In such a circumstance, the section plays a downbow, lifts the bow to recover the length of bow already used, and attacks the string again. At least a tiny articulatory silence will result.

18. You will see immediately that there will be spots in this passage (and in any other) that "do not fit" a simple alternation of upbows and downbows. Arbitrary adjustments are needed, from time to time, to make the bowing work at the most important and/or difficult points.

19. That is, with the axiom that downbeats generally are played downbow.

Example 4. "Sinfonia," measures 1–4.

will perform a trill at a subdued dynamic level (a notch below the notated loudness), exactly contradicting the composer's wish.

In each case you should know (1) whether the trill begins on the note, or above it, (2) the dynamic level needed for the trill, as it plays its part in the shaping of the melodic line, (3) where the trill itself is to end (i.e., at the beginning of the dot, most likely, in this music), and (4) how the turn at the end, if any, is to be played.[20] All this should be planned carefully before the first rehearsal.[21]

What about the winds? In general, the oboes and bassoons should use *articulation which has the same effect* as that of the strings. Attacks should have the character of those produced by the strings, and articulatory silences should have the same duration.

Watch the balance of the winds against the strings. Oboes are an important part of the sound of this music. When they are doubled with the violins, neither should predominate; rather, each should enhance the sound of the other. Ask them to be aware of each other—and then check the balance in the hall yourself!

The *Grave* is marked to be repeated. You may choose to play this repeat softly,

20. For detailed discussions of the trill and other Baroque ornaments, see especially Robert Donington, *A Performer's Guide to Baroque Music,* Frederick Neumann, *Baroque and Post-Baroque Ornamentation with Special Emphasis on J. S. Bach,* and Donington's article "Ornaments" in: Stanley Sadie, editor of *The New Grove Dictionary of Music and Musicians,* vol. 13, pp. 827–867.
21. Remember our suggestion (chapter 3, p. 31 n.2) that you may find it helpful to pencil into the margins of your score trill patterns you prefer.

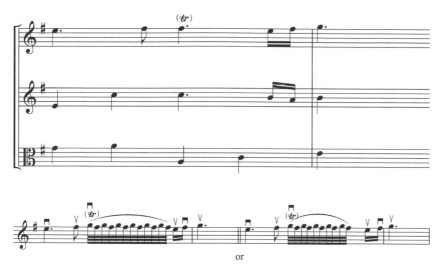

Example 5. A possible realization of the trills in the "Sinfonia," measure 9.

for contrast; in that case, you must decide (and mark) just where the necessary diminuendo should begin.

At the end of the *Grave* occurs the first of many "seams" (more-or-less dangerous transition points) in *Messiah*. As you approach the second ending of the *Grave,* be certain that every gesture is clear to the players; clumsiness at such a moment is especially risky, and can cause a complete breakdown. Whether or not you decide to use a *fermata* (Handel has not indicated one), be sure that your last beat before the tempo change ends with the point of the baton up. When you drop the stick, then, it comes down in the new tempo. The next section usually is taken in two, at perhaps ♩ = 88–92; the Violins I will have half a beat to estimate your new tempo.

In the *allegro moderato* you are likely to want separate bows for each note (*detaché* playing), beginning with a downbow. Just as in the *Grave,* however, the subtler question is how long you want each note to be—that is, how much space you want between each note.

Considering what we know of performance practice in Handel's lifetime, we can say with confidence that there is not a pitch in the first three bars of the *allegro moderato* that should be held out to its notated value. No two of these notes should have precisely equal weight. (Think which of them you hear leading to a succeeding pitch.) One could describe these three measures as directed to the half-note A-natural in measure 15; the shape of the line, then, commencing with downward motion to the B-natural in bar 14, and continuing through the ascent to the A-natural in bar 15, seems to give the phrase an S-curve contour (a familiar Baroque formation). Which of these tones deserve emphasis (and length)? Surely the first A-natural is quite short, for example, because of what follows; to play it full length would be to undermine the importance of the tied half-note. (You may decide, further, to mark the G-natural in bar 13 and the second F-sharp in bar 14, as the line ascends through the trill toward its peak.) In dealing with an orchestra, you can express the natural sweep of a melodic line just as you would with your chorus.

Working with this concept of the subject, the first violins will continue— "taking it as it comes"—occasionally making minor bowing adjustments which allow them to adhere to the rule of "the downbow on the downbeat." In measure 20, for example, they will need to compromise, probably taking consecutive up-bows on the B-natural and A-sharp; thus they can begin bar 21 on a downbow.

The second violins also start measure 17 on a downbow, as do the violas and the strings of the *basso continuo* in bar 21. Again, minor adjustments are necessary:

1. In the second violin part, you may want to "hook" the first two notes in bar 24, and then employ consecutive upbows for the G-natural and E-natural in the next measure.
2. Further on, the sound of the high G-natural in measure 29 may be better if you use consecutive upbows on the previous two notes (G-natural and D-natural).
3. In measure 36 the second violin should begin with upbows.
4. From measure 39, where begins the repetitive pattern of three eighth-notes leading to a downbeat, the first of those eighths should always be taken upbow.
5. In measure 95, the first violins should either take consecutive down-bows on the first two notes, or consecutive upbows on the last two.

In marking parts, is it required to indicate ⊓ or V for each new phrase? Perhaps not, but *it may be safest*. Remember that orchestral players, even in fine ensembles, may be short of rehearsal. Reassuring them about bowings could save you much valuable time.

When you approach a passage like measures 13–16, seeking unity and clarity of articulation and bowing, it may not prove necessary to rehearse each of the orchestral sections. *If you have the first violins play the subject correctly, the other sections will hear and imitate the note-lengths and phrasing of the violins,* leaving you rehearsal time for other passages.

The oboes, which double the violins here, articulate the motives and figures just as the strings do, maintaining the same spaces between notes, and defining the same melodic direction and sweep. The most one may have to do for them is to agree on occasional breath marks (although in this particular movement the silences created by your articulation patterns may be sufficient breathing-space).[22]

---

22. Remember that good double reed players can sustain very long phrases.

Be careful not to conceive this movement as "an introduction to the real (vocal) music!" It is complete and profound in shape and character, and has an integrity equal to the best of the other *Messiah* movements. You may have to make this point clear *even to the players,* some of whom may have come to regard themselves as mere *Messiah* accompanists. Get them to play with energy, concentation, and pride, giving every ounce of vitality to these lines—but *together.* (And remember: *don't* talk to them—*show them what you want.) They can make this movement sound fresh and new.*

No. 2: Comfort ye my people

For the opening of the second movement, which could be taken at approximately ♩= 50 in a divided-four pattern, one could begin the first violin part downbow, giving a little impulse to the attack of each of the four eighth-notes. Once again, you must decide how much space you want between these pitches. (And see how important a decision this is: this motive occurs in virtually every bar of the movement.) Separate bows will do well for the thirty- second notes. In bar 3, giving this thirty-second also a separate downbow, you could use consecutive upbows on the succeeding E-natural and A-natural; thus you come to the downbeat of bar 4 on a downbow. On the last beat of bar 3, the F-sharp and the sixteenth-note E-natural can be hooked, with the trill stopping on the dot.

The second violin, viola, and 'cello parts are quite simple, of course. Generally you will want a pair of bows per measure, except for the "echo" pattern.

Plan carefully how you will handle measure four (and the parallel bar 8). Consider particularly how long a pause you want on the final note of the "echo" motif each time it occurs, both in the voice and the strings. It is reasonable to delay briefly on both the second and fourth beats of each of these two measures; keep the baton virtually still during these pauses, or move it slowly where you want it to indicate either a *crescendo* or a *decrescendo.* Be clear and precise with each preparatory beat. (You will find it helpful, after the second count in measure 4, to move the preparatory beat for 3 in the direction of 2.) Insist on clean ensemble each time you re-start the strings. Make them listen to each other.

The "echo" in the last half of bar 4 can be played with the first two notes hooked on a downbow, leading then to an upbow for the final chord. (In any case, whatever bowing you use for a recurrent motif like this one should be maintained throughout the movement.) As the music continues, watch to be certain this consistency is sustained by the players.

From measure 30 you will want to decide how long and how forcefully you want each of the downbeat strokes played (remembering that they need not be identical in effect). Be certain the strings really speak *together* in each instance.

For the final measure, you probably should choose to follow the convention of delaying the two orchestral chords one beat; this permits the tenor to finish his phrase first, and avoids the implicit harmonic conflict on the first beat. There is good evidence in favor of making this adjustment; Haydn, in a letter to an

Austrian monastery (probably Zwettl, according to H. C. Robbins Landon, who has translated the letter, and assigns it to the year 1768) writes:

> In the accompanied recitatives, you must observe that the accompaniment should not enter until the singer has quite finished his text, even though the score often shows the contrary. . . . but I leave this to the harpsichord player, who would be very familiar with the convention, and all others must follow him.[23]

If this is to be your practice, place a *fermata* on the fourth beat of measure 36, wait there, and then synchronize the first beat of bar 37 (as a preparation) with the tenor: the orchestra will play the two chords (which would be best as upbow-downbow) on the second and third beats of measure 37.[24] Be certain that your preparatory beat for the orchestra is larger than the gestures you use when they are *tacet*—don't lead them astray with false cues.

Well performed, the effect conveyed by measures 30–37 should be that of the orchestra punctuating the declamation of the singer.

No. 3: Every valley shall be exalted

The energy inherent in the aria which follows contrasts sharply with the previous movement; the tempo, which should be bright *but secure*, could fall in the ♩ = 96–108 range. The bassoon in the *basso continuo*, which Handel marked *tacet* throughout the preceding recitative, moves in and out during the aria, joining always with the *ripieno*.

Decide how long the first two notes should be. How much space do you want between them? If you prefer them quite connected, a horizontal line over each of the two notes will help; if you wish a *little* more separation, put a dot over each of the horizontal lines. Taking each note on a separate bow (except for the marked slurs), the first three measures work out perfectly for the first violins.

In similar fashion, mark the amount of separation you want for the lower string parts, maintaining the character of the first violin line. (For eighth-notes, use just a staccato dot for separation; the horizontal line is unnecessary with shorter values.) The second violins can stay parallel with much of the bowing of the firsts if they take consecutive upbows on the second and third notes of the first measure, play the slur downbow, and then supply consecutive upbows again for the next two notes. The viola and bass lines take alternate bows, but the violas will want consecutive upbows for the last two notes in measure 3 (in order that all the strings play the pickup to bar 4 as an upbeat).

---

23. H. C. Robbins Landon, *The Collected Correspondence and London Notebooks of Joseph Haydn*, pp. 9–11. (Much of the time Haydn himself would have been the harpsichordist, of course.) See also Robert Donington, *A Performer's Guide to Baroque Music*, pp. 237 ff., and J. A. Scheibe in F. W. Marpurg, *Kritische Briefe*, paragraph 83.

24. This same situation will recur on several other occasions below, and your handling of it should be consistent, of course.

For the trill patterns that begin in measure 4 it is important to insist that the strings sustain the off-beat tones (the E-naturals in the first violins, for example) long enough that the audience members can hear the resolutions. Note that the rests break the pattern of alternate bows, forcing the strings to take consecutive upbows before and after each eighth-rest. In measure 6 Handel has marked the trill figures with slurs (perhaps because of the piano indication); if we take the first trill downbow, the pattern works out perfectly, with each of the string sections ending bar 9 on a downbow.

The accompanimental pattern which commences in bar 15 will begin upbow each time. If you want a little separation between the eighth and the quarter, write on the parts "middle" (of the bow) and "lift." (Note that the last of these eighth-note-and-quarter-note pairs, at the end of measure 18, must be played down-up, if bar 19 is to begin downbow.)

These motives, each marked early in the movement, recur throughout the aria, and should be handled with consistency. There are isolated problems:

1. In bar 26, decide how much separation you want after the pickup. (Your edition may show the first and second violins playing separated pickups against a slur in the violas.) The violin attack would be upbow, of course, and you might ask them to "lift."
2. In bars 34 and 35 the first violins could play consecutive upbows on the F-sharp and A-sharp, followed by consecutive downbows on the B-natural and the (pickup) C-sharp. This "fits" much better.
3. Consecutive downbows will be useful in measure 73, in order that the *fermata* may be emphasized.
4. In measure 74 be careful to cue only the 'celli, basses, and harpsichord. You may want to hold on the first beat of bar 75; certainly, in any event, you will want a *fermata* on 3 in that measure. Use 4, then, as a preparatory beat for cueing the full orchestra into bar 76.
5. In measure 81 consecutive upbows on the last two eighth notes start the next bar on a downbow; similarly, the last two eighths in measure 83 could be taken upbow.

No. 4: And the glory of the Lord

One often hears this movement taken too slowly, in too heavy a manner. Try a bright tempo—up to ♩ = 160 or so—and keep it buoyant. (Be sure to tell the orchestra whether you are conducting it in 3 or in 1.) Relate your tempo choice to your conception of the articulation of the vocal parts; decide how much space you want between notes, and match the strings consistently to the style of the singing.

The entrance at measure 14, then, should maintain this same energy and lightness, as should those at bars 33, 46, 50, 53, and 69. To keep the patterns consistent throughout the movement:

1. Both the violin sections must play the second beat of bar 73 downbow (which means the firsts must play consecutive downbows on the B-natural and the D-sharp).
2. At bar 83 you will want space after the second beat in both violin parts, with upbows on the third beat of the measure.
3. The first violins can begin bar 93 downbow, but they might take consecutive upbows on the high B-naturals in measure 96, so that the long note following will be a downbow. The second violins can use the same pattern in bars 95 and 96.
4. In measure 109 the bowing pattern in the violins could be down-up-up.
5. The final cadence, beginning in measure 135, should be marked with an upbow for each of the two pickup notes, of course. In conducting this passage, remember that a big, clear preparatory beat on the second count of bar 135—following small beats on the rests just before it—is all-important. Be sure it shows your tempo.

Take special care that the lower strings stay in character with the style of articulation you are seeking. 'Cello and bass players (particularly those in school orchestras) tend to play Baroque lines with notes too long and heavy. Don't permit the bass(es) to "growl." And watch the 'cellos, too: it is difficult for an inexperienced orchestra conductor to distinguish clearly between the sounds of these two sections. Correct the right people! Insist on a brush stroke[25] from the lower strings, and keep them under surveillance as you proceed, lest their playing become heavy again.

Be suspicious, in fact, particularly with school orchestras, that they will overplay the *tutti* sections. Waiting through solo-with-*continuo* sections, inexperienced musicians—including good players who are not familiar with Baroque style—often "pounce" on *ripieno* attacks. Keep them in check, and in good taste.

No. 5: Thus saith the Lord

First you will want to decide whether or not to double-dot the on-the-beat notes in the strings. Base this decision on the concept you form of the character of this recitative: how ponderous a sound do you want here, how much space between notes, and (then) what tempo? (We suggest approximately ♩ = 100.)

One way to bow this passage would be to begin each of the string fragments downbow, hook the dotted note that follows to the sixteenth (or thirty-second) thereafter, as an upbow, and end with a downbow on the strong beat. This whole concept, once established, would obtain also for the entrances through measure 9, and would be employed again from the pickups to bar 23 on through measure 29.

A second possibility for bowings would be a simple *detaché* alternation, begin-

---

25. The "brush stroke" is defined in the glossary and described in chapter 2, p. 13.

ning upbow each time. Listen to both these options, and make your choice. Similarly, in measures 10–13, decide whether you like the sound of alternate bows for these quarter-notes, or prefer the uniformity of treating them all downbow.

The sixteenths, commencing in measure 14, start with an upbow, of course, and should be *detaché*, played in the middle of the bow. This pattern changes in bar 19; here you may find it better to ask that notes be bowed in pairs throughout this passage, altering the spots where four notes are bowed together (bar 19 in the violins and violas, bar 20 in the second violins and violas, etc.). Maintaining that procedure to the cadential third beat in measure 22 will mean re-taking a consecutive downbow for the start of the dotted-note pattern. You probably will end measure 30, then, with an up-down bowing, in order to give extra strength to the attack on the final chord.

Be careful, by the way, not to discount Handel's own bowings too quickly, even when they appear inconsistent—as they do between the first violins and the second violins and violas in measure 20, for example. *Handel may not have wanted uniform bowing on every occasion.*[26] We have no single, decisive autograph manuscript for *Messiah,* and markings vary from score to score. Depend on the best editions available, study the alternatives, and choose.

Conduct this recitative as simply and directly as possible. The singer needs some *rubato* flexibility; stay with him during the measures when the orchestra is *tacet,* employing small beats. Stop the baton one count before the next preparation, and then use a large motion for the preparatory beat.[27]

No. 6: But who may abide the day of His coming?

You must decide whether to take the *Larghetto* sections in one or in three. (We recommend that you consider a flowing three, around ♪ = 104.)

Starting upbow, *detaché*, one can have the first violins play consecutive upbows in bars 2, 6, and 8, which will bring them to bar 12 on a downbow. Similarly, the second violins and bass instruments can take consecutive upbows in measure 3, and both seconds and violas consecutive downbows in measure 10. As the accompanimental pattern continues, it always begins upbow:

1. In measures 18 and 26, you may want to have the first violins play consecutive upbows, in order to prevent their making the final eighth note too heavy and prominent each time.
2. Bars 42–44 should be handled in the same way, with consecutive upbows in the violins in measure 44.

The "seam" in measures 58–59 is dangerous. You must conduct straight through bar 58 in the old tempo, without attempting to show in the last beat of measure 58 the new tempo at bar 59. The best chance you have to give the or-

---

26. For a detailed examination of this issue, see Dene Barnett, "Non-uniform Slurring in 18th Century Music: Accident or Design?" in *The Haydn Yearbook,* 15:170–199, 1979.
27. See above, p. 35.

chestra the new tempo is in the rebound of the first beat of bar 59. (If both you and the players are very good, you can try stopping the last beat of bar 58 at the top, dropping it faster *without* changing the length of that beat. If this feels risky to you, it will be.)

Once started, the *Prestissimo* may look difficult, but it is not really hard; the string players' left hands are not moving quickly at all. This can go cleanly in two at ♩ = 80 or so. The problem is to maintain ensemble. You will find it helpful to have the strings accent the harmonic changes on the first and ninth sixteenth-notes in each measure; by helping to emphasize the harmonic rhythm, these stresses will clarify the meter. As for bowings, the sixteenths are best taken *detaché*, on-the-string in the middle of the bow.

1. In measures 77–83 you may find that the first violins will handle the eighth-notes more delicately if they play consecutive upbows on the pairs of slurred eighths, coming to a downbow on the first beat of each bar. Thus the *piano*-to-*forte* patterns are clarified by the bowing. The lower strings can maintain a simple alternation. (Continue the slurred pattern in the first violins in measure 84, down-up-down-up.)
2. Resuming the sixteenths in bar 85, we come to bar 88 on a downbow; in the first violins, slur the first pair of eighths, and take the second pair upbow. Then you can return to the consecutive upbow pattern for measures 89–90.

These prototypes—the *Larghetto* pattern at measure 1 and the accented sets of *Prestissimo* sixteenths at measure 59—are models for the remainder of the movement. The transition back to *Larghetto* in bars 93–94 is easier than the seam at 58–59, for you can ritard into it through measures 91–93. The return to the *Prestissimo* in bar 115 is a bit safer this time because the violins do not commence playing again until bar 116. Stay with the old tempo straight through measure 114, and then hit the new tempo without pause (Handel indicated none) at measure 115.

The only important modification comes in measure 141; this time the quarter-note at the end of the pattern is *not* marked *forte,* and it may be best to revise at that point our consecutive-upbow procedure (from bars 77–83), beginning the motif downbow each time now, while continuing to slur pairs of eighth-notes. (Compare these two situations in examples 6 and 7.) An alternative for this passage (and for the same motif earlier) would be to take the eighths on separate bows, telling the players to use the upper third of their bows. This will keep the dynamic level under control. (In considering these alternative solutions, compare the markings *and* the direction of the lines in bars 141–146 with those in measures 77–84.)

No. 7: And He shall purify the sons of Levi

Consider how you want the "walking bass" to sound. Lightness is important in the 'cellos and basses, in order that they support the choir without

Example 6. "But who may abide the day of His coming," measures 77–84.

Example 7. "But who may abide the day of His coming," measures 141–146.

overpowering the delicate vocal lines, and so that they match up well with the violins and violas (starting in measures 2 and 4). In choosing a tempo which is in keeping with the concept of delicacy, then, you may find that your singers can approach ♩ = 104, which we would suggest as an attractive possibility. Do not subdivide here. Keep the pulse clean.

As for bowings:

1. The upper strings should begin the three-note pickup pattern upbow each time, *detaché*, including the last motif in bar 6.
2. *Detaché* is appropriate also for the *forte* lines which begin in bar 15.
3. In bar 17 the second violins could play the F-sharp and D-natural on consecutive upbows.
4. Similarly, in bar 20 the first violins can take the eighth-notes on G-natural and B-natural on consecutive upbows.
5. These standard patterns continue consistently to measure 34, where—in order to arrive at important spots on a downbow—the Violins I need to hook the first two notes of bar 34, and either hook the two sixteenths in bar 35 or take the final F-natural and C-natural in that measure as consecutive upbows. The violas should retake an upbow for the pickup to bar 36. Talk this spot over, perhaps, with your concertmaster, who will know what physical problems seem most important here.
6. The ending of the movement works out well if both the first violins and the violas play consecutive upbows on the last two notes in measure 55.

No. 8: Behold, a virgin shall conceive

Conduct the *basso continuo* here only if necessary; whether or not you do so depends primarily on the experience (in this style) of the keyboard player and the 'cellist. Can they follow the singer without you? With the upper strings *tacet* and the bassoons excused from the *continuo*, you need be concerned only about ensemble—particularly on the two last chords (which probably should be delayed until after the singer has finished, as in cases already discussed).

No. 9: O thou that tellest good tidings to Zion

This goes well in a bright (not fast) two—perhaps ♩. = 56–58. Depending on the edition, you will have the first and second violins doubled in all or part of the movement. Have them take it *detaché*, with the pickup upbow, of course; if you ask that they play the last two notes in measure 2 both upbow—in order to keep the downbow on the downbeat—the bowings follow naturally. As alternatives;

1. You may ask that the first and third groups of three notes each in measures 3 and 4 be slurred, with the lower notes kept separate.

G. F. Handel 75

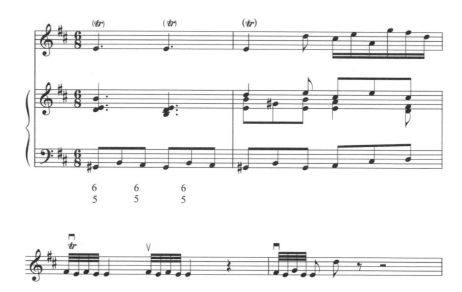

Example 8. Short trills in measures 10–11 of "O thou that tellest good tidings to Zion."

Example 9. Long trills as an alternative.

2. Or you may want the first group of three notes in each of bars 5, 6, and 7 slurred, with the last nine notes in each measure played *detaché.*

Probably you will want to keep this entire violin line as even as possible, preventing any pitches from obtruding. Decide before the first rehearsal whether you want long or short trills at measures 10 and 11. Examples 8 and 9 illustrate two possibilities: among other options, one might prolong the appoggiatura itself before beginning the trill.

The entrances that follow in measures 14, 18, 22, 25, 28, 32, 35, and on through bar 104 each begin upbow, and follow the same prototype. Note these special considerations:

1. Obviously where there are groups of three sixteenth-notes you will want to handle them just as you did this pattern in bars 3 to 8.
2. Decide how long to play the trill in measure 40.

3. You may want to take the last two notes in bar 43 as consecutive upbows.
4. The *piano* fragments in measures 44–47 should be taken lightly, in the middle of the bow.
5. In measure 71 the B-natural and D-natural can both be upbows, permitting the violins to arrive at the low G-natural on a downbow.
6. Note the slurring of duplets in measure 91.[28]
7. The slurs in measures 97–100 are taken downbow, for emphasis, with the other notes separate.

These standard solutions continue to serve after the entrance of the chorus in measure 106. The "seam" in bars 104–106 needs careful attention and rehearsal; measures 104–105 are, in effect, a cadenza, and must be given flexibility. You need to know approximately how much ornamentation the singer will use, so you can judge the motion of the *continuo* and the preparation of the *tutti* in bar 106.

You will need to make occasional bowing adjustments (consecutive upbows at the end of measure 108, for example) in order to maintain consistent phrasing. Plan again the length of the trills for measures 149–150, as you did for bars 10–11.

Some editions show this movement ending with two eighth-notes—one on the D-natural within the staff and the other an octave lower—with an eighth-rest at the end; decide if you want the lower D-natural. If you do, determine how you want it to sound, both in length and in energy.

Finally, when conducting in two be certain that the rebound of your downbeat is not as high as that first beat's starting point. The orchestra players, who are using only peripheral vision, need to see a clear difference between your first and second beats.

No. 10: For behold, darkness shall cover the earth

Most of us probably should conduct this movement in a subdivided four. Keep the four primary beat points well separated, and place your subdivisions next to those primary beats, so the players can tell where you are. Don't put all your beats in one central spot—especially in a subdivided movement.

A tempo of approximately ♩ = 80–84 can work well, and the bow changes are marked to occur at the same rate; the slurs indicate two sixteenth-notes per bow. Decide how much space you want at each bow change, and be certain that your choice is in keeping with the way your bass instruments are playing their eighth-notes.

At the middle of bar 10, you may want a brush stroke in the middle of the

---

28. And probably in measure 92, as well, though your edition may not show the slurs as continued in that bar.

bow. In any case, the strings should play lightly here, avoiding any overpowering of the soloist. As in earlier instances we have seen, the cadence pattern (in bar 23) should be begun upbow.

No. 11: The people that walked in darkness

You probably will want to begin this movement *attacca;* if this is the case, you can place a small *fermata* on the fourth count of the last bar of the previous movement, and then add a *fifth* count—in effect—to that measure as a preparatory beat for "The people that walked in darkness." (Be certain that you tell the orchestra members about that fifth beat in rehearsal, and that the motion you use for it is *upward.*)

This *Larghetto* aria opens with the strings in octaves, playing a clearly marked pattern of slurs and wedges.[29] The initial phrase (shown in example 10) is standard: slurring of groups of two or three notes, with separate pitches interspersed (the latter marked with wedges, in some cases), the whole covering about four measures.

Your concept of articulation, and of the articulatory silences between certain of these notes, is important to your selection of a tempo. The aria can flow well in four, perhaps around ♩ = 56.

There are a few adjustments to the bowing:

1. Note the need in measure 3 for consecutive upbows, in order that the next bar can begin downbow.
2. The pattern that begins in measure 9 is somewhat different, but the principle is the same. It is unlikely you would want to change to *detaché* bowing for measure 15, for example.
3. Beginning with the three pickups to bar 18, however, you certainly could choose to change to separate bows.
4. Measures 20–31 continue the original prototype, with its slurs. Separate bows, then, beginning with the last three eighth-notes in bar 31, would be useful for the *forte* passage to bar 33.
5. Starting with the pickup to bar 34, the slurred figures return; after that, separate bows can be used again from the low C-sharp in measure 38 to the next voice entrance.
6. These alternating slurred and *detaché* phrases continue in similar fashion to the end of the movement, a possible bowing for which is shown in example 11.

So long as your choices remain consistent with the slurring Handel has marked for the beginning of this movement, you have quite a lot of freedom to use slurs and wedges as you think best for any phrasing that seems effective to you. Experiment (before the first rehearsal, of course) with several possibilities.

---

29. See "wedge" in the glossary.

Example 10. "The people that walked in darkness," measures 1–4.

No. 12: For unto us a child is born

Once again your first decision must determine the character of the melodic lines and the balances of sound and silence within them. If the opening motif is to have a certain effervescence, you will want to shorten virtually all the notes somewhat. We suggest you consider taking the movement in four, approximately $\text{\textonehalf}$ = 108. (Whether or not you can do so will depend, in all probability, on the way your singers manage the sixteenth-notes, which must be clean and even at that demanding tempo.)

The first violins could begin with a downbow and a pair of upbows (the latter on the G-naturals), thereafter "taking it as it comes." (The E-natural pickup in bar 2 would be played upbow, of course.) To keep this phrasing consistent, the second violins could take their two G-naturals in bar 2—and the violas their first two D-naturals in both measures 1 and 2—as consecutive upbows.

Be certain that the 'cellos and bass(es) employ a light brush stroke throughout. Further:

1. To come to the cadence in measure 7 on downbows, the first violins could prescribe consecutive upbows for the last two notes of measure 5, playing the final sixteenth of bar 6 separately. The seconds would need to hook the dotted eighth and sixteenth on the fourth beat of measure 6.

2. The four-note accompanimental figures which begin in bar 8 could be taken on-the-string, starting upbow, in the upper third of the bow;

Example 11. "The people that walked in darkness," measures 59–63.

the two-note patterns in bars 12 and 13 would begin upbow also, and the quarters in bars 15 to 18 would alternate down and up in each measure.

3. The sixteenths that begin in bar 32 may be played separately, *detaché*, starting upbow. The violas could take the last two notes in measure 36 both upbow, in order to make all the sections come out downbow. Note

that Handel's wedges in measure 37 imply he wants some separation and a bit of an accent on each of these notes.

4. In bar 71 the firsts could take consecutive upbows on the tied C-natural and the first B-natural, and the violas consecutive downbows on the A- and G-naturals.

5. In measure 79, the firsts could take consecutive downbows on the A-natural and the low D, hooking (upbow) the last two notes in the measure. Each dotted-eighth-and-sixteenth pair in the passage which begins in bar 80 might then be hooked. Be certain you get as much separation as you want between the dotted-eighth and the sixteenth; use a line and dot under each pair, if you want more space—or ask (if your players are experienced) for "French overture style."

6. All three upper string sections will need to make some adjustment in bar 90 (hooking the last pair of notes, taking consecutive downbows on the first and second halves of the third beat, or playing consecutive up-bows on the last two notes in the measure).

Bowings for the closing measures of the movement work out perfectly for all the string sections. (You may want to take a little more time at the end of this chorus, since it is the end of the "Advent section," and No. 13 begins the Christmas segment.)

No. 13: PIFA (the "Pastoral Symphony")

This brief *Larghetto* is no interlude—no "throwaway;" brief as it is, it is still as important as any aria or chorus in *Messiah*. In a sense, this is an overture for the Christmas texts, which include the movements through No. 21, "His yoke is easy . . . ," the end of "Part the First."

There are *three* violin parts scored. If you have been using just one player on each of the *concertino* lines, you could have your assistant concertmaster cover the Violin III part. If you have had one desk play each part, you might ask the *outside* players on the two front Violin I stands to play the first violin part, with their two *inside* stand partners covering the Violin III staff; then the first desk of seconds could be responsible for the Violin II line. Just be certain that you maintain a distinct, audible contrast between this *concertino* section and your *tutti* force; if you have to hush the concertists—in order to sustain the dynamic level you wish—you risk causing them to produce a shallow, flimsy tone.

Slow tempos are often more difficult to conduct than fast ones. The PIFA can sag badly; we strongly advise you to regard it as a Siciliano movement, taking it in four, at ♩. = 48 or so. Don't wait on the musicians. Move them along! (Be especially careful that younger players don't slow down on the third eighth-note of each measure.) Watch that the "echo effect"—the repetition starting at the last beat of bar 2 and again at the last beat of bar 10—does not bog down: keep the stick moving steadily through those passages.

Handel's slurs are useful here; the bowings—with the first "echo" starting up-bow (on the fourth beat)—work out well. Some adjustments are needed:

1. The firsts will take everything "as it comes" (although this means be-ginning bar 5 on an upbow) until measure 6, where it may be best for them to play upbows on the last D-natural and the low G that follows it. Then they can take consecutive upbows again on the last two notes in bar 7.
2. For the seconds and violas, everything falls right until the last note of measure 5 and the first one in bar 6, both of which could be down-bows. The last note in measure 6 would be taken upbow, which brings the movement out right.

You may choose to ask the players for more bow here than they have been using on earlier movements. Be careful about dynamics, too. The "Pastoral Sym-phony" should have a "singing" character; if you make the strings play it too quietly, they may use too little bow to get good sound.

No. 14: There were shepherds abiding in the field

After the brief *secco* passage (No. 14a, in some editions), comes the *stromentato* "And lo, the angel of the Lord . . ." (No. 14b), with its sixteenth-notes shimmering in the violins. We recommend that you take this in four, at about ♩ = 80. The violins can provide this on-the-string, lightly, keeping the notes smoothly connected.

Try not to let this sound "busy." The slurs are fine, as marked; you will get a bit of separation between pairs of notes in the opening measures, because of string crossings, as well as the changes of direction of the bows. The downbeat of the first measure should be taken downbow, of course, and the alternation works out perfectly, then, to the final bar; there (where we have another example of the delayed-cadence convention) you will want an upbow first, with a down-bow for the final chord. We suggest you consider marking the 'cello part four-notes-to-a-bow, with a dot under each note; you will get a downbow followed by an upbow in each measure, with every note somewhat separated. (This is the *portato* bowing.)[30]

No. 15: And the angel said unto them

Here we have another *secco* recitative. (Maintain a sense of continuity through this whole succession of vignettes, avoiding delays at the end of each brief movement; thus you will minimize any tendency for the flow of *Messiah* to falter here.)

---

30. See above, p. 13.

No. 16: And suddenly there was with the angel

This movement (for which we suggest a tempo near $\quad = 104$) often sounds hectic in performance. Keep the sixteenths light, on-the-string, and in the middle of the bow. With the first note taken downbow the alternations follow logically to a downbow cadence. The lower strings can be played separately, grouped in pairs, or bowed *portato* in fours (as in No. 14 above).

A long *diminuendo* to the entrance of the soprano, followed by an equally patient *crescendo* to the final cadence, can be effective here (especially since this sets up the next movement well). The transition to No. 17 should be taken *attacca*, in any case.

No. 17: Glory to God

At the beginning of this movement, between the two trumpet parts, Handel at first wrote into his manuscript *in disparte* ("aside"—i.e., the trumpets should be placed offstage); later he crossed this out, and substituted *da lontano e un poco piano* ("distant, and rather softly"). There is *no* indication he wanted this same effect from the choir.[31]

Perhaps the biggest risk with this familiar chorus is that *everyone*—whether singer or instrumentalist—may tend to slow down on the quiet passages (bars 5 to 9, etc.). Hold to your tempo. (We favor something close to $\quad = 112$.)

The first violins can take both the second and third notes in measure 1 upbow; similarly, the seconds can play the two notes of the dotted pattern upbow in both bars 1 and 2, taking the first of their running sixteenths in measure 2 downbow. The violas and *continuo* strings could match this pattern by playing the dotted rhythms and the fourth beat of the second bar all upbow. This would bring all the strings to the first beat of bar 7 on a downbow. Another downbow on the first eighth-note, followed by an upbow for the first of the *portato* slurs, would carry them to the repeat beginning in measure 10. (These same bowings can serve through the cadence in bar 18.)

Each of the fugal entrances, commencing with that of the *continuo* bass in measure 18, should be played *detaché*, begun upbow. Minor adjustments are needed:

1. The second violins—to maintain the pattern—would need to take a second consecutive downbow on the first beat of bar 21, and upbows on the last two notes in measure 21.
2. The violas could take a second consecutive downbow on the first note of bar 24, in order to come to the cadence on a downbow.

Beginning at measure 31, the patterns set for the opening are still useful. (The pairs of notes in bars 35 to 37 should be taken downbow-upbow, since they con-

---

31. Alfred Mann, pp. 89–90.

stitute the opening fragment of the fugal motif.) All the string sections must make adjustments in measure 40: the firsts could take a second consecutive downbow on the first beat, the seconds and violas could play both their eighth-notes as upbows, and the *continuo* bass players could make downbows of the first two notes in the bar.

The primary consideration in the closing measures of the movement is the written-out *diminuendo* (*piano* on the last beat of bar 44, and *pianissimo* in bar 46). For this subdued ending, it will work well for the strings to use the tip of the bow; hence we suggest the bowings shown in example 12:

1. The first violins can take consecutive upbows on the last two notes of bar 44, and in bar 46. Then they can play all three of their notes in measure 48 on downbows.
2. The seconds can "take everything as it lies" to measure 46, and then imitate the bowings proposed above for the firsts.
3. The violas need downbows on both the tied A-natural at the end of measure 43 and the G-natural which follows it. In bar 48, both notes can be downbow, with the final D-natural taken upbow.
4. The 'cellos may play both the first two notes in measure 42 downbow, and then follow the viola bowing to the cadence.

Balancing the two trumpets against the strings, the choir, and each other is important here. Check, too, to be certain the articulation patterns played by the trumpets are consistent with the phrasing in the strings, and *vice versa*.

No. 18: Rejoice greatly, O daughter of Zion

This famous aria begins with a ritornello which—since Handel has marked it *senza ripieno*—is played by all the *concertino* violins in unison. There are three major sections to the movement; for the opening portion, a tempo of ♩ = 108 would do nicely. The middle unit (starting at measure 44) can be taken *meno mosso*—sometimes it is slowed to ♩ = 80, or further—and you can return to Tempo I on the third beat of bar 65, after the brief *cadenza* in bars 62 to 64.

With respect to bowing, the ritornello can be taken *detaché*, with each of the two-note patterns begun upbow. In measure 3, both the low F-naturals should be upbows, as should the B-flat and the G-natural on the third beat of bar 4. Everything else can be taken as it falls (including a downbow on the first A-natural in bar 6) through the slurred trills in bars 7 and 8 (except that you will need a pair of upbows on the fourth beat of measure 8, in order to come to the cadence in bar 9 downbow). Again, in measure 38 the second and third notes should both be upbows, as should both the C and F on the third beat of bar 41. The *continuo* bass will need to hook the dotted-eighth-and-sixteenth patterns in measures 5, 6, and 8, and take a fresh downbow on the third beat of bar 9; the first note in bar 23 should be a second consecutive upbow, too. An extra upbow is needed for the A-natural in measure 29, and the dotted-eighth-and-sixteenth

Example 12. "Glory to God," measures 42–49.

patterns in bars 33 and 40–44 should be hooked. The rest of the sequence follows logically.

This brings us to the "B section," which begins with an upbow A-natural (pickup) in measure 44. The opening G-natural in measure 49 can be taken downbow. Later in that same bar Handel added a brief second violin part, which can begin with an upbow on the B-natural. Meanwhile the firsts continue along: if you decide to use the dotted rhythms that Watkins Shaw suggests, you may want to slur the fourth beat in measure 52, making it parallel bar 51.[32] At bar 55, both violin parts should begin upbow, and in bar 58 both should take the low A-natural upbow. The *continuo* bass needs no bowing adjustments.

In the reprise of the "A section," beginning in measure 65, the original violin and *continuo* bass bowing patterns return. All violin pickups should be taken upbow through bar 85.

---

32. The Watkins Shaw edition suggests, as an alternative rhythm for bars 52 and 53, that all the eighth notes (save the last two in measure 52) be paired as dotted-eighth-and-sixteenths, so that these measures will parallel bar 51 (but it still does not recommend a slur for the fourth beat of measure 52). See Watkins Shaw, p. 85.

Some adjustments are needed for the balance of the movement:

1. Each of the three-note patterns in measures 86–88 can begin with a downbow, if you so desire.
2. The F-natural in measure 90—unlike previous pickup notes—should be played downbow, so that the violins come to bar 92 on a downbow.
3. The dotted pairs which begin in the violins at bar 92 can be separate strokes (each begun downbow), or they can be hooked.[33] (The *continuo* basses should follow whichever of these choices you assign to the violins.)
4. The first of the five-note patterns which commence in measure 96 should begin upbow (and thereafter they should alternate—the next starting downbow, etc.).
5. For the final passage, starting in bar 100, follow the guidelines established for the motifs early in the movement, taking each pickup note upbow. The two eighth-notes on the fourth beat of bar 107 (F-natural and A) should be consecutive upbows.
6. The *continuo* basses should hook the dotted pairs in measures 104 and 105, so that they come to the first beat of bar 106 on a downbow.

No. 19: Then shall the eyes of the blind be opened

This *secco* recitative should follow *attacca*. (Make certain the tempo of this—and every—recitative gives the diction a chance to communicate the text clearly.)

No. 20: He shall feed His flock like a shepherd

The motion here—for we suggest this movement be taken in four, at about ♩. = 52—is similar to that of the "Pastoral Symphony" (No. 13). As with that movement, you must be careful not to let it bog down: keep the stick moving (without subdivisions of the beat), and *don't* try to "help out" by waiting for the orchestra on the third eighth-note of each count!

Consider the special bowing problems here: since there are only two basic bow-directions—down and up—the simplest patterns always are those which divide the measure or the beat into *even* numbers of notes. Whenever one finds an *uneven* number of notes—say, three—in a beat, or a bar, one must make some sort of adjustment. In a 12/8 meter like this, such cases are bound to arise.

For the first violins, the first two measures are simple enough. Beginning upbow on the pickup, of course, they "take it as it comes" to the third beat of bar 3, where the three-note, dotted pattern makes the tied note an upbow; playing the sixteenth-note B-flat as another upbow will cause the tied F-natural to fall on a

---

33. Again the Watkins Shaw edition suggests an important change: this time that trills be added to all the dotted notes in bars 92 through 95. Page 87.

downbow. (Note that the tied length of the upbow C-natural helps to balance—and this is a subtlety we have discussed only in theory[34]—the amount of bow needed for the long downbow F-natural, several notes later.) Similarly, the three-note pattern in bar 6 reverses the bowing sequence; a pair of upbows for the G-natural and F-natural on the third beat sets it right again. Again, the three-note grouping on the second beat of measure 9 makes necessary a pair of up-bows on the two notes thereafter. Look, however, at the second violin part on the first two beats of bar 9: since there are *two* of these three-note patterns here, the alternation will work out automatically, and no adjustment will be necessary. The same thing happens to the seconds in measures 15 and 22. *Remember this method of determining bowings.*

We have discussed the first violin part through bar 9 already. Let us proceed further:

1. Consecutive upbows are appropriate (for the reasons we have been considering) on the third beat of bar 12, the second count of bar 15, the last count of measure 19, the first beat of bar 21, and the second beat of 22.
2. After the soprano entrance, the firsts could play extra upbows on the pickups at the end of measures 27 and 33, retake a downbow on the first beat of bar 37, and play a pair of upbows on the second beats of 44, 47, 51, and 52.
3. The final measures (of all the string parts) could go as shown in example 13.

For the second violins, similar adjustments are recommended:

1. Consecutive upbows are needed on the second beat of bar 1, the last two counts of measure 6, the last count of 7, 11, 12, and 15, and the second beat of 23. The seconds should retake a downbow for the downbeat of 25.
2. After the entrance of the soprano in measure 25, consecutive upbows are appropriate on the second beat of measure 27, consecutive down-bows on the E-natural and the C which follows it in bar 36, and pairs of upbows on the third beat of bar 37, the last beat of 40, and the last two notes of 43, of 46, and of 48. Consecutive downbows on the second and third notes of measure 52 would correct the bowing sequence which leads to the final cadence.
3. The bowing we suggest for that cadence is shown in example 13.

The viola part also requires the kinds of adjustments we have been making:

1. Consecutive upbows are needed on the final beats of measures 1, 6, 7, 9, 12, 13, 16, 22, and 23, the second beat of 32, and the final beat of 34, 36, 38, and 51.

---

34. See "Bowing: Central Concepts" above, pp. 12 ff.

Example 13. "He shall feed His flock like a shepherd," measures 53–56.

2. Bowing of the final cadence is shown in example 13.

The *continuo* bass part needs only the following:

1. Consecutive upbows will be helpful on the second beat of measures 9 and 15, on the tied G-natural and the following eighth-note in bar 19, and on the final count of 22.
2. Downbows should be retaken for the downbeats of measures 26, 45, and 51.
3. The final cadence should be bowed as shown in example 13.

No. 21: His yoke is easy

The final movement of Part I of *Messiah* should follow the soprano aria without delay. This chorus is very difficult for the singers, of course, demanding —as it does—virtuosic agility and control; it is the capability of your choir, then, that is likely to determine the tempo you choose. (We favor something close to ♩ = 104, if that is possible for you.)

At the opening of the movement, the choir is supported only by the *continuo*. Where the upper strings join the texture, in bar 8, they should play *detaché*, in the upper third of the bow. Generally, the off-the-beat pickups should be taken upbow, of course; in bar 10, however, the first violins need to take the F-natural pickup downbow. They also can play a second consecutive upbow on the sixteenth-note after the trill in measure 11. (We suggest taking the trill that is part of this motif on an upbow each time it occurs.)

Again in measures 15, 19, and 23, the firsts and seconds can take consecutive upbows on the second beat; in bar 29, they can do so on the fourth beat. In measure 37, the firsts should make the same adjustment. In measure 40, the seconds can hook the last two notes on an upbow. On the third beat of bar 41, the firsts should take both the dotted-eighth and the sixteenth downbow; in the same bar—and in measure 44—the seconds could take consecutive upbows on the second beat.

The violas need consecutive upbows on the second beat of bars 41 and 42, and the last beat of bar 45.

Through all of these measures, the *continuo* bass should play with a brush stroke, taking metrically weak pickups upbow, and adding consecutive upbows (where necessary) to bars with uneven numbers of notes, so that the first beat of each measure is taken downbow.

For the final cadence (the last three-and-a-half measures), each of the three upper string parts can begin with consecutive downbows on the dotted-quarter and the eighth in bar 48; the second violins will need to hook the sixteenths in measure 50 (upbow), so that all three sections will come out downbow on the whole-note. The *continuo* bass can begin bar 48 with a single downbow.

The alternations of *con* and *senza ripieno* in this movement present one danger: Handel clearly intends that these *tutti* passages constitute *forte* interjections, in contrast to the routine *piano* and *pianissimo* accompanimental patterns of the *concertino* instruments. At such points, the strings may tend to overplay (in an effort to carry out Handel's intentions), *may change the amount of bow they use, and may shorten the durations of the spaces between notes, thus altering their style of playing.* Be certain articulation stays consistent throughout the movement.

Here "Part the First" ends. If you are not taking an intermission at this point, you will want to make an extended pause.

PART THE SECOND

No. 22: Behold the Lamb of God

With this chorus, Handel turns Part II of *Messiah* immediately to the story of the Passion of Christ. There is neither overture nor *entr'acte*.

The omnipresent dotted rhythms need firmness of direction from you; one often hears performances of this chorus which become ragged (or interminable) —sometimes as a result of the desire of the choir members to sing this emotion-laden text too expressively. We recommend that you take it at a tempo near ♪ = 72, using a subdivided four in order to show the string players the length of the eighth-notes. (*There are many different types of subdivided beats.* Choose one which conveys clearly how much emphasis you want given to the off-the-beat eighth-notes.) On the fourth quarter-note in measure 17, you might consider modifying your beat pattern to a slow four, reverting to the subdivided mode where necessary.

As for bowings,[35] you probably will find it useful to hook most of the dotted-eighth-and-sixteenth pairs together. (Thus the opening measures of the first violin part would begin with an upbow for the pickup G-natural; the high G and F would be slurred, as would the E-flat and D-natural. After the downbow D in bar 2, each of the three dotted pairs would be hooked. The fourth measure would begin upbow, but the pickup G at the end of that bar would follow up-bow, bringing the downbow back to the downbeat on the first beat of bar 5.) Since the same motif penetrates each of the other string parts, this pattern of hooking can serve for them, as well.

You must determine, however, how you want this dotted rhythm expressed. Do you prefer a *legato* effect, or would you rather hear some separation within the lines? If you add nothing but the hooks, you should get a slurred, continuous stream of sound; placing dashes above the dotted notes should cause the players

---

35. Up to this point—and through the whole of the frequently performed "Christmas portion" of *Messiah*—we have given detailed and complete bowings for almost every beat of every measure. Of these choices, many have been obvious ones, and others have been arbitrary; moreover, we suspect that, by this point—if you have been following our discussion with your score—you have begun to understand the bowing process rather well, in terms both of theory and practice.

For the remainder of the work, then, *in order that our very completeness not become a hindrance,* we will suggest bowings for the characteristic motifs of each movement, so that you can apply those ideas to recurrent appearances of each motif, and will attempt to note and remedy special problem spots, but will not identify exhaustively every adjustment which might be made in one or another of the string parts. We trust this procedure will serve your needs.

to separate the notes a bit; substituting dots for the dashes should result in longer, more obvious silences within each phrase.

All these dotted rhythms could be played on separate bows—and Handel's musicians (using Baroque bows) may well have performed them that way—but the result would be less smooth, and the sixteenths would sound more insistent.

There are few other problems in this movement.

1. The very long, tied B-flat in the first violin part (bars 18–21) may be a concern. If you want an unbroken flow of sound here, ask them to "stagger the bowing" or "alternate," and they should make bow changes at varied moments. If you want this long note to end upbow, you may want to ask them to mark an upbow someplace near the downbeat of bar 20. (They will avoid making the bow change right on that beat, if you ask them to do so.)
2. The firsts should take the pickup at the end of bar 21 on an upbow. Then the same long-note procedure can be applied, as you wish, to the tied D-natural found in measures 22–26.
3. You may find it effective to ask the upper strings to play the first eighth-note in bar 26 downbow. This will bring all of them (*detaché*) on down-bows to the downbeat of 27. (You may want to have the firsts change bows a couple of times during the tied D-natural, so that they end that long note on a downbow; then they can retake a short downbow to fit into this pattern.)
4. For the final cadence, it may be best to have both sections of violins play their last dotted notes downbow, so that they can end downbow, as well.

No. 23: He was despised

This famous *da capo* aria, like the chorus before it, could be conducted in a subdivided four, but you may not find that necessary. (Our sense is that the strings may need less of an indication of the subdivision than they did in the previous movement.) We suggest that you consider a tempo of perhaps ♩ = 50.

The strings can play *detaché*, taking each of the off-the-beat pickups (in the three-note motif, and in longer figures) upbow. The trill in bar 2 will fall on a downbow, in that case and each time the motif returns. Note that the first trilled figure is slurred; while most recurrences of this motif are not marked with slurs, you certainly may choose to play them so (including the ones on the first beats of bars 26, 27, 35, and 36, which are not notated as trills in some editions).[36] You may prefer measured trills in this slow tempo; if so, you can have the musicians play a seven-note pattern—of six thirty-second-notes, leading to a slurred eighth—at each point on which the motif occurs. (See example 14.) Whatever

---

36. The Watkins Shaw edition, already frequently cited, suggests that trills be added in bars 26, 27, 35, and 36 and that all these three-note trill patterns be slurred, so that they are consistent with those in measures 2 and 3.

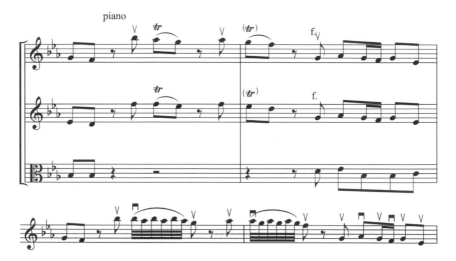

Example 14. Prototypical measured (five-note) trill figures in the aria "He was despised," measures 2–3.

choices you finally make about trills and slurs, be consistent. Be certain, moreover, that the players observe carefully the detailed alternation of *piano* and *forte* markings Handel wrote into this expressive and powerful movement.

Measures 49–50 are an important seam. Be sure to be precise in the gestures you use for the cutoff of the *fermata* at the end of bar 49, and for the preparation of the downbeat to 50. For the midsection of this aria, the orchestra members *do* need a subdivided beat. We recommend a somewhat faster tempo here, too—probably ♩ = 72, or so; and we seek to strengthen the thirty-second-notes in the string accompaniment. To this purpose, we recommend that *these* dotted patterns be played with separate bows, starting *upbow* and working near the tip of the bow. (If you prefer, the dotted pairs can be hooked, but this is likely to produce a less emphatic, less energetic image.) The last two chords of this section, before the *da capo*, should be taken upbow-downbow.

Remember that it is unlikely Baroque musicians would have performed the reprise of this aria exactly as they had presented it at the outset. Prepare your soloist, especially, to vary the ornaments the second time from those she incorporated originally.

No. 24: Surely He hath borne our griefs

Here again we have a movement you probably will want to conduct in a subdivided four, at something like ♪ = 100; subdivision will help the musicians maintain clean ensemble in a fabric which employs dotted rhythms *within* the

Example 15. Suggested bowings for "Surely He hath borne our griefs," measures 1–2.

Example 16. Suggested bowings for "Surely He hath borne our griefs," measures 6–7.

half-beat. Be cautious—especially in early rehearsals—to keep your beat pattern visually clear: place each beat in its own "geographic" area, and direct each subdivision into that same region. Use the lateral plane, as well as the horizontal one. Do not let your beats all focus on one spot.

We recommend bowing the characteristic rhythmic figure as shown in example 15, starting it with a downbow and hooking the internal dotted-sixteenth-and-thirty-second pair; thus the quarter-notes will come on downbows. Where the dotted pairs are consecutive (as in the last half of bar 2 in the first violins) you may choose to continue hooking the pairs. In bar 6—given the long (tied) note—you could balance the lengths of the up- and down-strokes in the firsts by hooking the final two notes (the G and F) rather than the B-flat and A-flat. (See example 16.) The second violin, viola, and *continuo* bass parts follow nicely. Measure 12 is similar to bar 5, save that the firsts should hook the final dotted pair, taking the final B and G as separate down- and upbows.

At measure 13 it will be clearer if you conduct a simple four-beat pattern, discontinuing your subdivision of the beat. (Obviously Handel is thinking of another sort of motion at this point.) In this section, it may be well for you to note in the orchestra parts the breath marks you have assigned to your choir, since the vocal lines are primary here.

Recommence subdividing, then, on the third beat of measure 19, for the dotted-sixteenth-and-thirty-second rhythm resumes there. The bowings for this passage follow the prototypes set for the opening of the movement. The notes on the last beat before the final cadence can be taken separately (down-up) for emphasis.[37]

No. 25: And with His stripes we are healed

Here all the upper strings are doubling the voices. That means you will want to give special attention to balance, making certain that neither the instrumental nor the vocal forces overwhelm the rest. Note the *alla breve* indications: consider ♩ = 108 as a possible tempo. (Handel marked this ₵ himself, yet "wrote bars of varying length."[38] Check the edition[s] your choir and orchestra are using, and determine whether you will conduct the movement in ₵ or 4/2; in either solution the half note is the beat.)

Both the subjects—the half-note line which starts in bar 1, and the quarter-note countersubject first seen in bar 7—should begin upbow. Otherwise, the bowing is routine; you need make only such adjustments as will maintain the clarity of the subjects and the cadences.

Decide how much separation you want between notes in the strings. You will find that a little space (especially in a movement which doubles instruments and voices) will give your choir a chance to make its consonants heard.

No. 26: All we like sheep have gone astray

Although this is one of the more difficult choruses for the singers, it is not particularly hard for the orchestra. We recommend ♩ = 108, if your choir can manage it.[39]

---

37. Note that in discussing dotted rhythms in the last two movements we have recommended quite different bowings: for the middle section of "He was despised," we favored separate bows for each note, while for "Surely He hath borne our griefs" we suggested hooking the dotted pairs. The distinction here is primarily one of expression (and, consequently of tempo, as well); it is our view that the dramatic force of "He gave His back to the smiters" is strengthened by our separate bows, while our slurs give No. 24 a rather more lyric quality. Remember that bowing is an expressive process, as well as a technical one. If you prefer a different character for a movement, you are likely to need a different bowing.

38. Watkins Shaw, already cited, p. 114.

39. This relates directly to the previous movement (i.e., here a quarter-note equals a half-note of No. 25).

Indicate clearly what articulation you want from the strings. (One way to do that efficiently is to let the orchestra hear the choir sing part of the movement.) As with the previous chorus, the extent to which the orchestra doubles the voices makes clarity of articulation doubly important; do not let your choir's consonants be lost in the strings.

The bowings are quite straightforward. The upper strings will want to begin the first motif upbow, of course; the countersubject at bar 6 should commence downbow, as could the octave figure at measure 23. Decide, in spots like bar 16, what you prefer that the two violin sections do about the effect of the sixteenth-notes: Do you want consecutive upbows on the fourth beat of the bar, or would you rather have them play the first beat of measure 17 upbow?

Note the wedges Handel has added (to measures 47–48 and 72–73) to gain additional emphasis for the homophonic chords on the words "every one to his own way." Note also the slurs under the accompanimental figures in the seconds and violas, beginning in bar 52; you may want to add equivalent hooks to the firsts and the *continuo* bass, or you may prefer to delete all of the slurring. (This inconsistency may stem from an old copying problem.)

The *adagio* in measure 76, at a proportion of perhaps 1:2, should begin exactly on the third beat of that bar. This is one of the spots at which the orchestra needs to know exactly what you and the chorus are doing, especially if you plan to stretch out the final phrase and cadence. Writing the choir's dynamics and breath marks into the orchestra parts here can save you a lot of rehearsal time. Each of the string sections can begin its line with a downbow on the dotted-quarter with which that line commences. Each can take the first quarter-note in bar 88 upbow, continuing to a downbow on the final chord. (The firsts will need consecutive upbows in bar 91.)

No. 27: All they that see Him, laugh Him to scorn

This is another movement it would be well to take in a subdivided four. Note that (like the PIFA, No. 13) Handel has stipulated three violin parts here.

The dramatic importance of the thirty-second-notes in this recitative is similar to that of the thirty-seconds in the middle section of No. 23; for the same reasons, then, we suggest beginning the first violin part upbow. (Taking the shorter notes downbow will emphasize them somewhat.) In bar 3, the firsts can hook the dotted C-natural to the B-flat, to maintain the pattern.

Given the *forte* indication, you probably will wish bar 6 to begin downbow; in that case, it may be best to hook the first dotted pattern in the first violins. Measure 8 can commence with a downbow, too. (Compare the slurs here with the separate notes in bar 9, and decide whether you want to edit either measure.) In measure 10, we can recreate the bar 1 effect by beginning this final phrase downbow; if you choose to make a big *ritard* here, it may be best to hook the last couple of notes in bar 10.

No. 28: He trusted in God that He would deliver Him

This is one of the choruses to which Bernard Shaw referred when—angered by "lumbering" tempi and "unwieldy choral impostures"—he growled that "Most of us would be glad to hear the work *[Messiah]* seriously performed once before we die."[40] We urge you to work toward a tempo approaching ♩ = 136, and to place special emphasis on diction here.

Once again, make certain the players understand what the choir is doing; mark the parts wherever this would be useful. Here, as in several of the movements we have seen already, the strings are doubling the voice parts. It will work well for them to play this *detaché,* with each of the entrances of the subject starting with an upbow (save the *continuo* bass, which begins downbow, of course); "taking it as it comes," then, the peak notes of the line and the cadence pitch each time will fall on downbows. (Note that the slurs marked over the sixteenths in the choral parts do not appear in the string lines.) Most of the countersubject statements should begin upbow, too, although you may want to make occasional adjustments.

You may prefer to strengthen the initial note of each entrance by marking the pickup downbow. That would be perfectly acceptable, but you would want to make a standard adjustment somewhere within the subject (perhaps hooking the two sixteenths together) in order to "make the bowing come out right."

Approaching the final cadence, the release in measure 60 will be more emphatic if you let both the third-beat dotted-eighth and the fourth-beat quarter-note be taken as downbows. The new tempo for the *adagio* should be established on the first beat (the quarter-rest) of bar 61. Be certain that the preparation beat moves in the right direction, and defines the tempo clearly. Each of the strings can attack the first note of the *adagio* with an upbow, then, and the rest will follow naturally.

No. 29: Thy rebuke hath broken His heart

This *stromentato* movement needs some patience and poise. Mark into the string parts the points at which the tenor will want extra time for a breath, or for phrasing (perhaps before the fourth beat of measure 7, before the third count of bar 13, and before the two final chords). Indicate any *crescendi* and *diminuendi,* too.

As to bowing, plan which attacks you want taken down- and which upbow—the spots above, for example—and make adjustments accordingly. You may prefer to have the bar 7 trills in the two violin parts played upbow. (Be cognizant that these two trills are of two different lengths.) Decide what sort of harmonic clash you want on the last fraction of the fourth beat, and edit the parts as necessary. Finally, choose whether or not you want the orchestra's cadence to

---

40. George Bernard Shaw, *Music in London 1880–1894,* vol. I, p. 116.

Example 17. Suggested bowings for "Behold, and see if there be any sorrow," measures 3–6.

coincide with that of the tenor; as we have said before, you may delay it until the tenor has finished, if you wish.[41]

No. 30: Behold, and see if there be any sorrow

You will have more control (particularly at the moments when you need it most) if you subdivide this *Largo e piano*. We suggest ♪ = 68 as a possible tempo.

The pickups of most of these accompanimental figures should be taken up-bow, for course. Everything can be separated, or—if you like—you can have a slurred effect in measures 5 and 14. (See the suggestions offered in example 17.)[42]

---

41. Unlike some earlier instances (the end of No. 2, "Comfort ye," for example), the harmonies of this cadence permit it to be performed either way. There are circumstances—particularly where you want to keep momentum going from movement to movement—when it may be deleterious to delay the orchestral cadence; in other cases—at a dramatic moment, for example—hesitation can be effective.
42. Watkins Shaw suggests trills (important with respect to the structure of the arioso) for the second beats both of bars 6 and—correspondingly—15. See Watkins Shaw, p. 142.

No. 31: He was cut off out of the land of the living

All the strings can begin this movement downbow. If your soloist sings the appoggiatura on the first beat of the final bar, the last two chords must be delayed; in any case, they should be played up- and downbow.

No. 32: But Thou didst not leave His soul in hell

This aria will go well in a straight four, paced near ♩ = 72. A deft brush stroke in the *continuo* bass can be the foundation of the alternation between violins and voice. The violin line itself can begin upbow, and follows thereon logically; our recommended bowings for the opening line are shown in example 18. (Note the possible trill on the dotted-eighth C-sharp in bar 2. Others can be incorporated for the G-sharp in measure 8, and the dotted-quarter D-sharp in bar 14.) All of the violin attacks should be taken upbow, since each begins with a pickup note. You may prefer that the final note—the low A-natural—be taken downbow; if this is the case, try hooking together the dotted-eighth C-sharp and the sixteenth-note B-natural. Thus you can avoid consecutive downbows on the octave A-naturals.

No. 33: Lift up your heads, O ye gates

This fanfare-like chorus, with its question-and-response text ("Who is . . . ?"), may suggest to you a clipped articulation with lots of separation between notes, both in chorus and orchestra. Look for ways of varying the articulation, as a means of highlighting the antiphonal character of the choral textures; you may want less separation for some phrases, and rather more for others. We try to avoid too fast a tempo here. Something close to ♩ = 116 may be about right.

The separation we are recommending implies *detaché* bowing, of course; the consecutive dotted pairs (in bar 3, for example) can be hooked, or they can be separated, as you prefer. (If you hook them, you might consider adding dots over each of the sixteenths, to keep the line from becoming too smooth—too connected.) Most of the motifs important to this movement appear during the first ten measures of it (and we provide possible bowings for this passage in example 19).

Once you have confirmed in your own mind how you want each of these motifs handled, most of the rest of the movement is predetermined, at least in concept. There are some adjustments to be made:

1. For the sake of emphasis of the text, you may want to take the dotted rhythms in measures 27 to 31 on separate bows, even if you have been hooking these earlier.
2. In bar 31, the firsts and seconds should take their initial notes down-

Example 18. Suggested bowings for "But Thou didst not leave His soul in hell," measures 1–5.

bow, in order to give the right stress to the downbeat of bar 32. Each time this motif returns the same solution is needed. (The pair of notes at the end of measure 39 should begin with an upbow, of course. See example 20.)

3. The lower strings in measure 39 (and the firsts, in bar 42) take up a figure which begins with three pickup eighth-notes. Consider placing

Example 19. Suggested bowings for "Lift up your heads, O ye gates," measures 1–10.

Example 20. Suggested bowings for "Lift up your heads, O ye gates," measures 39–42.

dots over each of those pickups (marking the first of them upbow) and treat the motif consistently each time it recurs later in the movement. See example 20.

4. In bar 62, the two eighth-notes in the first violin part can be hooked (upbow). The string crossing involved will give you plenty of separation, by the way.

5. The last three notes should begin downbow in all four string sections. Be certain the players (and the choir) keep the intensity high through these three chords. (Some players, like some singers, forget to "push through" important long notes.)

No. 34: Unto which of the angels said He

The only concern here is coordination of the soloist with the *continuo* section.

No. 35: Let all the angels of God worship Him

We suggest that you take this wonderful, but often-cut chorus in four, at about $\downarrow$ = 112. The bowing choices are not difficult; the upper strings begin upbow, of course, and the violin sections both need to hook their last pair of eighth-notes in bar 2 (or make some similar change), so that they come to the cadence in measure 4 on downbows. Few other adjustments will be necessary. (Both the firsts and seconds will need consecutive upbows on the last two notes of measure 36—the next-to-last bar.)

This is a good moment to remind you not to acquiesce thoughtlessly in "historic Messiah cuts." The oratorio, as it follows the Jennens libretto, is a continuity, both in textual meaning and in musical structure. (You will find that some cuts create enormous problems of transition between keys, for example—problems Handel solved movement-by-movement as he laid out the tonal relationships.) Even if you must excise some movements, for practical reasons peculiar to your situation, do not automatically cut ones that "are never done" (thereby continuing an evil tradition). *It is arguable that there are no weak movements in Messiah!* If a particular aria or chorus has been infrequently performed in your community, that circumstance is—as it stands—an excellent argument for your including that movement. *The very familiarity of much of Messiah urges us to fortify its freshness, and one good way to accomplish that is to restore to it some of its forgotten jewels.*

No. 36: Thou art gone up on high

For the opening melodic line, so typically Baroque in its curves and in its octave displacements, Handel has indicated *concertino* violins. Calculate what the effect of this will be, especially in terms of balance with the soloist and *con-*

tinuo body, and establish appropriate dynamics. The aria needs to flow; we suggest a moderate three, set probably at a tempo near ♩ = 100.

The bowing is straightforward. Beginning upbow, the violins can play separate strokes until the marked slurs in bar 7. (You will have to decide whether you want these slurs used in bar 8, too.) After an upbow on the high G-natural in measure 9, you will need consecutive upbows on the last two pitches in bar 10 (or some other adjustment). Note the possibility of a trill on the second beat of that measure.

Within the movement:

1. You can consider hooking each of the first two dotted pairs in bar 29, and again in 31.
2. The violin attacks in measures 15, 29, 56, and 105 start upbow; the others work better if begun with downbows.
3. The final cadence should be approached by taking the high G-natural sixteenth-note in measure 114 upbow. With separate bows, then, the downbeat D-natural in the last bar will be an upbow, and the final note a downbow.

No. 37: The Lord gave the word

Before conducting this movement, check your tempo (for which we recommend ♩ = 96–100), against the speed of the sixteenth notes. Keep your beat clear, particularly because of the *tutti* rest at the beginning of measure 3.

With respect to bowing this chorus, all the strings can begin downbow in bar 3. In measure 4, the firsts might take consecutive downbows on the two B-flats, while the seconds and violas could play consecutive upbows on their dotted pairs. From this point on, it is largely a matter of the string players "taking it as it comes."

1. Each of the four string sections might play consecutive upbows on the second beat of measure 11.
2. Dotted pairs and other figures can be hooked in any of the parts, wherever this is a useful adjustment.
3. In measures 21 and 22, it would be practical to hook the third-beat eighth-notes (on a downbow) in the upper string parts, adding a dot over the second of these notes in the latter case. This will bring all the strings to the downbeat of bar 23 on downbows.
4. It is only necessary, then, to add an extra upbow to the last A-natural in the second violin part.

No. 38: How beautiful are the feet of them

Handel tried several formats for this aria (including a duet version) and for the chorus which follows it. The G minor setting for soprano seems to have

Example 21. Suggested bowings for "How beautiful are the feet of them," measures 1–4.

been his eventual preference, and is the one now most frequently done.[43] Another of the *Siciliano* movements we have been seeing in *Messiah,* it can stay in
four (at something like $\quarternote = 40$, or $\eighthnote = 120$) if you will keep the flow of the dance
rhythm in mind. Watch the overall shape of the melodic line, respecting the
points at which the violins want a little time for phrasing (after the quarter-note
A-natural in the first measure, for example).

One possible bowing for the opening line is shown in example 21. Note that

<hr/>

43. See Alfred Mann, p. 87.

Example 22. Suggested bowings for "How beautiful are the feet of them," measures
20–24.

only the first of the quarter-eighth slurs is Handel's own; if you prefer, all the
later pairs can be bowed separately.

Going on, in measure 6 the F-natural pickup should be an upbow, but the
B-flat in the next bar should be a (consecutive) downbow; otherwise the violins
have to recover the entire length of the bow, if they are to have room to play
another note so long. The G-natural pickup in bar 8, then, can be another up-

bow. In measures 12, 13, and 14 the eighth-notes can be taken upbow, and in 15 the pair of notes on each of the first three beats can be slurred. A (second consecutive) downbow on the low G in measure 16 will be helpful in again evening out the bow strokes.

In the final *ritornello*, starting upbow at the end of bar 20, you may choose to slur the quarter-eighth pair on the second beat of measure 21, as Handel did (an octave lower) in bar 1, or you may have these played separately. Consecutive upbows on the last beat of that bar will keep the phrasing clear. See example 22 for a possible set of bowings for this passage. (Note the suggested trills, as well.)

No. 39: Their sound is gone out into all lands

If you followed our suggestion of $\flat$ = 120 for the previous movement, the relationship for this chorus will be easy: we suggest $\downarrow$ = 120; thus $\flat$ = $\downarrow$. You can take it in a straight four. Watch the balance at the chorus entrances at bar 13 and thereafter, marking dynamic changes into the orchestra parts if necessary. Be certain that the oboes (which are back with us in this movement, after a long rest) use articulation that matches that of the chorus.

Bowings are simple here. Both violin sections can attack the second beat in measure 7 downbow; other minor adjustments are necessary—in measure 22, for example, where the firsts should hook the dotted pair, and in bar 24, where again the firsts and seconds should attack the second beat downbow. The final cadence works out logically.

No. 40: Why do the nations so furiously rage

This movement can present problems for the inexperienced conductor. (If you have any concern about it, try writing the rhythm of the first couple of measures of the bass solo line under the opening bars of the movement, so that you can be thinking the melody and tempo of the solo itself before you cue the orchestra.) The tempo here will depend at least substantially on the needs of the soloist, of course; try something near $\downarrow$ = 144, if this seems comfortable.

Be certain that the dynamic variants you want are clearly indicated in the orchestra parts. Do not let the players pound out every note either; not every pulse is a downbeat here! Work to keep an even, shapely, forward motion through this exciting aria.

Bow everything separate. The sixteenths are almost constant in the upper string parts. Where an eighth-note (which, falling on the beat, will always be a downbow) interrupts the sixteenths, *mark the next sixteenth-note as a (second consecutive) downbow;* that will keep the bowing sequence right. (See example 23.)

Be cautious that the instrumental bass line does not become heavy. The upper strings will probably play this in the middle or upper third of the bow. (For the slurs in bars 12 and 13, they must be sure not to use too much bow; a smaller stroke will help produce a cleaner sound in this situation.) A few adjustments

Example 23. Suggested bowings for "Why do the nations so furiously rage," measures 1–4.

are necessary—in bar 27, for example, where the upper strings can take (second consecutive) downbows on the second beat.

The last seven measures are essentially an accompanied recitative, and are simple enough, assuming you know exactly what the bass soloist plans to do. You have an option in the final bar: you can play it as written, beginning with eighth-notes in both violin parts on the last half of the first beat, or you can change those two notes to sixteenths (dotting the eighth-rest on the downbeat); either choice is legitimate in the style of the period. Whichever rhythm you choose, the bowing for the last bar probably should be (1) a downbow, (2) an upbow hooking together the dotted-eighth-and-sixteenth, and (3) a final downbow. Move immediately to the ensuing chorus.

No. 41: Let us break their bonds asunder

A rock-steady tempo is required for this chorus. Do not take it too fast, for it gets much of its character from the consonants; consider ♩ = 120. You can infer articulation for the chorus from the wedges Handel has written for the orchestra. You probably will want to write in some dynamic variants, indicating the most emphatic of the fugal entrances, as well as the more relaxed passages.

The strings could handle this in the middle to the upper third of the bow, playing it quite energetically (*almost in a martelé style*). Start each section downbow, of course. Some adjustments will be needed:

1. Note the first violin part in measures 6 and 7. All this can be taken on separate bows, but you will want consecutive upbows (on the second-beat eighth-notes, for instance) in both these bars. The *continuo* bass(es) need a similar pair of upbows on the third beat of measure 7, as do the violas on the third beat of measure 8.
2. The new fugal line which first appears in bar 10 can begin with a downbow on the D-natural and two upbows on the B-natural and G quarternotes. The violas can "take it as it comes" from that point. The seconds and the firsts, in their turns (bars 12 and 15), can employ the same bowings.
3. The entrance of the first violins in measure 34 brings them to the downbeat of 35 on a downbow, and the second subject begins, then, on the next beat. Consecutive downbows (on the first and second beats of 35) and consecutive upbows (on the third beat of 35 and the downbeat of 36) are needed, so that the figure can be played just as it was before. (See example 24.)
4. If you want the strings to arrive at the downbeat of bar 52 on downbows, you could ask that each section hook the dotted-quarter-and-eighth pair on the first two beats.

No. 42: He that dwelleth in heaven

You have learned already how to treat these *secco* recitatives. The *continuo* group should delay the final cadence.

No. 43: Thou shall break them

The uniqueness of melodic shape in this movement makes it one of the best, most refreshing arias in the entire oratorio. Choose a tempo bright enough to have vitality, yet sufficiently broad to give the sixteenths time and substance. We recommend you and the soloist consider ♩ = 108. Give some thought, too, to the number of violins you want. (The part is marked *senza ripieno,* but that does not mean you must use every player you have.)

The highly decorated violin line virtually bows itself. Start it with an upbow, of course, and observe the slurs; every measure will work out right until bar 9, where you need to slur the dotted G-sharp to the A-natural (so that the low A-natural in the next measure will fall on a downbow). The string crossings (the skips to the low notes in the early measures) are not difficult, but—if you have a student orchestra—watch the intonation on these pitches. (If players have dif-

Example 24. Suggested bowings for "Let us break their bonds asunder," measures 33–38.

Example 25. Suggested bowings for "Thou shalt break them," measures 9–12.

ficulty, warn them not to use too much bow on the previous slur, and ask that they use care about bow placement for the low notes.)

These patterns are applicable throughout the movement. Only a few adjustments are needed.

1. After the three slurs in measure 21, the first two notes of bar 22 should be consecutive upbows. This same change is needed, for the same reason, in bars 62 and 72.

2. The last two notes in measure 34 should be hooked, just as was done in bar 9. At the end of the last *ritornello,* then, you could slur the dotted G-sharp to the eighth-note A-natural in the same way. If you want this final cadence to have a different effect, however, you can avoid the slur—in which case the first note in the last bar will be a downbow, and the final note an upbow—or you could mark them both as downbows. Try all three possibilities with your concertmaster, if you have an opportunity to do so.

No. 44: Hallelujah!

This, perhaps the most famous choral piece ever written, is not—as people who have never heard the complete oratorio generally assume—the end of *Messiah;* it is only the climax of the middle portion. The "Hallelujah Chorus" is difficult, in a sense, even though it is done—and sometimes done badly—by both able and unskilled choirs all over the world. It is precisely our familiarity with it that causes ensembles to take it for granted, to oversing it, to play it casually without thinking carefully about it, or to repeat bad habits learned in other years. And this is true for conductors, too; this movement offers a good moment for each of us to mistrust himself, and to check what it is we are doing with the baton. What exactly is coming out of the end of the stick? Is it clear? Is it showing what we want the singers and players to see?

Here is one of the most important tempo choices you will make in the entire work. It must be logical and musical, and it must sound fresh to singers, players, and listeners who already know this chorus well. We recommend something close to ♩ = 120, but your circumstances may suggest a different pace.

Most of your bowing decisions in this movement are forecast in the melodic elements that appear in the opening measures. The two "Hallelujah!" figures—the first, a dotted-quarter and three eighths (seen in bar 1), and the second, two sixteenths followed by two eighths (first found across the bar line of measure 6)—both begin downbow, here and later in the movement. The longer motif which begins with the half-note A-natural on the first beat of bar 12 also should start downbow; the two eighths (first beat of measure 13) can be taken on consecutive upbows, so that the final A-natural (third beat of 14) will fall on an upbow, too. All these bowings can be seen in example 26. If you concur with them, you will find it simple to apply them throughout the movement.

Example 26. Suggested bowings for "Hallelujah!" measures 1–14.

We suggest that the splendid passage which begins with the last beat of measure 33 calls for a new, more linear character. You may want to mark the orchestral parts *legato* at this moment. This is a good spot to show the players exactly where the singers will take releases (after the first "Christ," in bar 40, for example). The orchestra can take "breaths" with the choir, if you ask them to. The bowings shown in example 27 illustrate this point of view.

The enormous expansion that commences with the first "King of Kings"

Example 27. Suggested bowings for "Hallelujah!" measures 31–41.

statement in bars 51–52 tempts the singers and players to give too much too soon. Remind them that there are *six* repetitions of this phrase coming, as the soprano line ascends to the high G at 66–67, and they need to conserve energy, saving themselves (and their audience) for the peak. On the third beat of measure 67, when the orchestra joins the "King of Kings" rhythm, the strings begin with a downbow, of course; similarly, they take the third beat of bar 74 downbow, for here begins the same figure.

Only practical adjustments remain here and there. The pickup to bar 93 should be an upbow, of course, in order to end downbow. As we suggested at the end of the first part, if you are not taking an intermission at this point, you certainly will want (and need) to give your musicians and your audience an extended pause.

PART THE THIRD

To this point, *Messiah* has dealt with the specific events: the Messianic prophecies, the birth of Jesus, the first Passiontide, and the spreading of the Gospel. Part the Third is reflective, instead; in character, it is an elaborate song of thanksgiving. Shorter than either of the earlier sections—for there are only nine movements here—the final Part contemplates the implications of the Resurrection of Christ for the individual human being, and ends in an anthem of praise, the structural purpose of which is to transcend even the "Hallelujah!" chorus.

No. 45: I know that my Redeemer liveth

The impact of that "Hallelujah!" movement is cushioned by the intermission or pause after it, and by the stately motion and calm assurance of the aria which begins Part the Third. We recommend that you take this in three, beginning the *Larghetto* at ♩ = 80 or so, and enlarging the size of your beat at the *adagio* in measures 151–153 (and at any similar spots), in order to let the orchestra know that a broader tempo is coming.

The *concertino* violins are in unison here. The opening *ritornello* is usually taken *detaché* "as it comes." If they started upbow, the only adjustment we suggest is a downbow on the high G-sharp in bar 5. This means that all the three-note pickups (measures 5, 7, 9, 12, and 13) will start downbow. (If you prefer to hook all the dotted pairs, you will have to make other modifications. Handel appears to have slurred the pairs in bars 2, 4, 10, and 11 himself—as well as the eighths in 5—and yet he left similar situations in 7, 9, 12, 13, 15, and 17 unmarked.)

Once these prototypes are established, the bowing of the violin fragments in between the soprano phrases is largely predetermined.

1. Since Handel hooked the dotted pair in bar 2, you may want to do the same in bar 23; the three-note pickups (bars 28, 30, 32, etc.) should conform to the choices you made earlier, of course.
2. At measures 56–57, it is traditional for the soprano to ritard slightly, take a breath after the high G-sharp, and then resume the tempo; if you are going to follow this practice, write a breath mark into the string parts. (A breath is often inserted into the line after the first note of 63, as well.)
3. If you observe the slur under the triplets in measure 73, you probably should play the ones in 74 the same way. (In that event, you may as well slur the triplets in bars 140 and 160, too, as Handel did those in measure 14.)
4. The first bar of the hooked quarter-notes with dots under them (measures 129–132) should be played downbow.
5. If you did decide to begin the three-note pickups on downbows, and to slur the triplets in measure 160, the final cadence will work out perfectly.

Take your time before beginning the next movement, in order to let the beauty of this aria resonate a moment. This will increase the dramatic effect of the *a cappella* passages in the chorus to follow.

No. 46: Since by man came death

This expressive, powerful movement needs very careful thought, preparation, and rehearsal. We recommend a tempo near ♩ = 50 for the *Grave* sections, and something like ♩ = 136 (if possible) for the *Allegros*.

The seams in this movement can cause serious problems. There are the changes of tempo, of course, and there are rests at critical moments. What can you do to help?

1. "Hear" (in your mind's ear) the quarter-notes pulsing through the first phrase *before you give the downbeat*. This movement begins with a slow section, but *it should be clearly metric*, not arhythmic.
2. Be certain that the important quarter-note chord in the *basso continuo* on the downbeat of bar 1 is sustained for its entire length. This will help "set" the rhythm and meter of the *Grave* tempo in the minds of your singers, just as the choir enters.
3. The *Grave* should continue all the way through measure 6, right up to the first count of the *Allegro*. The *Allegro* must start precisely on the downbeat of measure 7, and *not before*.
4. In bar 16, try going back to the *Grave* tempo on the third quarter-note of the measure; this will let the *continuo* players (and everyone else) see two full beats in Tempo I before they enter in bar 17. Keep the stick moving through measure 16, albeit slowly. Do not stop and start.
5. Note that the *basso continuo* chord at the beginning of bar 17 is a half-note this time. Be certain, again, that you have the quarter-note clearly in mind as you move on into "For as in Adam all die."
6. Treat measure 22 just as you did measure 6: sustain the *Grave* all the way through the bar line, and do not begin the *Allegro* until the downbeat of measure 23.

Bowings should be *detaché*—well-articulated, *forte*, almost *marcato*. Be sure the players continue to use long strokes on the eighth-notes, as the lines unfold; do not let them play *only the surface* of these forceful passages. The upper strings should begin upbow in bar 7, and downbow at 23, of course. You will need consecutive upbows on the second beat of measure 8 in the second violin and viola parts, and in other measures where an odd number of notes occurs—including bar 15, where an extra upbow on the final eighth-note would be appropriate. (This same bowing can serve in measures 30 and 33. The firsts will need an extra up- or downbow in bar 35, as well.) Do not let the ending sag! Keep it strong.

No. 47: Behold, I tell you a mystery

You may find that the overall pace of this accompanied recitative works well for you at about ♩ = 56. While the first four bars can be taken freely, it is

Example 28. Suggested bowings for "The trumpet shall sound," measures 1–8. Violin I markings are here shown above the trumpet part.

important that you set a clear, regular four-beat for bars 5 to 7, in order that the orchestra can know precisely when you want the sixteenth-note pickups.

The strings can start with downbows, the second violins and violas changing direction, as necessary, on the tied notes. In measures 5 and 6 the first sixteenth in each pair can be taken downbow, but in measure 7 an upbow on the G-sharp sixteenth-note will allow them to finish with a downbow.

No. 48: The trumpet shall sound

Here is another movement for which it is vital that you "hear" the rhythm before you cue the orchestra.[44] Thinking both of your bass soloist and your trumpet player, try tempos around $\downarrow$ = 120–128.

The trumpet part itself is not difficult, especially when played on a D trumpet; it is exposed, and long, however, demanding stamina. Find someone who plays securely in the upper register.

We recommend you start the strings with an upbow, hooking the dotted-eighth and sixteenth together. The first beat of the first full measure comes downbow, then; taking another downbow on the eighth-note, and hooking the dotted pair again brings us to bar 2 downbow; repeating those patterns carries us on measure 3, and from there on everything can be separate. (See all this in example 28.)

If you begin the three-note pickups in bars 21 and 23 with upbows, all the patterns (with minor adjustments) will work out well to measure 30. Here the opening motif resumes; continue taking the lone eighth-note downbow, and hooking the dotted-eighth-and-sixteenth pairs on upbows, as you did at the beginning. From here on, you need only replicate the bowing patterns you already have established.

At bars 137–140, be certain the *basso continuo* and the trumpet player know exactly how the bass soloist wants to handle the *adagio*. The final *ritornello* contains no surprises. Neither does the voice-and-*continuo* mid-section of the aria (measures 157–213).

No. 49: Then shall be brought to pass

If you are conducting the *basso continuo*, decide how you want to time the final two chords. There are no other problems in this *secco* recitative.

No. 50: O death, where is thy sting

This superb duet (and its choral continuation, No. 51) is too often cut by conductors who fear the audience is impatient for the finale. With the aria (No. 52) which follows, it constitutes a useful tonal buffer—a diversion away from the key of "The trumpet shall sound," so that D major can sound fresh again for "Worthy is the Lamb"—as well as a logical textual continuity.

We recommend that the duet be taken in a straight four, at about $\downarrow$ = 92. If

---

44. In this case, you may even want to consider giving them *both* the first and second beats as preparation. (This will help them judge the lengths of the dotted eighth and the sixteenth before the attack.) A *very small* downbeat followed by a full-size second beat are all that is needed in such a case; be careful not to give *two* preparatory beats! (Although young conductors are taught to avoid extra beats, there are circumstances that justify them.)

Example 29. Suggested bowings for "But thanks be to God," measures 25(1)–30(6).

you broaden the tempo a bit at the end of the duet (measure 24), be certain to show the *continuo* group a clear fourth beat, so that they can time the eighth-note D-natural pickup at the point of the *segue* into the chorus.

No. 51: But thanks be to God

However you decide to handle bar 24, then, the tempo at the beginning of this chorus should be the same as that of the duet.

The movement can be taken *detaché,* with the upper strings starting upbow. The eighth-and-sixteenth figure which first appears in the first violin part in bar 29(5)[45] begins upbow, of course; consecutive upbows on the last two eighths in the measure will make this motif come out right with a downbow on the downbeat of bar 30(6). (All this can be studied in example 29.)

45. Both the Alfred Mann and Watkins Shaw editions, regarding Nos. 50 and 51 as a continuity, number measures straight through both movements; hence bar 25 is actually the first measure of No. 51, etc. For this movement only, our text will display the bar number used in the Mann edition, and will show the actual measure count for the chorus alone in parentheses.

These same figures recur during the remainder of the movement and can be handled in the same ways. The three-eighth pickup motif seen frequently should begin upbow. The dotted figures which occur in measure 51(27) can be hooked, if you wish, as can the pairs of eighths surrounding the dotted pairs. The final *adagio* itself should be begun upbow. (The seconds will need consecutive upbows on the eighths in the next-to-last bar.) Watch the clarity of your preparation beat, as always.

No. 52: If God be for us

The final aria of *Messiah* is much like a minuet, but be careful not to take this *Larghetto* too slowly. Consider conducting it in three, at perhaps ♩ = 108, or thereabouts.

The *concertino* violin line could begin with an upbow, and continue *detaché* to the slurs in measure 10, or it could start downbow and proceed on separate bows, hooking only the pair of eighths on the first beat of bar 8; which solution you choose depends on your sense of the shape of this passage. The complex rhythmic figure which first appears in bar 11 should commence each time with a downbow on the sixteenth note. (The rather similar pattern in measure 23 should begin upbow, however.)

The choices you have made to this point will guide your bowings for the rest of the aria. You will have to decide what to do about the apparent inconsistencies in the articulation of descending arpeggios: the slurred figure in measures 10 and 12 is sometimes, but not always bowed in this way later in the aria; compare for example, bars 42 and 44 with 134 and 136, and with 146. The violinists can change bow direction to sustain the very long notes in measures 124–129 and 150–155, if you want.

Some conductors broaden the tempo slightly at bar 150, moving into a full *ritard* in measures 156–158. The downbeat of 159 should be your cutoff for the *fermata* in 158; *stop your hand* at the bottom of that beat, and move again only when you and the soloist are ready to begin the *adagio;* then start your preparatory beat. Tempo I returns on the third beat of bar 162. The final *ritornello* (bar 163 to the end) is a reprise of measures 10 to 25, and can be bowed in exactly the same way *if you decide to retain the original slurs;* in any case, the sixteenth-note in bar 176 should be played upbow.

No. 53: Worthy is the Lamb that was slain

And so we come to the climax of Handel's masterpiece, a complex chorus built of massive chordal textures and intricate counterpoint. It is divided (as you must know already) into three major sections; the first a homophonic *Largo/andante* alternation, the middle a fabric of stately contrapuntal interchanges, and the last an elaborate, exultant Handelian fugue, paced at *Allegro moderato*.

We recommend that the opening *Largo* be taken in four, at about ♩ = 64. The

Example 30. Suggested bowings for "Worthy is the Lamb that was slain," measures 1–7.

andante, seven bars later, could go at ♩ = 108. This tempo change must happen precisely on the third beat of measure 7; the danger is that the conductor—through impatience or a wish to show the orchestra the new tempo too soon—will cut the second beat short, thus confusing the orchestra and chorus. *Think the eighth-note subdivision right through that beat,* and then shorten your motion to reflect the new tempo. Be certain also that your beat pattern is precise at the end of bar 11, as you move back to the *Largo.* Your fourth beat preparation must be clearly *up,* and both it and the downbeat should be in the new tempo. The bar 7 process is repeated at 19, and the transition to the *Larghetto* (measure 24) is much like bars 11–12.

The opening measures are displayed in example 30. As you see, we recommend that the dotted pairs in measures 2, 4, and 5 be hooked, and that consecutive upbows be taken—where necessary—to adjust (as on the last two counts of measure 5 in the first violin part). At the second *Largo,* we hook also the dotted pairs in bars 13, 15, 16, and 18. You probably will want to add dots over the eighth-note in each of these pairs. The remainder of the bowings for this section are straightforward.

"Blessing and honour, glory and pow'r" can go a bit slower than the previous *andante*, perhaps ♩ = 100, or so. Since the strings double the voices much of the time, it will be worth a great deal of rehearsal time to mark in dynamics for each instrumental entrance.[46]

Bowings here are uncomplicated: the principal subject (tenors and basses in bars 1 to 5), started downbow each time (no matter whether the first note is a dotted-quarter or an eighth), works out perfectly *detaché*.

Minor adjustments are necessary:

1. The first violins need an extra upbow on the C-sharp in bar 31, for example; the firsts—in order to come to the downbeat of 49 on a downbow—also could play consecutive downbows on the third count of bar 48, hooking the dotted pair on the following beat.
2. If you mark the A-natural on the fourth beat of bar 53 downbow (for all the strings), a pair of upbows on the first two eighths of bar 54 will be helpful, too.
3. The fragments—(a) an eighth, followed by four sixteenths, followed by an eighth, and (b) three eighths—which occur in the passage beginning at measures 61 and 62 should each be started upbow.
4. For the final *adagio*, the first violins and the *continuo* bass(es) should attack the final eighth-note in bar 68 with downbows. The seconds and violas start with upbows.

Once again you must plan carefully the transition to the next section. We suggest only a broadening of the pace at measure 69 (the *adagio*), not a new tempo; this choice works well musically, and is less risky. Practice *quickly* relating the tempo of this *adagio* to that of the next section.

For the *allegro moderato* we suggest a tempo of ♩ = 136–144, if this is appropriate for your musicians.

The *continuo* bass(es) begin downbow at bar 72; to make their line work out well they need an extra upbow on the F-sharp in measure 74, and a fresh downbow on the first eighth-note in 76. (See example 31.) The first violins can follow this prototype, in turn, at measure 92.

There is one inherent problem here, however: the movement builds to the *allegro moderato*, and beyond it to the choral exposition in measures 72 through 91, but all the forces drop away save the first violins and the *continuo* at bar 92. The effect can be disappointing. Part of the solution is the articulation; the firsts—without overplaying—must deliver this line very cleanly and convincingly.

These patterns will serve for each of the string parts, with occasional adjustments. The firsts will need consecutive upbows—perhaps on the third beat of measure 95—because of the effect of the two sixteenths; the seconds will have

---

46. In some fugal passages, you may find it useful to mark each new fugal entrance into the orchestral parts with *both* a bracket and an indication of the dynamic level you want.

Example 31. Suggested bowings for the final movement, measures 72–78.

the same problem in bar 100, and can take upbows on the third beat of that measure. Further:

1. Mark the orchestra parts in bars 107–108 with dynamics which reflect the fact that the chorus is tacet at this point.
2. Occasional dotted pairs (the dotted-quarter-and-eighth in the first violins in bar 113, for example) can be hooked; you may find you want a dot over the eighth in such cases.
3. If you agree that the first violins should begin bar 139—doubling the

fresh attack by the sopranos—with a downbow, you will want to mark consecutive downbows on the tied C-natural and the B which follows it. Another pair of consecutive downbows are needed (for the sake of bar 146) on the first two beats of measure 143.

4. The trumpets enter in at this point, and you will want to be sure they are using articulation which complements that of the singers.

5. When the timpani enters at bar 146, check the balance to be certain it is as you want it. Bar 158 may be performed as you prefer: the pattern ♫♫ ♫ ♫ may be played, the entire measure may be rolled, or the player may begin the roll and slow the rhythm of his strokes as you approach the final cadence.

Some fine conductors broaden the tempo somewhat at measure 151; others start a slow *decelerando,* as an approach to the final *adagio.* Whatever choice you make, be certain that your intentions are made clear in your baton, with reference to this passage, to the grand pause in bar 156, and to the closing measures.

8   J. S. Bach: *Magnificat in D Major, BWV 243*

We have been given fewer details regarding Bach's writing of his great *Magnificat* than of the composition of *Messiah*. Bach was installed in his post as cantor at Leipzig in the summer of 1723; it appears that he wrote this *Magnificat* for his first Christmas season at the Thomaskirche. That original performance was scored in E-flat major, however, and it was some time later that he transposed it into the key in which most of us know it now.

There was another unique aspect of that 1723 version. Martin Luther himself had authorized the continued use of this particular canticle—and in Latin, too—in the churches which joined his Reformation; it had become common practice however, for musicians to interpolate short, carol-like songs—in the vernacular—into settings of the *Magnificat*. Thus we find single voices inserting phrases of these German songs (rather like troping) into the Latin canticle. Bach chooses to do something rather more elaborate: after the second movement of his *Magnificat*, the aria "Et exsultavit spiritus meus," he interpolates a four-voice setting of "Vom Himmel hoch," in which the sopranos sustain the chorale tune on half-notes, while the rest of the voices sing imitative counterpoint. Similarly, after the bass soloist sings "Quia fecit mihi magna," Bach adds a four-part setting (for sopranos I and II, altos, and tenors) of the text "Freut euch und jubiliert." Two movements later, after "Fecit potentiam," the master—having thus inserted two choruses in the vernacular—interpolates a five-voice setting (rather homophonic, this time) of the angels' hymn "Gloria in excelsis deo", and he follows the aria "Esurientes implevit bonis" with another Latin addition, a soprano-bass duet on the text "Virga Jesse floruit." (His biographer, Spitta, reports that there was a small organ installed "above the 'high choir,' so that it was opposite to the great organ" in the Thomaskirche, and that this instrument was used only for festival services. He speculates that the Leipzigers' love for antiphonal singing on such occasions spurred Bach to add the four German-and-Latin interpolations, and that they were performed by a separate vocal ensemble, supported only by that small organ and a few instrumentalists—since the tiny upper loft would have permitted at most a few musicians; further, that the absence of any such facility in the Nikolaikirche would have precluded Bach's using these *addenda* at that site. It is Spitta's judgment, also, that geographical separation explains the fact that these four movements do not appear in proper order among the other twelve in the score.)[1]

---

1. Philipp Spitta, *Johann Sebastian Bach*, vol. II, pp. 369–374. An extensive discussion of the interpolation texts is included there.

While we cannot be certain why Bach transposed the original version into D Major, we can regard that key as more comfortable for his trumpets, and a happier choice for the brightness of the opening movement and the finale.

Choosing Performance Forces

Bach specifies what is for him a rather large orchestra (the so-called "festival orchestra") for the *Magnificat:* three trumpets in D, two flutes, two oboes, timpani, and *basso continuo*. All are used for the opening "Magnificat," the "Fecit potentiam" and "Gloria Patri" movements; varied combinations support the other arias and choruses.

Since this work, unlike *Messiah*, was intended for liturgical use, it is clear that a Baroque organ—or a larger instrument voiced for a Bach performance—should be used for the *basso continuo*. You may consider using harpsichord in place of the organ during the arias, however; we discussed these options in detail in chapter 6.[2]

We know that the choir Bach used at Thomaskirche would have been less than thirty—and perhaps half that number. You may choose (working in a modern auditorium, for example) to employ a larger vocal ensemble; bear the prototype in mind, however, and consider how your body of singers affects the style of the work. The size of your choir will influence the size of the your string forces, of course.[3]

Be cautious that your choir does not overpower the instrumental body (or *vice versa,* for that matter). What you probably want the audience to hear is a piquant blend of voices, strings, continuo, and (sometimes) winds; this is the nature of Baroque timbre.

It is possible to edit into the chorus movements the use of vocal concertists, if you wish. (Whether you want to do so will depend on both artistic and practical considerations.) As we said earlier, any such solo passages will tend to be virtuosic in character,[4] perhaps melismatic, perhaps chromatic, and probably lightly accompanied. If you undertake this sort of editing, be sure you are consistent with it through the entire work.

Performing Editions

In preparing to perform *Magnificat,* you will want to examine and study the *Magnificat* edition which is part of the *Neue Ausgabe Sämtlicher Werke,* pub-

---

2. See pp. 48–52 above, and see also the discussion on p. 62.
3. For specific recommendations touching the relationship of choir size to numbers of string players, see pp. 31–32 above.
4. See our discussion above in chapter 6, pp. 52–53; see further Wilhelm Ehmann for his "Performance Practice of Bach's Motets," *American Choral Review* 15:2 (April 1973) and "Concertisten und Ripienisten in Bach's H-Moll Messe," *Musik and Kirche,* 30:2–6; and also Alfred Dürr for "Performance Practice of Bach's Cantatas," *American Choral Review* 16:2 (April 1974) and *Die Kantaten von Johann Sebastian Bach.*

lished by Bärenreiter, and you may wish to use the complementary solo, choral, and instrumental parts as well.[5]

There also is the historic "Bach-Gesellschaft" edition, of which *Magnificat* is Volume XI/1,3.[6] This may be valuable to you for your research; a variety of old C-clefs are included, however, and it is improbable your singers and players would be comfortable with them.

Consult the most modern editions available to you, in any case. Good scholars always benefit from their opportunity to "stand on the shoulders" of predecessors.

ANALYSIS OF THE WORK

The main body of the *Magnificat* itself is composed of twelve principal movements (the last one divided by a tempo change into two distinct sections, which are treated in *attacca* fashion). And, as we have pointed out, Bach's original composition included also four German-or-Latin interpolations rarely performed these days.

No. 1: Magnificat

The work begins with a hybrid movement, part overture and part elaborate, contrapuntal chorus.[7] We recommend you consider a tempo of $\downarrow$ = 80 or so, taking it in three, with a rather light, buoyant beat.[8] Hand in hand with this decision goes your judgment about articulation: how much space do you wish between the notes of each of the motifs in this Baroque work? The full orchestra is employed here, so you will want to keep a close check on the balance between the choir, concertists (if any),[9] brass, woodwinds, strings, and timpani. Mark dynamics carefully at points where you believe balance will be problematic.

We favor *detaché* bowing here, with all the string parts beginning downbow, of course. Match the length of the string notes to the articulation of your trumpets. In measure 3, where the first of the sixteenth-notes occur, the Violins I should take the initial sixteenth downbow (as it comes); in the next measure,

---

5. Alfred Dürr, ed., *Johann Sebastian Bach: Magnificat*, ser. II, vol. 3 of *Johann Sebastian Bach: Neue Ausgabe Sämtlicher Werke*. (This edition includes the four interpolated movements we have discussed, transposed to be compatible with the D Major key Bach employed for his later version of the work.)

6. J. S. Bach, *Magnificat in D Major*, vol. XI/1,3 in *J. S. Bach Werke*.

7. From this point on you will find it important to have your full score of *Magnificat* at hand.

8. Remember that the size of your forces, their capabilities, the nature and acoustics of the hall, and other factors will influence your tempo choices. (See above, chapter 6, pp. 56–57.) The tempos suggested in these discussions are intended only as departure points.

9. As an example of the concertist possibilities in this movement, see measures 52–59; if the previous bars have been sung *tutti*, the set of melismatic, fugal entrances which commence with the soprano I line in bar 52 could be performed by soloists up to the tenor and bass cadences in measure 58. The *tutti* women can reappear on the first beat (overlapping the men) of that same measure, the *tutti* men returning one bar later. Echo passages can be treated the same way.

the high D could be a second consecutive upbow. The seconds and violas will need consecutive upbows on their second and third notes in both bars 3 and 4. For both the first and seconds, then, the final pickups in measures 5 and 6 should be upbows; for the firsts, the initial E in bar 8 should be an upbow, as should the last note in 12; and these parts follow without adjustment until bar 16; there the firsts can either (a) slur the two sixteenths on the second beat, or (b) take consecutive downbows on the two high E-naturals. As patterns recur, the firsts, seconds, and violas will want to play consecutive upbows in bar 18, as they did in measures 3 and 4. The second violins, then can play consecutive downbows on the first two notes in bar 19; no other changes are needed in the violins or violas. The firsts can commence bar 29 downbow, taking a second consecutive downbow on the high B-natural in bar 30. The *continuo* bass bowing follows naturally from the start.

You know now how to treat each of the basic motifs. Bar 33 recalls the beginning, and the bowings are essentially the same.[10] Be certain that the dynamics you have incorporated maintain the balances you want. For the remainder of the movement:

1. The off-beat entrances the upper strings have in measures 47 and 51 should begin upbow, of course.
2. All three of the upper string sections can begin downbow at bar 66 (the first violins taking consecutive downbows on the two B-naturals in that measure), or the firsts can start the bar upbow.
3. The violas need to attack bar 69 on a (consecutive) downbow.
4. Measures 76 to 90 replicate bars 17 to 31.

No. 2: Et exsultavit spiritus meus

Again you must determine how much space you want between the opening notes in the Violins I, since this determines much about the sound of the movement. (We favor a fairly long bow stroke for each of the first three eighths, with a slight separation between them; you can indicate this preference, if you share it, by underscoring each of these notes with a dash.) Give consideration to a tempo $\flat$ = about 120.

Bowings for this movement are quite straightforward. The primary materials are established in the first dozen measures. (See example 32.) All the downbeat attacks (bars 1, 3, 7, 9, 15, 17, 23, 27, etc.) should be taken downbow, of course; most of the rest should be bowed "as it comes," following Bach's own markings. Let us check two specific spots:

1. You can handle the off-the-beat entrances in measures 39, 42, 44, 64, 66, and 70 just as you bowed the same motif in bar 12.

---

10. Spitta points to resemblances between this movement and the concerto form—with its recurrent *tutti*—in his analysis, already cited, vol. II, pp. 374–375.

Example 32. Suggested bowings for "Et exsultavit spiritus meus," measures 1–14.

2. Note that Bach has *not* slurred the first two notes in measure 77, though he did connect them in bar 11, and in similar cases later— including the next-to-last bar.
3. Occasional adjustments are necessary also in the *continuo* bass line. Each time they should be consistent with your treatment of the original motifs, discussed above. The second note in bar 29—the first E-natural—might be a second consecutive downbow, for example. We suggest that both the D and F# in bar 58 be taken upbow, as should the low A in 76.

You may want a *ritard* at the end of these movements, by the way. We try not to do anything ostentatious in this respect, however, preferring a broadening, rather than a braking effect.

The first of the insertion-movements ("Vom Himmel hoch")—should you be interested in performing them—comes at this point. If you hope to reproduce the impact these had on Bach's congregation, you will want a separate ensemble to perform them, geographically removed from your main body, and perhaps above the audience (surprising them with unexpected music "vom Himmel hoch").

No. 3: Quia respexit humilitatem

This lyric *Adagio* balances a soprano soloist against your *oboe d'amore* (or first oboe), both of them supported by the *basso continuo*. We recommend you take this in a subdivided four, at a tempo near ♩ = 40–48 (♪ = 80–96). Depending on the ability of your singer to sustain line (and breath), it could go as slowly as ♪ = 60; what is needed is a pace that is reflective, but not halting.

The *continuo* bass line—with the three-sixteenth figure slurred each time—practically bows itself. You may want to mark as upbows both of the A-naturals in measure 18.

An important, tricky "seam" joins this movement to the chorus which follows it. If you regard the relationship of "Quia respexit humilitatem" to "Omnes generationes" as proportional (as we do), with ♪ (approximately) = ♩, then "finding" the right tempo for the "Omnes" in the heat of performance will be relatively easy. Take care to weigh your needs in "Omnes . . ." as you plan with your soloist the pace of "Quia . . ." Build a modest *ritard* into the final measure of the aria; this will shape the end of that movement with some grace, and it also will permit you some flexibility with the exact tempo of the chorus (by "erasing" memory of the previous pulse).

No. 4: Omnes generationes

This powerful chorus may be less a hymn of praise than a dramatic image, "grave and mighty in its rush and flow" yet not "wild or vehement."[11] Its tempo, as we have said, probably should be set in approximate proportion to the preceding aria; try ♩ = 80–90.

Give thought, as usual, to the articulation of the notes and the space you want between them. You can begin each of the two principal motifs (the two violin parts display them in bars 1 and 2) with a downbow, marking a fresh downbow every time either of them recurs; since these two subjects comprise virtually all of the movement, there are few adjustments to make. *Watch for points at which an odd number of notes occupy a beat or a measure:* at such spots you can hook a pair of sixteenths, or mark a fresh up- or downbow; don't edit *every* such example, however; check to see whether the pattern reverses itself again within a two-bar span, and—if it does—you can leave things to work themselves out. Taking this approach, you probably will want upbows on both the sixteenth-notes in the *continuo* bass in bar 1, a fresh downbow on the low C-sharp in 5, and hooked pairs of sixteenths on the third beats of bars 9 and 10. Where pickup figures made up of odd numbers of notes occur, as in bar 13, start them with upbows. Apply these same criteria to the upper string parts.

At bar 21, be certain the players give the quarter-notes full bow strokes. Decide, also, whether you want the *fermata* in bar 24 played up- or downbow, and

---

11. Spitta, already cited, pp. 378–379.

mark all four parts in measure 21 so as to achieve that result. After the *fermata,* each of the upper string parts should commence upbow. The seconds will need an adjustment here. (Hooking the second and third notes in the final measure would work.) The *continuo* bass part needs nothing but consecutive upbows on the pair of sixteenths in measure 25.

There is one conducting problem: at bar 24, the *fermata* actually occurs on the second count; your cutoff of the *fermata* will be the preparatory beat. (In effect, you are adding a fifth count to this measure.) Take care that this cutoff beat is at the exact tempo you want for the phrases that follow.

No. 5: Quia fecit mihi magna

The bass aria involves only the *continuo* group. Take it in four, at perhaps ♩ = 68. The bass(es) can begin downbow; each time the original motif returns (bars 6, 10, 13, 17, 24, and 30—generally on the second beat), recommence it downbow. No other adjustments are needed.

Since the orchestra is not involved, the soloist and the *basso continuo* can manage this sort of movement alone, if they are well prepared. If you do conduct the aria, you will want to broaden the tempo a bit for the most important cadences (bar 29, for example, with a return to the original tempo on the *second* beat of 30). Just be certain your musicians know what to expect, both from you and from the soloist.

The optional insertion-chorus "Freut euch und jubiliert" follows here (if you include it in your performance).

No. 6: Et misericordia

Muted upper strings (the violins doubling the two flutes) join the alto and tenor soloists for this movement. It can move nicely in four, but you may want to use a twelve-pattern at the outset and at cadences important enough to deserve *ritards.* The biggest technical problem with beating compound meters is visual: be certain that the geography of your pattern is spacious enough that the players know where you are; especially in this context you should avoid bringing the beat point always to the same spot in front of you, for that will confuse them; whether you use a "Christmas-tree" pattern, or some other format, make your preparatory beat come from the traditional side (the twelfth beat from the right, for example).

If your choice is to begin this movement in twelve, be certain that this does not tempt you to take it too slowly. We recommend a tempo near ♩. = 40 (or ♪ = 120) to your consideration.

Mark the string parts carefully to indicate where the flutes will be breathing, so that the violins can phrase their lines correspondingly. Ask them to work for very smooth bow changes (this is an example of *legato* technique), and expect them to play precisely with the left hand—for accurate rhythm comes from fingers, not the bow.

Example 33. Suggested bowings for "Et misericordia," measures 1–4.

With respect to bowings, the *continuo* part needs no adjustments. The bass(es) will prefer to play everything separate, because of string crossings; in this *barcarolle*-like rhythm, one might just ask that the off-beat eighth-notes be graceful and modest, and not stressed.

The upper strings can "take it as it comes" with few modifications. There are decisions to be made: Do you want the third-beat notes in bar 2 of the Violin II part played separately, as marked, or slurred, as they are in the parallel case in bar 9 (and as they are in the first violins at the same moments)? Where will you adjust the viola part? (Perhaps with consecutive upbows on the E-naturals in measure 2.) Once the first four measures have been established as a prototype (see example 33) the rest of the movement follows naturally.

Through the rest of the movement the on-the-beat attacks can be taken downbow, and the others upbow; do not let those pickups (bars 16, 23, and 25) become accented. (This generally is a matter of the players being completely ready for the entrance, so that they do not "grab" the note.) The closing measures, begun downbow at 32, will come out on an upbow; the players can change direction to a downbow to fade out—if that is what you want them to do.

Example 34. Suggested bowings for "Fecit potentiam," measures 1–3.

No. 7: Fecit potentiam

Setting exactly the tempo you have rehearsed is crucial in this demanding chorus. Recall the initial tenor line to find that tempo; "hear" it in your mind during the silence between movements, and use that mental image to pace the preparatory beat. The "right" tempo will depend on the capacity of your singers, of course. Certainly the movement should be in four; for us, an ideal choice would lie somewhere near ♩ = 80.

Decide how much space you want between the notes of the primary motifs. The flutes, oboes, and strings should approximate the style of articulation you set for the singers. The dotted pattern on the fourth beat of bar 1 in the upper strings can be hooked conveniently, as we indicate in example 34; this will make the downbeat of bar 2 fall on an upbow, but you can mark a second upbow for the pickups on the last half of the second beat. (If you prefer, of course, the same dotted figure can be bowed separately, to end downbow.)

This motif continues in the strings until measure 21. At that point, the first sixteenth should be taken downbow, with the dotted-eighth-and-sixteenth hooked, as before; again the bar will end upbow (as illustrated in example 35).

Throughout the first section of the movement the *continuo* bass line continues what is shown in the examples. The player(s) will take the octaves on separate bows (because of string crossings), and then will recover a bit of the bow to play the first sixteenth as a consecutive upbow. Caution the bass(es), if necessary, to emphasize the first note of each of the octave skips.

The beginning of the *adagio* constitutes another hazardous seam. The cutoff beat (after "*superbos*") is the fourth count; stopping the stick for the length of the *fermata*, if you want one, drop the baton straight down *in your Adagio tempo* for the (risky) silent downbeat of measure 29. The first danger here is that someone will enter early, of course; the second is that you will give too abrupt—or too fast—a preparatory beat, confusing your musicians about your intended tempo.

Example 35. Suggested bowings for "Fecit potentiam," measures 21-23.

Write in breath marks after the first count of measure 32, if you want a break there, so that (the *adagio* having begun) your players will phrase this spot cleanly with your singers. You probably will want the strings to use fairly full bows; if so, tell them "smooth connections, and *colla voce.*" The half-notes in measures 29 and 32 should be taken downbow, of course, in all four string parts. Everyone is likely to need a bow change on the final *fermata.*

When it is performed, "Gloria in excelsis Deo" (the third of Bach's four insertion-movements) follows here.

No. 8: Deposuit potentes

Bach is fond of madrigalisms; this aria about the "putting down of the mighty" begins with vigorous, *descending* F-sharp and C-sharp minor scales and continues with rising patterns once the text starts to speak about "exalting the humble and meek"; the unison violins reiterate these images throughout the movement. Take this aria in three, at perhaps ♩ = 92; since all the violins are together here—and as a safety gesture, for exposed sixteenth-notes can be tricky—you might even give tiny first and second beats, before delivering the full-size preparatory beat on the third count.

The violins need to play this soloistically. For this reason, we suggest taking the initial sixteenth downbow! (The pickup to bar 3 can be more traditional, however.) With hooks for the dotted pairs in measures 2 and 13, the rest of this opening passage follows logically enough. (See example 36.) The succession of long notes in measures 16 to 22 can be a problem, for they can "use up too much of the bow," so we recommend starting the pickups with alternate up- and downbows: the A-natural in bar 16 taken upbow, the D in 18 downbow, the high C-sharp in the next bar up and the one in 20 downbow; thus the effect of the long notes is dissipated. The low C-sharp in measure 23, then, can be an up-

Example 36. Suggested bowings for "Deposuit potentes," measures 1–14.

bow. The same principles apply for the rest of the movement, with a couple of exceptions:

1. In measure 48, after the last of a series of long slurs, the final G-sharp within the second beat should be a second consecutive upbow, in order to keep the pattern oriented properly on into bar 49.
2. If you begin bar 65 with a pair of downbows, the violins will end the movement on a downbow. (Do not hook the dotted pair on the first beat of bar 66.)

The *continuo* bass line can be taken largely "as it comes." An adjustment of some sort is needed occasionally (consecutive upbows at the end of bar 7, for example).

No. 9: Esurientes implevit bonis

The *staccato* notes in the flute lines are the signals of the grace and character of this aria. This lovely movement needs to flow lyrically from beginning to end, and we suggest you conduct it in four, at a tempo near ♩ = 60.

Be certain you get good balance between the two flutes, and between them and the *basso continuo*. Focus carefully on the quality of the *pizzicato* sound, too; the bass might need to be reminded to "listen," especially on the final E-natural.[12]

Measure 35 is touchy. The soloist may want to treat this "*inanes*" freely; understand what the singer plans, and then deliver the preparatory (first) beat of

---

12. It has been said, by the way, that the stark, unaccompanied E-natural in the *continuo* bass at the end of this movement is Bach's whimsical way of "sending the rich away empty."

35 *a tempo*, for *the second beat must be back in rhythm*. If you broaden the final beats, time the last note carefully, so the bass will know exactly where you are.

The last of the four insertion-movements, "Virga Jesse floruit," belongs at this point, if you wish to perform it.

No. 10: Suscepit Israel

This lovely chorus offers some problems. First, be certain you know the plainsong *tonus peregrinus* yourself, so that you can help the oboes interpret the shape of their line, if necessary. Second, while potentially this is one of the most beautiful movements in choral literature, balance and pitch problems here can be significant. Your cues should be sympathetic (supportive particularly of the second sopranos, for whom some entrances are tough).

This moves nicely in three. The tempo could be something close to ♩ = 54. The *continuo* bass line should be performed with a "brush stroke," evenly and lightly, with every note consistent in length; begun downbow, it unfolds logically, with no adjustments needed.

No. 11: Sicut locutus est

This familiar *alla breve* movement can be taken in two, with the tempo set at about ♩ = 68.

There are no orchestral problems here, of course. The *continuo* bass part needs few, if any, bowing adjustments; it may be best to leave it to the player(s). Only be certain that the singers and the *continuo* share the same concepts of articulation and space between notes.

No. 12: Gloria Patri

And so we come to the final movement. In the opening section, Bach employs three great flourishes of triplets to extol Father, Son, and Holy Spirit; each of these passages ascends, resolving in a *tutti* (the trumpets are included only the last time). We recommend that you take this in a simple four, using a tempo near ♩ = 60. Some conductors attempt to "help" the singers in the triplet passages by trying to show in their beats some sort of subdivision; we suggest that *you can assist them most effectively by making your beat very clear*. The more gestures you use in moments like this, the more you are likely to get in the way!

Within this section, the first detail you must handle is the articulation of bar 1: How long do you want each of these three pitches to be, and how much space is there to be between them? You probably can save time by getting your flutes and oboes to play the first measure together cleanly, while the others listen; then the strings can imitate the result. (Nothing will be gained, however, by sharpening the articulation you are getting from the instrumentalists, if your singers are imprecise.) You may or may not want a brief *tenuto* on the fourth beat of measure 1 (and of bars 6 and 11); either way, be especially insistent about the

Example 37. Suggested bowings for "Gloria Patri," measures 15–20.

clarity of the *tutti* release on the downbeat of measure 2 (and of the ones in bars 7 and 12, as well).

Everything is *detaché* here. The strings start downbow each time, with the continuo bass(es) changing bows during the tied notes. The *tutti* at bar 15 needs adjustments, and we have suggested some in example 37. (The trumpets return here—on high notes—for their first entrance in five movements; cue them, and be certain they conform to the style of articulation already established by the rest of the ensemble.) Instruct your first trumpet, first oboe, first violins, and first sopranos what style of trill you want on the third count of measure 18; prepare everyone for the approximate duration of your fermata in bar 19, and calculate the duration of the silence that follows it against the resonance time of the hall. Taste counts here.

Do let that silence "ring" for a moment. Then, for "sicut erat in principio," make your tempo exactly "as it was in the beginning."

Each of the families of voices and instruments is back here—sometimes playing together, sometimes alternating—in this section, which makes balance problems more sophisticated. Stay alert to this, and have someone listen out in the hall, as well.

Bowing choices for the rest of the work parallel those made for the opening movement, of course. To deal with the new circumstances, we suggest a few adjustments:

1. At measure 27, the first violins can begin upbow, while both the seconds and the violas commence downbow.
2. While both violin sections can attack bar 33 with downbows (which will give the firsts an upbow on the tied note in 34–35), the seconds need consecutive downbows on the two G-naturals in 33. The violas begin downbow, of course, at measure 34.
3. Each of the upper string sections comes to bar 40 on a downbow; the violas continue "as it comes" to the end, while the seconds need an-

other downbow on the next note (the low F-sharp). The firsts can either (a) take another downbow on the low D-natural in measure 40, or (b) play consecutive downbows on the A- and B-naturals (the fifth and sixth notes) in bar 41.

4. The *continuo* bass line needs consecutive downbows on the second beat of measure 41.

The final *ritard* could begin late in measure 40, or near there. With three levels of rhythmic activity present (quarters, eighths, and sixteenths), you will want to subdivide your beat in bar 41.

Note the final fermata, comparing it with the closing chord of the first movement. Bach's having written a fermata over the final *rest* of the opening movement—not over the first-beat chord—may imply that he did not want the so-called "emergency brake" *ritard* in that instance; for the final movement, his having notated the fermata over the final *chord* would justify a different interpretation. In any case, the appearance of a fermata over a final rest in a Bach score is unusual, and deserves your attention.

9   Antonio Vivaldi: *Gloria (in D)*

Through the mists that still rise from the Venetian lagoon we see a flash of bright red, and the outline of a rather proud, almost patrician face. This is *il Prete Rosso,* the Red (-headed) Priest, one of the great figures of eighteenth century music, and—of them—probably the one about whom we now know the least. As one of his biographers has written:

> He was famous and feted during his lifetime, and his music was performed and plagiarized throughout Europe. But soon after his death, or even a little before, he passed into a state of neglect that seemed final. His works disappeared from concert programs, and even in his own country his name was omitted from the gazettes, histories, and biographical dictionaries.
>
> A century elapsed. Then in Germany came the rediscovery of Johann Sebastian Bach, who had been the victim of a similar fate. . . . One of the first concerns of the new admirers of Bach was to gather, with a view to publishing, the manuscripts scattered in public and private libraries. In the course of this work they came upon a collection dating from 1739 [of Vivaldi concertos transcribed by Bach]. . . .
>
> Who was this Vivaldi, whom Bach had honored . . . ?[1]

We know even less about the creation of this famous *Gloria* of his. Ordained a priest, Vivaldi in 1703 became a teacher and eventually music director of the conservatory of the Ospedale della Pietá in Venice, and it is generally assumed that the *Gloria* was written for a special service (or perhaps a concert) in the Pietá church sometime during his years there, and performed by the young musicians under his tutelage.

Like Bach's *Magnificat,* this *Gloria* revolves around the key of D Major (and for many of the same reasons, including particularly, we suspect, the nature of the trumpet). Closely related keys—the relative minor, the subdominant and its relative minor—lead away to the more distant C Major and F Major; from there Vivaldi takes us back through the parallel D Minor and A Minor to the original tonic, confirming it by setting all the last three movements in that key.

And like most other composers of his era, Vivaldi borrows—not just melodies, but entire contrapuntal fabrics—from himself and from contemporaries. Thus the "Cum Sancto Spiritu" movement of this work, its crowning glory, reappears with minor modifications as the finale of Vivaldi's *Chamber Mass;* some scholars believe, what is more, that both these paraphrases are derived from the closing movement of an earlier (?) *Gloria* by one Giovanni Maria Ruggieri;[2] since we have no certain dates of composition for either of the two Vivaldi

1. Marc Pincherle, *Vivaldi, Genius of the Baroque,* pp. 13–14.
2. See, for example, Antonio Vivaldi, *Chamber Mass,* edited by Vahe Aslanian, p. III.

works, however, it is dangerous to assume which of these three pieces came first. In the end, moreover, it is the beauty and power of the given work at hand that matters now, two and a half centuries after the death of *il Prete Rosso*.

Choosing Performance Forces

This *Gloria* is written for an orchestra comprised of trumpet, oboe, strings, and *basso continuo*. All appear in the opening and closing movements, and in the "Quoniam tu solus Sanctus" (which is a reprise of the first movement). In general, Vivaldi has the strings support the internal choruses; solo instruments and continuo share the arias and the duet with the singers. You probably should use a Baroque organ for the *continuo* unit here (though a harpsichord could serve if no organ is available to you).

As to numbers: it is unlikely that Vivaldi heard the work performed by a chorus of modern size; the work is flexible, however, and your circumstances may lead you to employ a choir of sixty or more. Link the proportions of your string section to the scope of your vocal forces, as we have suggested in earlier chapters.[3] *Do not* let orchestra costs or other difficulties cause you to understate the weight of the strings in this balance of instruments and voices, by the way; the characteristic timbre of the Baroque is one of equality of media; the impression that a handful of instruments are *accompanying* a chorus is probably not the one you want to convey.

Performing Editions

The "state of neglect" from which Vivaldi suffered for a century or more[4] delayed a standard edition of his works; as a result, there is little agreement on a definitive version of the *Gloria*.[5]

At the moment, we recommend that you study the 1961 edition by Mason Martens.[6] Consider carefully also the edition by Clayton Westermann, which is based on a full score, vocal score, and orchestral parts held by the Biblioteca Nazionale in Turin.[7] Perhaps the piano-vocal score best known in this country is the one by Alfredo Casella;[8] it is thought by some to be substantially altered

---

3. See pp. 31–33 and 62.
4. Pincherle, pp. 13–14.
5. In 1970, Ricordi published an accurate edition of the *Gloria in D* as an element of the late G. F. Malipiero's *Le opera di Antonio Vivaldi*, the great "collected works" project begun in Rome in 1947. (The new editor is Francesco de Grada.) This edition replaced the 1941 Ricordi version, edited by Casella, which is mentioned below. Unfortunately, the 1970 edition is not readily available in this country.
6. Antonio Vivaldi, *Gloria*, edited by Mason Martens, Walton Music Corp., New York, 1961. This is a vocal score, but a full score is available on rental basis. (We use the Martens edition for the measure numbers cited in this chapter.)
7. Antonio Vivaldi, *Gloria*, edited by Clayton Westermann, Edwin F. Kalmus, New York, 1967. This is a full score.
8. Antonio Vivaldi, *Gloria*, edited by Alfredo Casella, with an English translation by Joseph Machlis, G. Ricordi, Milan, 1941, and Franco Columbo, Inc., New York, 1958.

(even "romanticized"), and its vocal and instrumental parts are "not compatible with those of other editions."[9] There are other versions as well.[10] The most recent scholarship is always worth your attention.

ANALYSIS OF THE WORK

Like the Bach *Magnificat,* this Vivaldi *Gloria* is divided into twelve movements. Along with some eight choruses, there are arias and a duet for soprano and alto soloists, and one movement (the eighth) in which the soloist and the choir are treated responsively.

This is a work which a *good* high school orchestra can do nicely. The writing, which sounds brilliant enough, nevertheless is not virtuostic; it does not demand playing in the upper positions, for example, nor are the bowings complicated.

No. 1: Gloria in excelsis Deo

Vivaldi begins with a bright, effervescent *Allegro* for *tutti* orchestra which serves the function of an overture. Decide what sort of articulation you want in this style; specifically, consider how much space you want between notes. We recommend that you consider taking this at $\downarrow = 120$ or so, asking your musicians for rather short, light articulation; try to keep the octave leaps from sounding ponderous or pompous. Know exactly where you want this tempo to be. Do not allow the players (or permit yourself) to rush to the next downbeat; *this is a movement which can gain momentum,* particularly with inexperienced players. And since this is one of the three *tutti* movements, check the balances carefully.

Although the opening may look difficult to someone not used to working with strings, this is not the case; on-the-string, *detaché* in the middle to upper half of the bow (the first note played downbow, of course), the bowing is quite straightforward. Fresh downbow attacks are necessary at such points as measures 7, 16, and (the middle of) 28; otherwise, the players can "take it as it comes" (that is to say, the strokes alternate without adjustments).

Your major responsibility in this passage, with respect to the strings, will be to see that the articulatory silences (the spaces between the notes) are consistent from player to player and section to section. You may want a somewhat shorter, lighter stroke—especially from the basses—at bar 16, as the choir enters. Conversely, a slightly heavier stroke may be appropriate in the intervals between choral phrases: measures 36–37, for example. (Try to establish in the minds of

9. David Daniels, *Orchestral Music. A Handbook,* 2nd edition, Scarecrow Press, Inc., Metuchen, N.J. and London, 1982, p. 316.
10. Lee Barrow, "Editions of Antonio Vivaldi's Gloria", *The Choral Journal,* 21:22–23 [November 1980].

your musicians distinct *piano* and *forte* dynamic levels, but expect the orchestra to adjust these slightly, reflecting whether or not the choir is singing at a given moment.)

Make certain both the choir and orchestra maintain a sense of shape and direction through these somewhat repetitive passages. (If you do not know where you want the energy and peak of each phrase, you can tire out your musicians rather quickly in this movement.)

Plan the length of the *fermata* in bar 67 carefully, and be certain that your preparatory beat is in the exact tempo you want for the final phrase. The bowings for the ending of the movement, then, work out perfectly.

No. 2: Et in terra pax hominibus

The second movement can be more dangerous. Note that the choir is singing—at a slow, sustained pace, with many chromatic adjustments, as the line evolves—almost without a break. If they do not bring enough concentration to this movement, or if they permit their energy to sag, you can run into serious tempo and/or intonation problems. Train them with this risk in mind.

We recommend that you consider taking this *Andante* in three, at about $\downarrow$ = 60. Mark dynamics into the orchestra parts; there are many repetitive figures, and the players need to have some idea where the most important cadences are, and how sections relate. At bar 55, for example, you may wish to emphasize the sudden shift to D Minor with a lower dynamic level; again, at measures 61 ff., a long, slow crescendo to bar 65, followed by a diminuendo to measure 69, may help to set up the approaching E Minor section.

At the beginning, although all the string parts can be taken with separate bows, you might consider—as an alternative—having the violas pair their repeated eighths in a *portato* bowing. (See example 38.) This may give more shape to their accompanimental line. (The repeated notes in the bass can be kept separate, however.) As another alternative, you may want the violas to play separate bows in measures 3 and 4, to match the violins. It is not necessary, by the way, to use consecutive upbows in the first violins in bar 1 in order to make that four-note motif "come out" downbow on the first beat of bar 2; they can play the downbeat properly as an upbow. In bar 5, then, the violin figure should begin upbow, as should the off-beat motif which appears initially in the firsts in measure 11.

With these bowings established for the basic string figures, the remainder of the movement employs them as prototypes, almost without adjustments. (You may want a pair of upbows in the upper string parts on the second and third beats of measure 89, in order that the last note will begin downbow.)

And be certain you make clear in rehearsal—especially since this is a slow movement—how long you plan to hold the last *fermata*, so the strings can anticipate the proportions of bow necessary. (Do not mislead them by treating this cadence casually in rehearsal, only to extend it dramatically in performance!)

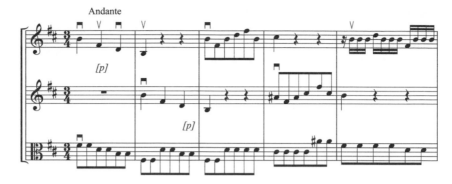

Example 38. One set of possible bowings for "Et in terra pax hominibus," measures 1–5.

They can change bows quite smoothly, if necessary, to give the final chord as much duration as you need.

No. 3: Laudamus te

This is another of those movements[11] which best may be begun with an extra preparatory beat—a very small downbeat, followed by a standard upbeat—that will set the length of the pickup sixteenth in the minds of the violins. A tempo near ♩ = 108 should work well for you.

The solo entrances here can be tricky, especially for young or inexperienced singers. Train them to depend on your cues. Then be consistent in signalling them.

One of your primary responsibilities is to build a clear aural concept of duration and articulation for this movement, a concept which *may* be different, to some degree, from that of the *Andante* which preceded it. With respect to bowings:

1. The violins, beginning upbow, can take it as it comes as far as measure 17, where the low G-natural should be a second upbow. Consecutive upbows are also needed on the last two notes in bars 41, 63, and (if you want to end on a downbow) perhaps 123. The final trill (in measure 124) should start from above.
2. The violas will need extra upbows (in order to keep the patterns oriented traditionally) in bars 6, 17, 41, 67, 114, and (on the two sixteenths in) 124.
3. Similar adjustments can be made—depending on the size and nature of your bass forces—in the *continuo* lines. (An extra upbow at the end of bar 6 would be appropriate, for example.)

---

11. See p. 114 n.44.

No. 4: Gratias agimus tibi

There is a potential conducting problem in this brief movement: be certain that—after the first *fermata*—your cutoff and the preparatory beat are the same motion, so that you do not confuse the players. (You can help in this spot by writing a breath mark into the parts.) This movement can be set at about $\downarrow = 60$.

Beginning downbow, the strings can take this as it comes. (There is no problem with playing the *fermata* notes upbow.)

No. 5: Propter magnam gloriam

This *Allegro* should not be rushed; taken in four, at a tempo of $\downarrow = 92$, or something near that pace, it can be very effective. Balance can be a problem in this movement; all the players and singers need to be made aware of the various fugal entrances—especially those which, like the alto statement in bar 9, may easily be covered by higher voices. It will save rehearsal time if you will mark dynamics in all the parts in such spots.

The bowing style here is much like that in the first movement. You may want a bit more separation between the quarter notes than between the eighths which follow; it is typical of the style, too, for some silence to occur within the dotted pattern (for example, between the D-sharp and the C-sharp in bar 2 of the second violins). Since the instruments and voices are doubled, part by part, throughout the movement, you will want to edit breath marks into the strings; if you do not do so, you risk having the players undermine all your careful work on choral phrasing.

1. The main subject can be taken *detaché*, hooking the dotted rhythm—probably with a dot over the eighth. (Another instance of this particular marking is included in example 39 below.) To save rehearsal time, indicate this bowing each time the subject appears in the strings. And you can gain quick unanimity of style here if you have the sopranos—already trained to your preference—sing this line for the orchestra at the first rehearsal; the players will be able to imitate their articulations.
2. Occasional adjustments are needed in accompanimental lines; the violas (bar 5) and the first violins (bar 6) need hooks—with dots under them—over the dotted figures, for example. Mark the final measures so that all the strings will come out on the same bow stroke.

No. 6: Domine Deus

We think it probably best for this *Largo*, with its *siciliano* rhythm, to flow in four, rather than twelve, at perhaps $\downarrow. = 52$. Plan to talk with your soprano and your oboe player about the placement of trills; experienced musicians are likely to recognize spots where they should add trills to those already marked in the score; these decisions are entirely up to you and them, of course. There are "echo" options, too—bars 8, 29–30, and 41–42 are three instances—and these should be discussed. Further, some passages which are reprised later may be ornamented differently the second or third time (conveying the impression of impromptu variations). All this is well within the prerogatives of conductor and performers in Baroque style. Do insist, however, that the work of both soloists be consistent.

At the bottom of the texture, the *continuo* bass line should be played quite lightly. (A "brush stroke" is appropriate.) Do not let the bass become heavy and stodgy, and—above all—do not let it drag.

In a limited situation, you may find it necessary, lacking a capable oboe player, to use a flute or a violin. This is permissible—even if it is not preferable—in the Baroque era.[12]

No. 7: Domine Fili Unigenite

This famous, marvelous chorus can be performed in double-dotted fashion, if you favor that option, as we do. (There is substantial evidence that double-dotting is historically stylistic for such movements.) In any case, we recommend that you consider taking this in a lively three (as bright as $\quad = 144$, if you can keep your forces well in hand at that pace). Beware of rushing, however!

As we have said before, it will help your balance problems and save much rehearsal time if you will edit breath marks and dynamics carefully into these contrapuntal doublings.

Hooked bowing, binding each sixteenth (or thirty-second, if you are double-dotting) to the longer note which follows it, is appropriate for the dotted rhythms here, and probably is easier for your string players. It can be used, as shown in example 39, for each of the orchestra parts. With respect to the longer note values:

1. The second violin part should be played *detaché*, beginning downbow.
2. In measure ten, the tied half-note in the first violin should be played downbow.
3. Each of these figures should be begun and bowed consistently whenever it recurs in later bars of the movement.
4. For the final cadence, you may want the first note in each string part in measure 95 marked downbow; this will bring all the strings to the final chord on downbows. Be certain your violins and violas know whether or not the pitches in bar 97 are double-dotted.

---

12. In the event you must use a violin solo in place of an oboe, you can adjust the *detaché* bowing by slurring (probably with dots under the slur) certain of the quarter-eighth pairs, where this is necessary to keep the downbow generally on the downbeats; this is appropriate in bars 1 and 5, for example.

No. 8: Domine Deus, Agnus Dei

It is important that you *shape* the bass line with which Vivaldi begins this movement just as carefully and expressively as you would any melodic phrase. Do not assume that your players—even in a professional orchestra— know as much about this style as they may know (for example) nineteenth century interpretation. Give careful thought to the connection and articulation of the bass part, to its harmonic orientation, and to the location and relative value of its cadences. You will want these players to keep their bows flowing, to avoid the heaviness that can result from too much pressure. Ask them to think in terms of melodic phrases—not individual notes.

We suggest taking this in four, at about ♩ = 58. Be quite sensitive to the balance of the alto soloist against the choir and orchestra, subduing the ensembles without completely smothering the timbres of the strings and the *basso continuo*.

1. You probably will want to take the three pickups in bars 1, 3, and 4 on upbows. In the related patterns that follow in measures 15ff. occasional adjustments are needed; in general, as we have been saying, upbeat attacks should be taken upbow, and downbeats downbow.
2. The chordal pattern which first appears in the upper strings in measure 13, and which doubles the choral parts, should be begun upbow. After a downbow, the last two notes in that bar should both be upbows. This bowing, which conforms to the syllable stresses in the text, can be used in bars 15–16, 18–19, and 23–24, as well.

With younger choirs, the common danger in this movement is that the singers may not make timely entrances on the eighth notes in bar 13 and the similar cases that follow. Make certain they concentrate on these attacks.[13] Be cautious, also, that the momentum of this *Adagio* does not bog down in the repetitive antiphonal entrances in the latter half of the movement.

No. 9: Qui tollis peccata mundi

We prefer—while taking this movement in two—to maintain the same pace (that is, ♩. = 58) as the preceding *Adagio;* it certainly can be conducted in four, however; just be sure you tell the orchestra which meter you are employing. Be cautious to make your cutoffs after the *fermatas* in measures 2, 4, and 7 very clear, with each of them a preparatory beat which sets the tempo of the phrase to follow.[14]

---

13. Your edition, if it follows the best sources, may not show any dynamic level for the choral entrances in bars 26, 28, 31, and 35. You will want to edit these passages.

14. The dynamic markings for this movement are editorial in most published versions of this work. Decide whether to retain or alter them. (One alternative is to begin at measure 8 a gradual *crescendo* to a *forte* at the end of the movement.)

Example 39. Suggested bowings for "Domine Fili Unigenite," measures 1–10.

One shifts either to three or six at measure 8, of course. Mark the breath points for the choir into the string parts in advance, as we have been suggesting.

Our choice of bowing is to start each of the string parts downbow in measures 1, 3, and 5—although this violates the traditional rule about pickups—in order that each of the *fermatas* can be attacked downbow. If you prefer that the strings end the movement on a downbow, you can add an extra upbow somewhere in the final phrase, of course.

No. 10: Qui sedes ad dexteram

This elegant alto aria can be taken at or near the pulse used for the previous movements (♩. = 58). We recommend you consider a somewhat brighter tempo, perhaps ♩. = 68; you may want to start conducting it in three, shifting to one as the movement continues.

The phraseology of the string parts varies quite a lot. Try to make clear to the orchestra the shape of each passage. There are many hemiolas; some people like to conduct them, and that is acceptable if it is done skillfully enough that it is helpful to the performers. Good musicians will play hemiolas effectively, if they realize the device is present.

The strings should play this rather lightly, on the upper third or middle of the bow; do not let the *forte* marking encourage dragging or heaviness. Starting downbow, the players can take everything as it comes, with a few adjustments.

1. The eighth-quarter figure, which first appears in the violins in bar 8, should begin downbow; this pattern penetrates all the parts in measures 16 ff.
2. Approaching the end of the movement, and certain of the internal cadences, you may want to have the strings take consecutive upbows somewhere, in order to have them end on the same stroke.

Insist that the dynamic contrasts implicit in the transitional interjections and the *ritornelli* be clear. Much of the charm of the aria depends on this effect.

No. 11: Quoniam tu solos Sanctus

This is a reprise of the musical material of the first movement. Tempo, bowings, and general treatment should be the same.

No. 12: Cum Sancto Spiritu

The closing movement of Vivaldi's great work—like the final *Allegro moderato* of *Messiah*—has a built-in structural problem: at what seems to be a high point in the fugal development, the texture suddenly thins out, and the audience can lose interest; energy and articulation are more necessary than ever at such points. Give the dynamics, articulation and phrasing of this spot thorough consideration, and make it a principal concern in your rehearsals. If the articulation is interesting enough, and played cleanly, it should not be necessary to alter (what we are told are) Vivaldi's dynamics to make the passage effective.[15]

This *Allegro* must have a stately quality, in our judgment. Begun at too fast a tempo, the quarter-and-eighth passages may take on an awkward, cumbersome character. Consider conducting this in four, at something close to $\bf J = 104$.

The fugue begins with only chorus and *basso continuo*, adding instruments in dramatic fashion in bar 12. The orchestra members need to hear and imitate the articulatory style of the singers, then, as they undertake the same lines. The reappearance of the trumpet in bar 18, on a high A-natural, adds excitement to the evolving form.

We suggest bowing the opening *continuo* bass line *detaché*, hooking the dotted-half and quarter together, with a *staccato* dot over the quarter note. (This choice can serve throughout the movement as a prototypical approach to this main subject.) The rest of the bass line can be taken as it comes to bar 6, where only keyboard is used.

---

15. See above, p. 119.

At measure 12 all the strings enter, playing the countersubject the sopranos introduced in bar 2. Begun upbow in all four parts, this passage can be taken on separate bows; only one adjustment—hooking the dotted-quarter-and-eighth figures in measure 13—is needed to come to bar 15 downbow. The second violins need a second consecutive downbow on the first beat of bar 16; the dotted rhythm which follows in the same line should be hooked, and articulated just as in the main subject. (In this instrumental passage it is important that the players know from your markings where the important voices are.)

Just as the dotted-quarter-and-eighth figure in measure 13 should be slurred (with a *staccato* dot over the short note), so the same figure should be hooked when it occurs in the violas in measure 20, in the first violins in bars 25 and 33, in the seconds in bar 30, in the *continuo* bass in measure 38, and elsewhere. (This hooking is useful because it protects the player from having to recover on an eighth-note duration—at this *Allegro* tempo—the same amount of bow used on the previous dotted-quarter.)

Besides these basic patterns, isolated adjustments are needed from time to time:

1. The G-sharp in bar 28 of the first violin part should be taken downbow.
2. The dotted-half-and-quarter figures in the firsts in measure 37 should be hooked, with dots over the quarter notes. (Here again the instruments are doubling the choral parts, through the "Amens" in bars 41 through 45. Be certain to mark the orchestral parts accordingly.)
3. Other adjustments are needed, or may be preferred. How specifically must you mark the rest of these notes—especially the half- and whole-notes? That depends particularly on the age and experience of your players; they will tend to take a downbeat after a rest—as in the first violin part, bar 63—with a fresh downbow. It is always safest, however, and most efficient in terms of rehearsal time, to mark the parts carefully and thoroughly.

In the final measures the familiar subjects reappear. The second violins, beginning downbow in bar 72, come out downbow on the last *fermata;* if you want the other three string parts to do so, you might mark the first two quarters in measure 75 (for the firsts, the violas, and the *continuo* bass) as consecutive upbows. Since you may want to hold this final chord of the *Gloria* for quite some time, the players should be ready to change bow directions. Do be conscious, however, in making this artistic decision, of the endurance required from the trumpet player.

Perhaps your performance will give your audience a clearer view of that partly obscured genius beside the Venetian lagoon. For the beauties of the *Gloria* he deserves that.

Part Three: *Conducting Three*
               Viennese Classical
               Masterworks

10 Franz Joseph Haydn: *Missa in angustiis (Nelsonmesse)*

We turn now from three towering Baroque creations to a parallel representation from the Viennese Classical era. The Haydn, Schubert, and Beethoven masterpieces we are about to examine are just as accessible to choruses and orchestras of standard size and instrumentation. We will address the same elements of historical and biographical interest, together with possible performing forces, and editions appropriate to your use.

Again we will move through each movement, giving suggestions about tempo choices, specific bowings, and interpretive decisions. The modest system of technical language we employ can largely be found defined in the glossary, and much of it is discussed in detail, as you know, in Part I of this book.

Elements of Viennese Classical Performance Practice

It is convenient to base our consideration of Viennese Classical works on the music of the founder of the style, Franz Joseph Haydn. The evolution from Baroque to Classical is marked especially by the disappearance of the *basso continuo* as the harmonic foundation of the texture. Joseph Haydn played a major role in this development; in his post-choirboy years he earned a part of his livelihood playing serenades outdoors in Vienna, and no doubt found it very inconvenient to haul a keyboard instrument to these engagements. His string quartets—so fundamentally different from the Baroque trio sonata—were his workshop from his youth on, as he turned away from the *continuo* and figured bass. Church music always tends to be conservative, however, and so we find even his late masses include organ parts which reinforce—but no longer constitute the whole essence of—the harmonic flow through the texture. In the *Nelsonmesse* the organ reinforces and supports, and it sometimes handles solo responsibilities, but it does not assume the structural importance it has in, say, the Baroque works in earlier chapters.

How should this music *sound?*

The Austrian churches for which Haydn's masses were intended are filled with hard, reflective surfaces; there is much marble and glass; above all this there are domes which contribute to (in the case of Eisenstadt's Bergkirche, for example) a 4½ to 5½-second echo. Rapid passages played *legato* become unintelligible; in fact, any full nineteenth-century *legato* turns to cacophony within a single phrase. "Lighter, shorter, listen!" would have to be our watchwords, were we in such settings. In these churches tempos must be a bit slower, and strings of quarter notes must be performed as eighths separated by eighth rests. More than in American concert halls, many of which tend to be acoustically "dry," connections between notes are provided by reverberation, rather than by *legato*.[1] Articulation, then, has to be a constant matter of concern to us in performing this music. Here we should not permit the full Romantic *legato*, as we know it now; separation was taken for granted by Haydn's players—and his singers! *Detaché* bowing was standard, and the *wedge* (∧) was one of his favorite markings: it denotes separation like a modern *staccato*, less emphatic than Haydn's accent (>).[2] His *staccato* was even shorter.

"Lighter, shorter" is not intended to make the music sound superficial. It is to lend it clarity, and forward impetus. Heavy, muddy performance of Viennese Classical repertoire will lead inevitably to slowing of your tempo, and to dull, lackluster phrases.

By contrast, what happens when you teach your ensemble the real Viennese Classical style can make a magical transformation in the musical outcome. And that style is too often taken for granted: just as many trained musicians have not been taught the indispensability of ornamentation in Baroque music, so too few really understand the expressiveness and intellectual sophistication of the Classical idiom. To touch briefly, but—we hope—emphatically on a few points that apply directly to the *Nelsonmesse:*

1. Use rests and *fermatas* to give the music time to breathe. Don't rush new attacks, and don't be rigidly metronomic at the most important "seams" (that is, the transition points).
2. Remember that eighteenth-century treatises[3] cautioned against playing notes of equal notated value as if they must be all alike in duration. Notes of equal value are not always equal in character—that is, in musical value.
3. In accompanying solo passages, be willing to give some extra space at cadences, and treat them as opportunities to fit into place brief (unwritten) ornamentation. Be tasteful, certainly, but not hidebound; we know such *cadenzas* often were improvised in Haydn's day.
4. In that same way, try to make the music sound spontaneous. Encourage your musicians to sing and play as if even they do not know what's coming next. We rehearse works so much that we lose a sense of the unfolding of the rhetoric, of the impact on the mind of the listener of repeated—repeated—repeated words, and the like. There are surprises, and you must not give them away.

---

1. Most concert spaces in the larger Austrian palaces tend to be rectangular, with hard surfaces, so that reverberation is a serious problem in many of them, as well. In this respect, the famous Haydnsaal in the Esterhazy Palace at Eisenstadt, which has wonderful acoustics, is a notable exception.
2. See the glossary.
3. See, for example, C. P. E. Bach's *Versuch über die wahre Art das Clavier zu spielen,* which Haydn knew well.

5. Above all, do not make this music sound or appear childish. It was the life's work of Haydn, Beethoven, Mozart, Schubert, and others whose intellectual weight and artistic gravity cannot be doubted. They were artistically sophisticated.

To regard these predecessors of ours as naïve, or to see the great Romantic composers as somehow more profound than their Classical fathers, is to ignore the testimony of those Romantics—to ignore the express evidence that Brahms and Wagner and Stravinsky and all of us owe much of our conception of music to these towering Viennese masters.

Determining Classical Tempos

The acoustical circumstances we have just described affected Haydn's tempo decisions, as we have said. It is clear that an *Allegro,* for example, does *not* connote as fast a tempo as the same indication would in later style periods. Markings which appear in the *Nelsonmesse* were understood to be more modest in pace than the same indicators would be conceived to be in the late nineteenth century.

Be guided in these tempo decisions by that consideration, and by the inter-relationships which exist between the various movements of the larger work: "stand back and look" at all those relationships before you make final decisions about any of them. Richard Strauss is said to have believed that a "macro-tempo" existed even between whole symphonies. Whether or not this is the case, there is little doubt that *proportional* pacing of the components of a single work makes sense to the listener, and makes good ensemble easier for you and your musicians.

In the *Nelsonmesse,* for example, a *guiding pulse* of 120 is central to the au-thors' choices: we choose that as the tempo for the *Allegros* of the Gloria (both of them), the Pleni sunt ceoli, and the Osannas. The Benedictus we set at half the 120 ($\downarrow$ = 60). The Qui tollis we shade slightly slower than that, and the Dona nobis pacem a bit faster ($\downarrow$ = 126); the other tempos are close to multiples of 60, as we will point out movement by movement. This kind of overview helps to resolve a lot of questions about the meaning of the Italian tempo terms and their modifiers.

Watch carefully the time signatures, as well. Haydn is quite specific, for ex-ample, about his use of the *alla breve* symbol in this work, in other masses, and in all his writing.

Other Rehearsal Considerations

Earlier in this book[4] we suggested specific ways you can teach Baroque style to your musicians. We warned at that point that most orchestras still "lean

---

4. See pp. 57–58.

heavily on standard nineteenth-century selections," and that they "may tend to perform everything in lush, Romantic character, with long, *legato* bows and a lot of vibrato; often they overplay the *tutti* passages." The same dangers apply to the Classical works that follow, and the same rehearsal procedures we suggested to teach Baroque style can serve you well to teach Viennese style.

Haydn in the 1790s

In the last decade of the eighteenth century, Joseph Haydn was standing at the pinnacle of the European musical world. After he had spent a career working as a liveried servant (but the Kapellmeister, nonetheless) of the fabled Princes Esterhazy in their splendid Austrian and Hungarian palaces, the death of Prince Nicolaus "the Magnificent" in 1790 had essentially freed him to accept Johann Peter Salomon's invitation to compose and conduct for a time in London. During two stays in the British capital (1791–92 and 1794–95) Haydn became aware of his true international standing; treated by the British royal family to the sort of attention modern-day "rock stars" receive from the media, honored by Oxford University, and lionized by English audiences, he came fully to realize the stature his life as a composer had earned him. When he returned to Austria in the late summer of 1795 to live out his life, he knew he was honoring his homeland by choosing it.

What a transformation! Later Beethoven himself, making a pilgrimage to Haydn's birthplace in Rohrau, would express his surprise that such a great man had been born in a dirt-floored farmhouse. Underfed and regularly flogged by choirmasters in Hainburg and then Vienna (the standard lot of common boys in that period), Haydn determined early to work hard and learn how to make a livelihood as a musician. His years as a choirboy in the Cathedral of Saint Stephan in Vienna gave him solid experience with great choral literature of the Renaissance and Baroque eras, but he apparently received almost no formal instruction there. His voice was of solo quality, and his youthful musicianship earned him distinction, so long as his soprano voice could be trusted. At last it gave way, though, and he was out of a job about age 17.

Haydn came of age on the streets of Vienna. Working as a valet, an accompanist, a music teacher, and a freelance musician, he gradually built for himself both a profession and a reputation. Educating himself by reading (one of his most important influences came from the *Prussian Sonatas* of C. P. E. Bach, and from the latter's text *Versuch über die wahre Art das Clavier zu spielen*)[5] and observing what was effective in both street serenades and brief courtly engagements, he was fully prepared for an important, permanent appointment when that opportunity came in 1761 from Prince Paul Anton Esterhazy.

---

5. Haydn said later, "Who knows me well must have found out that I owe a great deal to Emanuel Bach, that I have understood and diligently studied him." Karl Geiringer, *Haydn. A Creative Life in Music,* p. 32.

Haydn was 30, and daily for the next three decades he wrote string quartets, symphonies, masses, sonatas, concertos, and operas, all for the Esterhazy palaces at Eisenstadt, Eszterhaza, Vienna, and elsewhere through central Europe. He was generally isolated from the competitive artificiality of the imperial court circles in Vienna, which proved a great advantage. Late in his life, he wrote that he could "make experiments, observe what produced an effect and what weakened it, and was thus in a position to improve, to alter, make additions or omissions and be as bold as I pleased. I was cut off from the world; there was no one to confuse or torment me, and *I was forced to become original.*"[6] His art was a matter of great pride to the Esterhazys, and the princes put Haydn and his musicians on display at every opportunity as the years passed. He remained, nevertheless, a super-servant.

Then came London, and the international public esteem. Returned from those trips, he was given honorific status by his fourth prince, and his responsibilities as Kapellmeister were reduced essentially to little else but producing an annual mass for the princess's name day. The six masses he wrote beginning in 1796 are among his greatest masterpieces, and it is one of these to which we address ourselves now.

The *Nelsonmesse*

Haydn's *Missa in angustiis* (roughly translatable as "Mass in the tight, or limited time") has been known by many names. This ambiguous Latin title could have referred to the geopolitical dangers Austria was facing from the Napoleonic challenge, to Haydn's own ill health (apparently a result of fatigue from the enormous labors leading up to the premiere of *The Creation*),[7] to the brevity of the period in which he wrote the work,[8] or perhaps just to some private frustration felt by the master at that time: as a result of the recent dismissal by Prince Nicolaus of the wind players formerly part of his retinue, Haydn now was having to write for a much more modest orchestra than he had for the *Missa in tempore belli*. All these public and private anxieties may lie behind that word *angustiis*.

Why the work is popularly referred to as the "Nelson Mass" is just as uncertain and even more complicated. Absent the discovery of some new evidence we will never know. The autograph score in Vienna makes no reference to Nelson. At the time Haydn was writing the *Missa in angustiis*, Admiral Lord Nelson was confronting a French fleet supporting Napoleon's military expedition to Egypt; this campaign culminated in the famous Battle of the Nile, during which Nelson's forces effectively destroyed the French squadron. As a result, Napoleon was

---

6. Conversation of Haydn with his early biographer Griesinger, translated in Karl Geiringer, p. 72, see above. (Italics added.)
7. The premiere of *The Creation* had taken place in Vienna at the end of April.
8. Griesinger, cited by H. C. Robbins Landon in *Haydn: Chronicle and Works,* vol. IV, p. 325.

forced to abandon his plan to conquer Egypt. Austria was allied with England at the time, and the outcome of the battle was the cause of much relief and rejoicing in Vienna.

The autograph score[9] indicates that Haydn completed the work on the last day of August in 1798. Nelson's victory had occurred on August 1, but it was probably mid-September before the news could cross the Mediterranean and reach Vienna. The mass had its first performance in a service about a week later. Clearly the *Nelsonmesse* title was not Haydn's own intention; it could not have been, for he was bound by his duties to write it in honor of Princess Esterhazy, and it was completed before word of Nelson's victory was received at Eisenstadt. At least three other possibilities come to mind: (1) some expression of thankfulness *(Gott sei dank. . . .)* for the destruction of the French fleet may have been made by the prelate at the service, and that may have led those present to refer to it by this "German" title; (2) when the Nelsons made a "state visit" to Vienna and then to Eisenstadt in September of 1800 two years later, one of the tributes paid the international hero (by then a "media star") might have been the announcement of a work named (renamed) in his honor (although the princess might have preferred to keep it "hers"); or (3) since we understand this *Missa* was used liturgically in the admiral's presence, it may be simply that it came to be known locally as "the mass we presented when Admiral Nelson was here." At best, all one can do now is speculate.[10]

Whatever one calls it, this is the third of the six "late masses" that Haydn composed after his London visits, and it was written in Eisenstadt the summer after *The Creation* premiered in April 1798 in Vienna. Like all the others, it was created for specific liturgical use, and not as a concert piece, though that is how it most often is performed in America now. Its proportions are standard; it is not the sort of *missa brevis* to which Mozart complained he was limited (by the archbishop of Salzburg), nor is it too long to be practical for service music (as is Bach's *Mass in B Minor* or Beethoven's *Missa solemnis*). In America it continues to be the most-performed of Haydn's masses.[11]

Choosing Performance Forces

Haydn's orchestra was a superior one from the time of his original appointment by his first prince, and it grew better, player by player, as the years passed; there are evidences that—beyond his day-to-day burden of administration —the orchestra was a joy to him. As an example, one need only contrast his string quartets from the 1750s to the later outburst of virtuosic violin writing

---

9. This can be found in the Musiksammlung of the Österreiches Nationalbibliothek, Vienna.
10. To add to the confusion, the autograph score is in fact entitled *only Missa*, and most modern printings capitalize the A ("Angustiis"), although Haydn himself—using the phrase *in angustiis* in his *Entwurf-Katalog*—did not. To add to this muddle, the work is generally known in England as both the "Coronation Mass" and the "Imperial Mass," and in France as the latter.
11. This is somewhat to be regretted, for the *Missa in tempore belli* (the *Paukenmesse*), the *Harmoniemesse,* and the others deserve high regard, as well.

in quartets from his early Esterhazy years to recognize the trust he placed in Luigi Tomasini, the leading player. (In later years, Haydn would stand godfather to Tomasini children.) You will find demanding string writing in the *Nelsonmesse* that reflects his confidence in Tomasini and his colleagues.

Prince Esterhazy's (much-needed) economizing having eliminated (even after the great success three months earlier of *The Creation*) the full wind complement Haydn had been using, the master seems to have argued for and won princely permission to pay freelance trumpet players; thus he was able to score the new mass for soloists, choir, three trumpets in D, tympani, strings, and organ.[12]

Haydn's biographer G. A. Griesinger wrote to Breitkopf & Härtel in late 1802 that the edition of the *Nelsonmesse* about to be published should add wind parts to cover passages which Haydn (short of players, as we have said) had assigned to the organ; this was poorly done by a Breitkopf employee. A later Esterhazy Kapellmeister added clarinets. (Today older, unscholarly publications of the work reflect these and other editorial misjudgments.) For our part, the present authors agree with Robbins Landon's assessment that Haydn's "use of the solo organ and trumpets with kettledrums is a stroke of genius." Even Haydn probably could not have improved on the 1798 orchestration, once he had conceived and implemented it. One of the most interesting features of this mass is its unique instrumentation; and thus we urge you to employ it.[13]

The best evidence available implies to the authors that Haydn had 18 to 23 singers in the choirloft for the *Nelsonmesse*.[14]

This work was being performed late in Haydn's life, *after* the first presentations of *The Creation*. Whatever the reduced numbers available to Haydn due to princely budget cuts, it seems clear that the Handel concerts in London had influenced him, that he admired larger forces, and that this was—after all—the name day of the consort of Prince Esterhazy. Moreover, we know the Eisenstadt choirlofts are commodious enough to hold comfortably at least that 18–23 range. The rosters of instrumentalists at Eisenstadt suggest Haydn probably wanted a string body of about 4-4-2-2-1. In a modern hall, with less reverberant

---

12. Robbins Landon assumes "a bassoon or bassoons doubled" what he calls "the *basso continuo*," but does not cite evidence that—in spite of the princely cutbacks—Haydn employed these player(s), as he did the three trumpeters. Landon, cited earlier, vol. IV, p. 427. The present authors recognize that this would be possible, but do not encourage you to use a bassoon for such "*continuo* duties."
13. *If* circumstances require that you perform *Nelsonmesse* without organ you might want to use the optional woodwind parts in the Henle edition recommended below. In such an event beware of older editions that may be inaccurate in these and other parts.
14. Schenbeck, in *Joseph Haydn and the Classical Choral Tradition,* basing his calculations on extant choral parts and other factors, concludes "Haydn's choir numbered no more than thirty, and probably closer to fourteen"; p. 257. At pp. 365 ff. Schenbeck acknowledges, however, that "Haydn was so impressed by the large choirs he heard at the Westminster Abbey Handel concerts that he determined to reproduce this effect in the public performances of his own late oratorios." For the "Nelson performance" in 1800, nevertheless, Schenbeck says (p. 312) that Haydn paid only eight singers, but he personally believes much larger forces were used for Vienna performances.
 Landon lists individual singers, but is less direct about choral numbers. Landon, cited earlier, vol. II, pp. 39 ff.

acoustics than the Eisenstadt churches, you could justify a much larger body of musicians; 50 to 60 singers, for example, would imply a string body of approximately 8-8-4-4-2.

Organo e Violone simply means the usual doubling of 'celli and contrabass, plus the organ; the latter (perhaps because of the absent woodwinds) is given brief solo passages, beyond doubling other parts throughout. The instrument itself should be Baroque in style, much like the instruments one would use for the Bach and Handel works we have studied.[15] The same watchwords—"lighter, shorter"—discussed above apply to the organ, as to the singers and players.[16] Your soprano soloist must have a flexible voice with the security of a coloratura in the top register. Haydn has given her major responsibilities: there are commanding high notes and melismas, especially in the Kyrie and Credo movements, and a high *tessitura* in the Gloria; in the Et incarnatus section she must offer a warm sound of great beauty. The bass solo in the Qui tollis Haydn wrote for one of his favorite singers; what is needed here is rich size in the voice, but without any loss of lyric flow. To choose a contralto, look at the important solo at measure 10 of the Agnus Dei. The tenor must mesh nicely with these three voices in circumstances that are largely ensemble singing. Finally, a second soprano is necessary only briefly (and may be a chorus member) to complete the solo quintet at bar 43 of the Christe eleison.

In the Eisenstadt choirlofts Haydn probably placed his soloists to one side or the other—facing out over the balcony railing behind one of the string sections —for acoustical purposes. You may choose to seat them in front of the orchestra, beside you, or behind the orchestra in front of the chorus; do what seems best for the hall in which you are performing.

Some conductors mistake that Haydn is "easy" for the orchestra—that the parts are simple. To the contrary, it has been the authors' experience that his music can prove to be less predictable than Mozart's, and therefore somewhat more difficult in places. Haydn's string scoring—while masterful—requires a special level of concentration because the motival figures he writes, as they reappear, often take varied bowings. He changes the linear setting of some figures so that the players, expecting to "take it as it comes," find some spots will not work out routinely.[17] (Haydn was a good violinist himself, and knew exactly what he was asking Tomasini and his colleagues to do; sometimes he chose to let a phrase evolve in a certain way in a symphonic movement, or to reinforce word stress in a vocal circumstance. These intricacies pop up in both instrumental and choral works.) In any case, it may be a mistake to "force" a figure

---

15. It is possible to know precisely what sort of organ was used for the *Nelsonmesse* in 1798; the instruments installed at the Bergkirche and the Stadtpfarrkirche in Eisenstadt—having been reconditioned—are still in use today. You and your organist should consult Schenbeck's detailed discussion, cited earlier, pp. 360–363.

16. One contemporary source speaks directly to this, advising the organist to "take the notes off short." See above, p. 361.

17. A typical case: a fine player, getting ready for a rehearsal at the Classical Music Seminar at Eisenstadt, once remarked genially, "Good! We're rehearsing Mozart. We can relax a little this morning."

into a rigidly consistent bowing pattern; moreover, unless you have a good musical reason for doing it your way, these are good spots to discuss with your concertmaster and principal players.

Performing Editions

The authors have conducted from the full score published by G. Henle and edited by Günter Thomas, and we recommend it to you.[18] For performance parts, we suggest you consider Robbins Landon's 1963 edition[19] and the version published by Carus.[20] Other editions, some carefully done, and some less so, are available as well.

ANALYSIS OF THE WORK

At this culminative stage of his career, Haydn's style is mature and settled. His late masses form a continuity, one influenced certainly by his symphonies, operas, string quartets, and (most recently) *The Creation*. Each of these sacred masterworks has its individual characteristics, of course, but Haydn is not attempting anything radical—and certainly not in a liturgical setting meant for the princess's name day! Working in this genre earlier in his career he had found a vehicle of expression that represented a framework within which he could be free to explore. Looking from mass to mass across Haydn's catalog today one sees many similarities of key (Glorias generally in D major, for example), and tempo, and (to a lesser extent) of orchestration; yet there remains a vibrant originality—one which many famous composers could not match at Haydn's age (for he was past 66 when he wrote the *Nelsonmesse*).

The *Nelsonmesse* is emphatically *not* a choral work with deferential orchestral accompaniment! It is a balanced whole in which the singers, *like the other instruments,* have musical responsibilities no more nor less important than those of the strings, brass, timpani, and organ. At the same time, the text was liturgically important to the clergy and the congregation in these services, and that means the orchestral *colla parte* passages must be subservient to the intelligibility of the text. These are important considerations for you: the acoustical balances you seek, your emphasis on materials introduced in the orchestra (rather than the voices only), and the temporal proportions you create all should emerge from these conceptions.

Some have spoken of these late masses as "symphonic" in character. Robbins Landon has written that Haydn ". . . continued the symphonic form under this new guise: *for the late Haydn masses are in their fundamental construction symphonies for voices and orchestra using the mass text.*"[21] We strongly agree. To say

18. Günter Thomas, editor of Haydn, Franz Joseph, *Missa in angustiis.*
19. H. C. Robbins Landon, editor of Haydn, Joseph, *Mass in D Minor.*
20. Wolfgang Hochstein, editor of Haydn, Franz Joseph, *Missa in Angustiis,* Carus-Verlag.
21. Landon, *The Symphonies of Joseph Haydn,* p. 595. Emphasis his. His full consideration of this topic is on pp. 594 ff.

so is *not* to say, however, that these structures are replicas of textbook forms.[22] Like the late sonatas and quartets of his successor Beethoven, the form of each of these mature creations of Haydn's arises out of its own rhythmic, melodic, and textural identity; Haydn did not impose a rigid template of some sort on his late masses, any more than he did his late string quartets. As we look at each movement, we will discuss these structural issues further.

Kyrie

Again, determining an appropriate pace for any passage depends on the acoustics of the performance hall and the capabilities of your musicians, as well as the indications in the score of the intentions of the composer. That reminder given, for the opening movement in D minor we recommend a tempo of $\rfloor = 96$. If you have the "guiding pulse of 120" in your mind, think 60, halve that to 30, divide that into triplets at 90, and shade that higher to the 96 we suggest. (This sounds complicated, but practice makes it reflexive.)[23]

Treatises written in the eighteenth century make clear that tonal designs (not themes) are the principal architectural influence on the musical forms of Joseph Haydn and his contemporaries.[24] That applies here: implications of sonata design are manifest in this first movement. The first section, orchestra alone, begins in D minor; the chorus enters with the same materials; and, after the soprano solo entrance, the tonality shifts to the relative major, just as it would in a sonata allegro design. The Christe eleison elides into a choral fugue, and—in a modulatory development section, driven especially by ascending step-progressions (bars 65 ff. and 83 ff.)—the original tonality returns (through a "retransition" in measures 96–98) to a recapitulation at bar 99. (Notice that Haydn thickens the orchestral writing considerably in this reprise.) Once again there is fugal development, but this time there is no real departure from D minor, just as would be the case in a sonata allegro movement in one of Haydn's string quartets or symphonies.

This is a movement of great dramatic power, beginning with the D minor arpeggios and the low D naturals in all three trumpets. What are we to think of these emphatic repeated notes, emphasized by their wedges? This is not "nice" music, and it is not "pretty." (Two years later Beethoven—seeking the same sort of rough, unrefined sound—would deliberately cast in C the first theme of the first movement of his first symphony, thus driving the violins down to an open-string G-natural, so that the players *could not use vibrato*.) Haydn could have settled for a single trumpet, too, but instead he doubled the three with a tym-

---

22. See also Landon's citing of Martin Chusid's attempt to demonstrate that the *Nelsonmesse* is a compounding of three "vocal symphonies," an analysis which the present authors regard as prescriptive, and somewhat contrived. Landon, cited earlier, vol. IV, p. 427.
23. For a first movement, you can always carry a metronomic tempo on stage with you.
24. Ratner, "Harmonic Aspects of Classical Form," *Journal of the American Musicological Society* 2 (fall 1949): 159–168.

panum! Robbins Landon calls these trumpet phrases "menacing,"[25] implying that they represent the approach toward Austria of the Napoleonic forces. At the least, this is not traditional church music, but quite a revolutionary timbre that the 66-year-old Haydn is creating.[26] Let us see how these trumpets reappear later.

The strings begin downbow, of course, playing *detaché*. The groups of three quarter notes (multiple stops in the violins) that begin in the third measure should each commence downbow. In measure 23, and thereafter, the three pickup notes at the end of the bar should begin upbow. The "trumpet pattern," which first appears in the lower strings in measure 22 and in the Violins I in bar 43, should always begin with a downbow on the downbeat and a second downbow on the first of the two sixteenths. For most of this, the strings take the bowings "as it comes," as usual.

The running sixteenths that begin in measure 33 in the violas, and in measure 38 in the violins, should be taken slightly off the string. This applies again in the first violins at bar 54, and each time thereafter. (The "lightness" of which we have been speaking is the point here, of course: the violinists certainly could play this passage on the string and not detached, but in so doing they would be outside the character of Haydn's style, creating balance problems in the texture, and—ultimately—problems maintaining tempo, as well. At measure 80 this separation and lightness is particularly important during the ascent of the first violin line.) Both violin notes in measure 82 can be taken upbow.

Note the use of wedges in spots like the opening chords, and—especially— the running sixteenths in the violins in bar 38: Haydn could have written *staccati* here, with a *diminuendo* to the bar 39 *piano,* but this is not that sort of chic elegance. It is power! That *piano* comes without warning, and a *diminuendo* would *give the surprise away.*[27] (There are a great many *subitos* in this music that we would call "Beethovian" if it were not that Haydn had been doing it already.)

As you rehearse the fugal passage, which begins at measure 54, have the chorus listen to the orchestra alone, and then vice versa. This will (1) lead the singers to use shorter articulations and (2) lead the players to pick up the accents created by syllable stress in the text. (This procedure can be of help in other movements, as well.) Where the instrumentalists have repeated notes, as in bar 125 in the violins, be careful again to keep their playing light. The *appoggiaturas* (the first note in bar 126, for example) must be played on the beat, as a sixteenth, and slightly stressed, with the following note shortened.

Gloria

There is another major problem with editing here, rather like the confusion over the woodwind parts. Haydn's first version of the soprano solo had

---

25. Landon, cited earlier, vol. IV, p. 431.
26. It has an operatic quality, as will the Verdi *Requiem* in its own time.
27. Page 150.

her singing the same *pitches* in bar 5 as the choral sopranos (and the first violins), but with the syllables of the complete *Gloria in excelsis Deo* phrase. Apparently to protect or at least accommodate a weaker soprano at a later performance (and there is much speculation who that might have been) Haydn himself changed to the notes shown at measure 5 of the G. Henle edition. He made the same change at bar 175 in the Quoniam, apparently for the same reasons. (He did *not* make parallel alterations in either the choral sopranos' part, *or* in the contralto soloist's entrance at measure 56, so we know what he preferred.) In a similar way, he shifted the tenor to the lower octave for the last note of bars 19 and 24.[28] We recommend that you utilize the original, higher pitches.

The wedges in the strings at measures 1 and 2 (marked *piano* to stay in balance with the soprano soloist), together with the antiphonal solo-choral passages (first the soprano against the choir, and then the solo quartet against the *tutti*), establish the character of the Gloria.

An appropriate tempo for the opening *Allegro* would be ♩ = 120, what we are calling the "guiding pulse" of this work. The *Adagio* (the Qui tollis) we would set at ♩ = 56 (shaded down to just a bit less than half the *Allegro*), and then we would restore Tempo I for the return of the Allegro at the Quoniam. The violins should begin the movement with good separation, slightly off the string, in order to enunciate clearly Haydn's wedges here. Lighten the sixteenths in the lower strings in bar 3, as well. The rhythmic motif Haydn establishes in the solo soprano line in measures 1 and 2 can be played by the violins with consecutive upbows on the second and third notes of measure 3.

At bar 15 the first note in the violins should be light, with the next note—the A-natural—taken downbow. In bar 32 begins a modification of this figure; we suggest playing the slurred notes downbow, and the intervening unslurred notes upbow. (Consider the rhythmic effect of these upbow wedges!) These patterns recur throughout the movement.

Haydn's writing has been called "an art of motion."[29] Rhythm is masterfully handled here: see the syncopated *sforzandi* motif in the choral entrances beginning in measure 33; now compare that with the metamorphosis of the first violin line from bar 15 into syncopated *sforzandi at the level of the eighth note* starting at measure 33; *these tug against the choral accents at the level of the quarter note*. Examine Haydn's dramatic use of syncopation and of *subitos* in this movement (and on throughout the *Nelsonmesse*).

In the Qui tollis the choir picks up the repeated-note figures of the strings in a series of chant-like entrances. Haydn's dramatic alternation of dynamics here serves the text very well. In this section the strings should play any eighths not marked with wedges with a "brush stroke." (Review this concept of "lifting," if need be.)[30] Where there are two pickups, begin them downbow, and

---

28. For a detailed discussion of this matter, see Landon, cited earlier, vol. IV, pp. 428–429. For his specific recommendations, consult his Schott edition, cited earlier.

29. Robert Sondheimer, in his *Haydn; A Historical and Psychological Study Based on His Quartets* (a flawed book, but insightful on this one point about design), pp. 27–28.

30. Page 13.

where there are three, upbow. Have the first violins begin the "turn figure" (bar 4) upbow each time. The *fz* motif in bar 115 begins downbow. The Violin I part in bars 151–156 is a bit complicated: each *fz* gets a downbow; the first two notes (and the turn between them) in bar 153 are taken on a slurred upbow; the two thirty-seconds in measure 154 are slurred back to the preceding *fz;* the next four sixteenths are slurred on an upbow; bar 155 is bowed in exactly the same way (with the second beat still downbow, though without the *fz*), and the six sixteenths in the middle of measure 156 are slurred together. The rest of the Qui tollis is straightforward.

This is a ternary form with a substantial coda. After this *Adagio* "B section," the Quoniam reprises the opening Gloria. (Bowings follow the same patterns.) The sixteenths in the Violins I in measure 176 can be taken on the string, slightly detached; the better your players, however, the more this sort of passage can be played off the string. Then at measure 192 Haydn begins a wonderful fugue (the coda) which amplifies the words "in the glory of God the Father, amen." There is a shift from the D minor of the Kyrie to the D major of this Gloria. We can guess at explanations of this change that are based on the text; there is no doubt, however, that Bach, Haydn, and Beethoven all chose D major for Glorias, and that it is a happy choice for trumpets.

Syncopation is again a major feature of this great fugue: the entrances of the subject are deliberately ambiguous at the beginning; they are thetic, but set the weak word "in." At measure 214, then, he shifts ("de-syncopates") the text, with the *"glor-"* syllable falling on the downbeat. Note, by the way, that Haydn reinforces important entrances of the fugue subject (particularly in the lower voices) by doubling them with short, single notes in the trumpet and timpani! (The last such case strengthens the soprano entrance in bar 224, disadvantaged as it is by the tessitura of the violins at that point.) This is craftsmanlike orchestration by a master who has been judging balances for decades.

One final clue to the movement's structure: consider the D pedal point at bar 15, which recurs not in the Quoniam itself, but—after a *dominant* pedal at bar 224 —at measure 231. Sustained for seven measures, it returns again three bars later.

As to bowings for the fugue, the players generally can "take it as it comes" (keeping a downbow for the first beat of every measure), with the strokes slightly detached. The orchestra should be reminded that this is *colla parte* writing; the text is important, and once they play the initial subject they should lower their dynamic level to let the words come through.

Credo

The autograph refers to this spirited counterpoint as *"in canone."* Perhaps because the text itself is a precise and formal statement of belief, Haydn has chosen to use this strict and formal compositional procedure for a setting. Until measure 77 the high voices are kept one bar ahead and placed a perfect 5th above the altos and basses; then a single homophonic phrase emphasizes "God's descent from heaven."

Example 40. Suggested bowings for the *Nelsonmesse* Gloria, measures 151–156.

This does not imply that the pace should be pompous or ponderous, however. Haydn has indicated *Allegro con spirito,* and marked it *alla breve;* we suggest that a tempo ranging from ♩ = 88–92 (close to the triplet multiple of 30 we suggested above)[31] is stylistic.

Begin the string parts with a downbow and take the last two notes in the first

---

31. Page 158.

bar on the upbow; then keep subsequent downbeats on downbows in this re-
curring motif. The quarter notes should be well separated.[32] In the passage beginning at measure 41, the eighth notes should be off the string. In general the
quarters in the lower strings should be somewhat lifted. Bowings in this section
are straightforward.

The stately Et incarnatus which follows begins with one of the most beautiful passages Haydn ever wrote, introduced by the strings, stated fully by the soprano soloist, and reprised *forte* in rich homophony by the choir. For this *Largo*,
♩ = 52—a bit slower than halving our "guiding pulse"—would be appropriate.
The accented Crucifixus (note the wedges) is underlined by a return of the
trumpets' repeated-note motif from the Kyrie; for five measures the rhythm and
timbre that Landon calls "menacing" recurs here. There is an arresting solo trio
which ends with a dramatic *fermata* at measure 126; then the full ensemble
(consider carefully again the wedges in both strings *and voices*) portrays the interment of Christ. The repeated notes in the string parts (measures 93–94, for
example) can be taken with a sharply articulated brush stroke. In measures 95–
97, the violins' three slurred pickups at the end of each bar should be taken
upbow.

The jubilant *Vivace* that announces the Resurrection should be paced at something like ♩ = 108–112, somewhat slower than the "guiding pulse" itself. It is first
of all the capability of your violins that determines how fast this can be set. (If
one were to overdo this tempo, however, the effect could sound frenetic, rather
than joyous.) It is unusual that the Et resurrexit commences in B minor. Bach
and most other composers set this text in a major key. It appears that Haydn is
saving D major for measures 146 ff., to emphasize "Christ's coming in glory."
Be careful that the strings—concerned with the technical demands here—keep
their articulation light. Most of this should stay slightly off the string. Starting
at bar 167, the two-sixteenth, two-eighth pattern should always begin upbow.
Again at 172, be certain the repeated notes do not become heavy-handed. The
syncopated quarters in the Violins I beginning at measure 182 (and later again
at bar 225) should always be taken downbow.

This is a four-part sectional form: the Credo, the Et incarnatus, and the Et
resurrexit are brought to a close by an extended emphasis on the crucial text
"and the life of the world to come, Amen." There have been a series of important
"Ands" through this movement, and the last of them is a dramatic half-note
from the choir at measure 200, an *"Et"* left hanging in air. The soprano's *Et vitam
venturi* at bar 201 is one of the glories of Haydn's liturgical settings. Note that
Haydn marked the strings *piano*, but *with* wedges; he wants the accompaniment
here sharply defined, *secco*. We recommend that you continue the wedges up to
the marked slurs in bar 211; without question, Haydn's orchestra would have
known to do so.

---

32. For a review of this general topic, and of the technical terms used with orchestra players in
these circumstances, review chapter 2 above, pp. 12 ff., and the glossary.

Sanctus

The Adagio needs a stately, unhurried tempo, and ♩ = 48–50 (a bit faster than the pace you get from tying together three beats of the 120 "guiding pulse") would be the authors' choice. This means quite a slow beat pattern, however. To conduct in a standard four at this pace can look imprecise; yet—since the ensemble moves in quarters in bars 1 to 4—to beat it in eight would look too "busy." We recommend that you use a "stopped four" here (that is, starting the "prep" stroke for each beat on the intervening eighth), which has the advantage, by the way, of signaling to your musicians the precise speed of the eighth notes they will begin to perform in measure 5. Keep your hand moving slightly during the *fermatas* in bars 2 and 4, until your cutoffs, and be certain to give clear prep beats in bars 3 and 5, as well.[33] At measure 7, note the *portato* bowings. Keep them light.

The *Allegro* of the Pleni sunt coeli comes, then, at the same ♩ = 120 you remember from the *Allegro* of the Gloria (and the Quoniam), our "guiding pulse," which you should be able to recall quite dependably. The string treatment here is much like that of the Gloria.

The congregation has come a long way in this mass: the musicians' opening arpeggio in bar 11 reverses here (as it ascends to "heaven" in D major) the descending D minor motif from the first measures of the Kyrie. There is much tone-painting in Haydn; note his treatment of the phrase *in excelsis,* for example.

Benedictus

You can begin this movement in two at ♩ = 60, returning to the Allegro at ♩ = 120 for the Osanna reprise.

Haydn makes the character of this *Allegretto* quite clear from the beginning in the *subito* alternations of *piano* and *forte* blocks, of slurs versus wedges, and of orchestra, soloists, and choir. The important contrast between the slurred pairs of notes and the shorter, wedge-marked figures commences in bar 3; then the wedges become quite emphatic by measure 24, offering you a chance to distinguish the *tutti* choral interjections from the generally *legato* solo lines. This dichotomy continues through the Benedictus.

The arched symbol over the violins in bars 1 and 2 is probably just a phrase marking, not a bowing. If you do not tell them otherwise, your string players are likely to take alternate (down, then up) bows. Either way, the lower strings—with their two-note slurs—need to be heard through the texture, and the violins need to move gently toward the F-natural peak of their line; again, the contrast between these smooth connections and the subsequent wedges is the important point.

---

33. Note the "rolled" chord in the right hand of the organ part in the first measure (of the G. Henle score), and notice further that Haydn gives no such indication for the left hand. We believe this editing to be correct.

The figure that appears first in measure 4 at the *forte* marking recurs frequently, and should always be begun downbow. The three thirty-seconds in bar 5 can be hooked to the downbeat F-natural, if you wish; this pattern should be consistent with measures 7 ff., of course. The *sforzandi* in bars 22–28 should come downbow, with intervening notes hooked as needed. In general, otherwise, the strings should bow "as it comes."

At bar 50 note the change in the bowing of the lower strings: the patterns now are four notes long, rather than two. The accompaniment under the soprano solo at bars 65 ff. becomes almost *secco* again. As the movement unfolds, with the soloists taking their turns, these figures continue to appear, and your earlier bowing choices can be replicated.

The unison statement in repeated notes by the choir, beginning syncopated in measure 72 on the sub-mediant triad (the Neapolitan of the coming dominant chord), reminds us of the opening trumpet figure in the Kyrie. This phrase proves to foreshadow an arresting, vivid trumpet call at bar 122 (one thinks of the fanfare in Beethoven's *Leonore Overture No. 3*), rhythmically different from the beginning, but clearly related. It is a spectacular moment.

One *very* important feature here: in bars 122–128 in the Henle edition the small-note timpani alternative the authors consider to be Haydn's intention: while the autograph score shows only the first beat quarter notes in bars 122, 125, and 127, the authentic parts in the archives at both Eisenstadt and Klosterneuberg show the timpani doubling the trumpets' rhythm throughout those seven measures.[34] The trumpets dovetail with the choral text, and then the full strings reinforce the trumpets' triplets with urgent wedges, driving to a powerful half-cadence.

Its resolution finds us back in D major for the second Osanna, which mirrors the *Allegro* in the Sanctus in every respect (save the absence of the Pleni sunt coeli). This Osanna tempo surely should match the first one, and so should the bowings.

Agnus Dei

Haydn returned to the G major he used for the Et incarnatus to begin this movement. He moves through the relative minor by bar 30 to a distant, tentative cadence on an F-sharp major chord (!) at measure 41.

We recommend beginning this at the same tempo as the last *Adagio:* the opening of the Sanctus was set at ♩ = 48–50, and we would suggest 48–52 in this case, using the same "stopped beat" gesture here for the first measure, and then easing into a divided three in the second bar in order to assure rhythmic clarity in the strings.

The opening of this movement is a "violin aria," much like solos Haydn wrote

---

34. H. C. Robbins Landon, in a discussion with one of the present authors. See also his comments in Landon, cited earlier, vol. IV, p. 429.

for Tomasini in his string quartets, and offers a last moment of reflection before the energy and assurance of the Dona nobis pacem. If you want to emphasize this aspect of the movement, a reasonable option would be to cut your strings down to one-on-a-desk, or even fewer, at the beginning of the Agnus Dei, returning to *tutti* strings at the bar 19 *forte*.[35] This return to full orchestra will give emphasis to the change in character which takes place at that point: the soprano entrance in measure 19 is recitative-like; treat it—with its orchestral interjections—as such, until the florid violin line returns in bar 24. Be certain you give the violin line its share of primacy here; it must have composure and tranquility. The dotted rhythm in measures 19–21 should be played each time with a downbow on the first sixteenth, the next two notes hooked upbow, and the final note in the pattern downbow.[36]

For the *Vivace* of the Dona nobis pacem the authors recommend a tempo of ♩ = 126, a notch faster than the "guiding pulse" of the earlier *Allegros, providing your strings can handle that pace*. Note Haydn's use once again of syncopation to lend power and excitement to the contrapuntal entrances. The first violins (doubling the altos) can start with an *upbow* here: the fugue subject's opening half-note always begins downbow. Similarly, the violas (although they can begin with a downbow) can take a second downbow on their fourth-beat B-natural, which will give emphasis to their syncopated half-notes, and the Violins II can take their measure 44 tied-A-natural downbow, so that they will reach the high A-natural in measure 46 on a downbow, as well; Haydn has them doubling the sopranos. The lower strings can employ a brush stroke for lightness and separation.

This is a whirlwind for your violins. They begin playing as separate Violin I and Violin II sections, but by measure 47 the firsts and seconds are scored in unison. You will remember that the Violins II are generally not quite as virtuosic as Violins I; this movement demands a lot of them, if you are to use all of them on the written part.

Another problem for the firsts—an unusually difficult one—begins at measure 57: these isolated pairs of slurred sixteenths happen so quickly that it is difficult to play them without "smearing them" or losing their metric (between the beats) clarity. The players can take consecutive downbows at the beginning of bar 57, so that the first of these sixteenth-note pairs in each bar is always on a downbow. Use the same bowing when this figure returns at measure 90, and at 105.

Keep the choir's energy up all the way to the end, right to the wonderful moment at measure 102. This interruption, with its stunning *subito piano,* is just the sort of surprise we have warned you not to give away. Take time here—extra time! If you're performing in a live hall, make certain the reverberations die

---

35. This is consonant with Haydn's *Tasto solo* marking (that is, "play only the bass line") instruction at measure 1, canceled by his *Organo* ("now full organ") at bar 19. See Schenbeck, cited earlier, p. 161.
36. You have seen this same four-note figure, with this same suggested bowing, earlier in this book: see Handel's "Surely He hath borne our griefs," example 15, p. 93.

away before you move the baton. Then demand a full measure of energy again, and urge the ensemble on to the final cadence.

In this joyous prayer for peace, after the earlier pleas for "mercy" in the Agnus Dei, Haydn is making a theological point: he is confident of salvation, both in this world and the world to come. Beethoven will end his own *Missa solemnis* with the same sort of expression of confidence.

11 Franz Schubert: *Mass in G Major, D.167*

Still a teenager, Franz (Peter) Schubert in early 1815 already was a sparkling fountainhead of original melody. The wellspring of lyricism from which choral works, string quartets, and an unprecedented flow of songs already had bubbled was by now fast becoming a geyser. In time that geyser would prove to be the primal font of German *lieder,* and its torrent would pour into much of the music of the West in the nineteenth and twentieth centuries, influencing both the concert halls and the popular tunes of the streets. The teenager was gifted, and the gift was a unique one.

Young Schubert wrote every day. A former choirboy at the Habsburg's Royal Chapel (Hofkapelle) in Vienna, he had both a clear sense of what was felicitous for the voice and a special love for poetry. He read Goethe and Schiller, together with—as the years passed—a wide range of other poets; studying their works often moved him straightway to compose. On any one day he might produce two or three songs, and some days as many as six or eight! Before his nineteenth birthday he had written around 200 *lieder.*[1] These are not "student works," in any sense of that cliché: *Gretchen am Spinnrade, Rastlose Liebe, Heidenröslein,* and *Erlkönig* are among them. At age 18, Franz Schubert was creating vocal literature that is heard today on every recital stage. Perhaps no composer in music history has created as much fully mature music while an adolescent, even the venerated Mozart.[2]

Two of his brothers played the violin, as did Franz, and his father was a 'cellist. With Franz shifting to viola, they often joined in chamber music, and that started him writing string quartets. In school, he had the luck to participate in what seems to have been a very capable student orchestra, competent to attempt Viennese Classical symphonies; what is more—as what we now would call the ensemble's concertmaster—young Franz apparently was permitted to conduct on occasion. Salieri was among those who guided his musical studies.

Schubert was Viennese, Catholic, a singer, and an orchestral player: it seems natural then that among his earliest major works would be masses for the Austrian churches. In 1812–13 he wrote at least four individual *Kyries,* before fash-

---

1. At the time of his death, just ten years later, there would be well over 600 of his *lieder;* exactly how many is a matter for scholarly disputation.
2. An assessment of Mozart's output will show that little of what he wrote by his eighteenth birthday is performed with any frequency today, with the *Exultate, Jubilate, K.165* a notable exception. Quite a number of Schubert's early songs, by contrast, are heard with great regularity.

ioning a whole mass (D.105, in F) late in 1814. Grateful that this first complete ordinary had been well received the previous autumn, he spent the first week of March 1815 composing another—the *Mass in G Major, D.167*—for soprano, tenor, and bass soloists, chorus, string orchestra, and organ. His second symphony (*D.125, in Bb*) was in progress at the same time, and would be finished late that month.

Perhaps the first impression one gets from the *Mass in G Major* is its blend of that melodic gift of his with the overall style of the great Viennese Classical masters—the style especially of Haydn, Mozart, and (then 45-year-old) Beethoven.[3] In the Hofkapelle Schubert was made familiar with the liturgical music of the time, as well as that of earlier eras. As we have said, in his school orchestra he played and sometimes conducted the instrumental works of his great Austrian predecessors, and from his boyhood he was aware of the new creations coming from Beethoven's pen. In that context—as in any Viennese Classical work—the directness and clarity of the *Mass in G Major* are manifest; moreover (in the Benedictus trio, for example) its maturity is surprising. Audiences are invariably responsive to it.

Choosing Performance Forces

Of the earliest performances of the Handel, Haydn, and Beethoven works in this volume, scholars now know quite a lot, as you have seen—specific dates, places, musical forces, and all. Of the creation of Vivaldi's *Gloria* itself we know essentially nothing. Of the Bach *Magnificat* and the Schubert *Mass in G Major* we know a bit more, and—beyond that—can make some reasonable assumptions.

Schubert spent much of his youth around the parish church his family attended in Lichtental, a village outside the walls of Vienna. He was tutored by one Michael Holzer, the choirmaster there, and sang in the parish choir. We are told that Schubert's first mass, the F major one (*D.105*), was premiered in that church in the autumn of 1814, apparently gaining an enthusiastic reception.[4] It seems fair to assume that the choir of which he was a member (probably a typical Austrian parish choir of the period) sang that new mass as service music. The young composer may have sung in the choir; at any rate, his brother Ferdinand Schubert seems to have been the organist. We know from the recollections of one of Schubert's friends that a young woman in whom Schubert had a romantic interest at the time, one Therese Grob, had an attractive soprano voice, and that the solo part was intended for her. The orchestra players probably

---

3. The authors have no real interest in the old, artificial arguments which endeavor to designate individual composers as "Classical" or "Romantic" (or "Modern," for that matter). We do agree with Maurice J. E. Brown that the forms Schubert designs are those of the Viennese Classical world, and that "his mature work grows more conventional." See Brown's article "Schubert, Franz (Peter)" in *The New Grove Dictionary of Music and Musicians,* vol. 16, p. 778.
4. Brian Newbould, *Schubert. The Music and the Man,* pp. 131 ff.

would have been members of the parish, or nearby residents. Josef Mayseder, conductor of the Court Opera Orchestra, no less, was the *Dirigent.* Salieri himself attended, and is reported to have been very pleased with the outcome.

At least partially because he was buoyed up by the Lichtentalers' response (and Salieri's) to his first mass, one assumes, Schubert produced the *Mass in G Major* half a year later. It may even have been commissioned, in some sense. (Young composers of any century like to write music that is likely to find performances, of course.) Of the first presentations of this second mass we know nothing. There seem to be no extant records.[5] It seems a reasonable conjecture that at least an early performance (if not indeed the premiere) took place in the Lichtental church. One biographer speculates, indeed, that the soprano solos were again sung by Therese Grob, and that this is why the soprano gets two entrances in the Agnus Dei, instead of one, to the detriment of the tenor.[6]

All this suggests that you could properly perform the *Mass in G Major* with the forces typical of a village church of the period, say 16 to 20 singers, an orchestra of about 4-3-2-2-1 strings, and organ. Schubert himself seems to have contributed trumpets and timpani later.[7] The woodwinds the composer's brother Ferdinand apparently added a quarter of a century later are not Franz Schubert's creation. If you have available a larger choir, given an appropriate performance space, you could employ forces much like those we suggested for the *Nelsonmesse:* that is, up to a maximum of 50 or 60 singers, and a string body of approximately 8-7-5-5-3.

Clearly the numbers Schubert must have used for his early masses—about the same size as those employed by Haydn, or even smaller—link this mass to the whole Viennese Classical mass tradition.

Performing Editions

In preparing to perform this work you should consider the 1995 version edited by Franz Beyer for Breitkopf & Härtel;[8] this publication has been based on autograph parts in Schubert's own hand found in recent years in the famed Klosterneuberg Monastery. A voice-and-piano version (with available rental string parts), edited by Alice Parker and Robert Shaw, was published by G. Schirmer in 1954.[9] The original nineteenth-century Breitkopf & Härtel edition of the master's collected works still is—at this time—the only complete Schubert *Gesamtausgabe;* it is generally available in a reprint by Dover.[10] (The

---

5. Maurice J. E. Brown, *Schubert. A Critical Biography,* p. 236.
6. Brian Newbould, cited earlier, p. 136.
7. These would be a legitimate option, depending upon your circumstances. The authors regard the original string version as appropriate to the overall character of the work.
8. Franz Beyer, editor, *Mass in G Major, D.167, for Soloists, Chorus, Orchestra, and Organ.*
9. Alice Parker and Robert Shaw, editors, *Mass in G (Major).*
10. Eusebius Mandyczewski, editor, *Messe (in G) für vier Singstimmen, Orchester, und Orgel.* This edition has been reprinted by Dover Publications as *Mass in G Major, D.167.*

G. Henle *Neue ausgabe sämtlicher Werke,* which is in progress as of this writing, has not yet offered the *Mass in G Major,* but the earlier *F Major* mass is finished, as are later works.) Other publications of the *G Major* should be compared bar by bar with the Breitkopf versions.

ANALYSIS OF THE WORK

Because the *Nelsonmesse* was the first of the three Viennese Classical works you were to study in this book, its stylistic characteristics were given a particularly detailed, extensive examination. The *Mass in G Major* was written not by a sophisticated and mature master at the peak of his creative powers, but by a youthful genius; it is not forty-five minutes in length, but twenty-five. Its orchestra is smaller, and its structures less complex.

These characteristics make it a good choice for a young conductor in circumstances which permit one to work with choir and orchestra for the very first time. It is also a good choice for someone for whom available orchestral resources are limited, or for an audience with little experience of serious music.

Reading the earlier chapters of this book has changed you. We expect it has given you a new familiarity with bowings, with certain rehearsal procedures, and with orchestral communication techniques. That makes your and our job easier now. Many of the points made to you in chapter 10 would be redundant if repeated in chapters 11 and 12; further, the authors assume you will recognize many Classical features and factors for yourself, and so (just as the Bach and Vivaldi discussions were briefer than the Handel chapter) the Schubert and Beethoven chapters will be less detailed than chapter 10. Talking with and managing the orchestra will remain a principal focus, along with some details of tempos and bowings.

Kyrie

The first movement of Schubert's mass is a straightforward ternary structure parallel to the form of the Greek text.[11] The opening section is in G major, moving to A minor for the beginning of the solo-centered *Christe eleison;* it becomes modulatory, passing through C and E cells on its way back to G major for the reprise of the opening *Kyrie eleison.* The choral writing is largely homophonic.

It is always something of an inconvenience when a choir has to begin a work without an introduction. Depending on the confidence you have in your singers, you could solve the problem of starting the Kyrie by (1) having a 'cellist or violinist give a soft *pizzicato* G-natural to the choir, (2) by having the organist play the note, after she or he has provided the A-natural to which the orchestral play-

---

11. For a detailed discussion of overall conducting problems with this movement see Robert W. Demaree, Jr., and Don V Moses, *The Complete Conductor,* pp. 202 ff.

ers tune, (3) by depending on a singer in the upstage center of the choir to give the pitch after the orchestra is ready, or (4) by trusting the choir to take their pitches from the same A-natural to which the orchestra relates.

Be cautious that you do not label this orchestra as merely accompanimental. While there is much doubling here, and the second violins tend to fill in harmonies, the firsts often have important counter-melodies (see measures 8 to 16, for example). Consider the ornaments indicated for the strings only: the trills, the *fortepianos, sforzandi, pizzicati,* slurs, and other expressive markings. Schubert is giving the orchestra a texture and sound different from that of the choir, and doing so with clear intentions. *Make certain your string players understand those responsibilities and that they realize you do not regard them as a mere background for the singers.* Be sure the text has clarity and intelligibility, for it is all-important liturgically, but do not lose the value of Schubert's orchestral writing, and do not let your players infer that you have less esteem for them than for your singers.

We recommend you set this *Andante con moto* at ♩ = 76 to 80. You will be able to determine most of the bowings yourself. We suggest for the Violins I consecutive downbows in measures 1, 3, 5, and 6, and a pair of upbows to begin bar 4. The trills in the early bars should start on the D above the written C-natural, and should be performed with strength. (Remember that such ornaments are—as we have said before—dissonant accents.) For the violas, try hooking the last two low D-naturals in bar 4; mark two downbows for measure 13 and a pair of upbows in measure 14.

For the repeated notes in the upper strings starting in bar 30 we recommend the brush stroke—off-the-string playing. These patterns recur throughout the movement, requiring only minor adjustments. For the next-to-last bar, mark a pair of upbows after the initial downbow, so that all finish downbow.

As the movement concludes, there is an important tenor entrance in measure 90, which announces a brief codetta. You may want to increase the tenors' dynamic level slightly into the final cadence.

Gloria

The *maestoso* modifying this *Allegro* seems to caution against too fast a tempo. This movement might be started either in two or in four, at ♩ = 60–64 or ♩ = 120–128, depending especially on the technical security of your violinists' sixteenth notes. If the orchestra is an experienced one, taking it in two is the preferred choice; if not, you may have to take the first measure in four. The singers should "think in two," even if you need to start in four for the strings.

One of the features that this mass setting owes to its Viennese heritage is its stylistic use (as you saw in the Kyrie) of such markings as the *sforzando* in measure 17 and the adamant repeated orchestral *sforzandi* of the movement's closing bars. Schubert's youthfulness may be visible in the enthusiasm shown by the *ff* dynamics at bars 7 and at 28, but these indications do lend to this music (in contrast to the richness of the sound of the Kyrie) real vigor.

Again we find a Gloria set in D major, apparently everyone's favorite choice for this text. Again, too, we find a ternary form; Schubert—like Haydn—casts the *Quoniam* section as a reprise of A, with a modulatory middle section which sets a pair of soloists against the *Miserere nobis* chanting of the choir. Schubert holds the choristers down to *p* for this passage, saving the *f* for the return to the original tonic at the reprise in measures 62–64.

Mark the strings to begin with consecutive downbows, and ask for separation on the quarter-note chords; the first sixteenth in each of the patterns in measure 3 should be taken downbow. Both violin sections should commence bar 8 upbow; both should take consecutive downbows at the beginning of bar 9, and consecutive upbows in bar 10. These patterns continue to appear. In the *Quoniam* ask for emphatic and consistent *sforzandi*.

We prefer not to *ritard* the end of this movement, but to maintain the tempo, unrelentingly, to the final release.

Credo

Our recommendation here is a tempo of $\boldsymbol{J}$ = 60–62. You can relate this pulse easily back to the 60/120 of the Gloria.

The charming *sempre staccato* walking-bass lends a march-like quality to the opening of this movement. Ask the low strings to play this with light strokes, off the string. (You may elect to ask your choir for a matching *marcato* in these passages, but there is no such indication from Schubert.) For contrast, the violins and violas should play *legato*, minimizing the effect of the changes in bow direction.

A complicated editorial issue: at bar 16 some of the older editions[12] show a *sforzando* on the first beat, followed by *diminuendos* in either or both of bars 16 and 17. With the whole ensemble already at *pp*, if those *diminuendos* after the *sforzando* at bar 16 are Schubert's own marking, what was the composer's thinking here? Ordinarily an *fz* is a one-note emphasis, and no *decrescendo* should be needed later in bar 16, let alone in the violins in bar 17. The Franz Beyer edition[13] (which has the choir commence the Credo at *p* and the orchestra at *pp*) includes the *sforzandi*, but *considers the "crescendos" actually to have been accent marks* in both bars 16 and 17, which makes much more sense.

Give the violins encouragement at measure 49: their melodic line floats unexpectedly and beautifully above the choral fabric. This contrapuntal octave line is an especially lovely example of Schubertian lyricism, set in place to give emphasis to the *Et incarnatus* text, and made lovelier by the *legato* interruption of the marching *staccato*. Note that Schubert is calling particular attention to this line when he marks it *piano*, for the other choral and orchestral parts remain at their original *pianissimo* dynamic! Shape this phrasing carefully.

As a contrast, then, come the *fortissimo* and the *staccati* of the dramatic

---

12. See above.
13. Franz Beyer, cited earlier.

Crucifixus and *Et resurrexit*. The strings should all take this off-the-string until the *ligato* marking. The eighth notes at the *Et resurrexit* should be taken on the string, with clean bow changes. Ask the lower strings for very sharp, clear articulation of the syncopations in bars 127–128.

Measure 137 is another one of those temporal highlights discussed in the previous chapter: take plenty of time with the *fermata* to "let the music breathe." Then you can return to the original texture and dynamic level at the reprise. (The edition the authors prefer shows a three-bar *cadenza*-like line in the strings after measure 137, which is indicated as present in the "first version," but the editor does not include those bars in the measure-numbering.)[14] The parallel octaves between tenors, basses, 'celli, and contrabasses in measures 141–142 are apparently Schubert's own scoring; if you prefer, you could change the tenors' E-natural (in 141) to a B-natural (as does the Parker-Shaw edition).[15] (When one recalls measures 16–17, it is less clear how to view the orchestral *diminuendos* in measures 154–178, since the strings again have been at a nominal *pp* since measure 138.)

Like the Kyrie and the Gloria, this Credo has been a ternary form. It seems time for Schubert to give us a different structural design.

Sanctus

A compact Sanctus and Pleni sunt coeli, just nine measures in length, serve almost as an introduction to a more extended (though brief) Osanna in excelsis. For this two-part form, Schubert contrasts trilled *sforzandi*, wide arpeggios, and multiple-stop chords in the strings with homophonic chords in the chorus, all marked *ff*. The Osanna, on the other hand, begins with strict *forte* contrapuntal entrances, with voice and string parts doubled; the last eleven measures shift the chorus back to homophonic chords punctuated by resolute dotted-note rhythms in the strings.

You could well take the Sanctus in four at ♩= 84–88, or even a shade faster to 92, and then double that pace at the 2/4 sign, treating the previous quarter notes as eighths; that is, in two at ♩= 84–92.[16]

The strength of the opening *Allegro maestoso* comes first from the jagged arpeggios in the strings, and then from the V_2/IV dissonant attack by the choir. It is probably best for the fourth beats of the beginning measures to be downbows. (After starting bar 1 downbow, of course, retaking a downbow [on the first thirty-second note] will make the fourth beat a downbow also.) The *sforzando* trills in bars 2 and 3 should also be taken downbow, from above (as in the opening measures of the Kyrie); the *nachschlag* at the end of the trill should be *measured* (that is, the two ornamental sixteenths should fill the last eighth

---

14. See above.
15. Alice Parker and Robert Shaw, cited earlier.
16. As we pointed out in the Haydn *Nelsonmesse* chapter, this sort of convenient multiple helps you maintain in the performance atmosphere the tempos you intended to set. Page 151.

of the second beat). The remainder of each of the two measures could be bowed up-down-up-up-down. Hook the dotted patterns in bars 4, 5, and 8; the rest of the notes should be taken individually, "as it comes." The *nachschlag* at the end of bar 9 should be played as two sixteenths leading to the eighth-note pickup (almost like two grace notes).

For the Osanna *fugato:* mark a pair of upbows at the end of any bar which has an odd number of notes in it. Hook the dotted pairs in the last 13 measures of the Osanna, and then take the final chords on three consecutive downbows.

Benedictus

This lyric solo trio, with its canonic entrances, is a quick glimpse of the mature Schubert (already, at age 18) at his best. Three "verses" of a *"lied"* follow each other in succession: first the soprano alone, and then the tenor accompanied by congenial contrapuntal figures in the soprano line; finally Schubert gives the *"lied"* to the baritone, accompanied by what was the soprano's counterpoint (now in the tenor voice) and a new soprano *obbligato* rises gracefully above the tenor and baritone. Take this in two, about ♩. = 50–52.

The orchestral role *is* accompanimental here, but attention must be paid to the rather intricate markings—accents, *sforzandi*, and *pizzicati*, as well as the balancing of dynamics.[17] Note that the soprano solo is supported by eighth notes in the orchestra, the tenor-soprano duo by sixteenths, and the trio by triplet-sixteenths all the way to the cadence in bar 54.

We regard the "slurs" here as phrase marks, not bowings. Taking separate bows for each set of triplets, with the whole of bar 2 on a single bow, brings us to the cadence in bar 3 on a downbow. Begin measure 4 downbow again, of course.

Start the violas, 'cellos, and basses *downbow* in bar 2, and begin the three-note groupings in bar 4 (Violins II and Violas) upbow, but commence bar 8 downbow. Ask these sections for a brush stroke for the *pianissimo* repeated-sixteenths which appear in measure 20. You may want to slur the two sets of triplets at the end of bars 30 and 33. The triplet-sixteenths that appear in measure 36 should be taken off the string.

The final three chords before the *Allegro* should be bowed down-up-down. The second Osanna, then, is a mirror of the first, and will of course be taken at the same tempo as before, with the same articulation and bowings.

Agnus Dei

For the final movement Schubert constructed a "double *ritornello*" design in miniature. There are three strophes for the soloists and chorus, intro-

17. This may be a good moment to remind you again of the importance of asking for good tone quality on the *pizzicati.* String players may sometimes take *"pizz"* sound for granted, but they should not.

duced and separated by something of a *pathetique* passage in the first violins, supported by the rest of the orchestra. The violin line is not just an introduction; it establishes the character of the Agnus Dei, and each time it returns the Violins I deserve their "moment." Make certain they understand that you regard this *ritornello* as equal in importance to the vocal passages.

Each of the three solos is answered *(miserere nobis,* and then *dona nobis pacem)* by the supplicants of the choir, speaking for the congregation. Schubert's process is modulatory (as was Haydn's in the *Nelsonmesse*), with the movement beginning in the relative minor, the orchestral *ritornello* returning at measure 15 in B minor, and then returning again at measure 29 in A minor; the composer's key scheme brings the chorus back, at the end, to the original G major. We recommend you conduct this movement in four at ♩ = 64–72, using a "stopped beat"; that will effectively show your musicians the eighth-note subdivision. Whether you choose the lower or higher end of this tempo range depends—among other factors—on the ability of your soloists to keep a flowing line at a slower pace, and on the acoustics of the hall.

Bowing for each part can be taken "as it comes" from the beginning of this movement. Note the *fp*s which first appear in measure 3: How long does the *forte* of each *fortepiano* actually last? Probably the *f* is one eighth in duration and the *p* lasts a sixteenth (shortened to half its notated length—a sixteenth—as in an *appoggiatura*). Make certain the last notes of these phrases (the C-natural in bar 3, for example) are sounded enough to be heard.

The repeated sixteenths (starting in measures 8 and 22) should be taken off the string with a brush stroke. For bar 35 mark both the third and fourth notes as downbows. In bar 40 have the Violins I and the lower strings retake downbows for the high G-natural. Elsewhere follow the established patterns to the end.

In the final analysis there are more shared features than differences between Schubert's *Mass in G Major* and Haydn's *Nelsonmesse*. Though the *Mass in G Major* is much briefer and less elaborate, the legacy of Viennese Classical style is clear; the younger master's writing is disciplined, not radical. In the final movement Schubert's penitent and subdued prayer for peace is quite a change, nevertheless, from Haydn's confident, joyous Dona nobis pacem, written just seventeen years earlier.

12 Ludwig van Beethoven: (Choral) Fantasia, op. 80

This unique work offers you a wonderful opportunity to conduct Beethoven with orchestra. The *Ninth Symphony* and the *Missa solemnis* are hardly works to be attempted by those who are unused to confronting orchestras. The *Fantasia* makes more modest demands, on the other hand; its orchestral parts are standard, the choral demands are not strenuous, and for you its technical difficulties will not be great.

One of its most striking aspects is that it features a solo pianist of high calibre. Every conductor—young or old—knows an excellent pianist (for there seem to be so many of them these days!), and in this work the player at the keyboard faces the greatest demands. You could schedule the *Fantasia* (which requires 20 minutes or less) as part of an impressive concert made up entirely of masterworks you have studied in this volume: say, (1) the Bach *Magnificat* or the Vivaldi *Gloria*, (2) this *Fantasia*, positioned like a concerto, (3) an intermission, and (4) the Haydn *Nelsonmesse*. (Your concert would be little more than one-third the length of the one at which the *Fantasia* was premiered, as we are about to recall.)

Beethoven at the Midpoint of His Career

By the first of December of the year 1808 Ludwig van Beethoven, composing and performing in Vienna, had succeeded Franz Joseph Haydn (dwelling in retirement in the Gumpersdorf suburb nearby, with only six months to live) as the most important composer in the Western world. Mozart had died seventeen years before; Franz Schubert was just twelve, and a schoolboy in the neighboring village of Lichtental. In Beethoven, the rough-hewn master born in distant, provincial Bonn, the Viennese Classical style was about to mount another peak.

This had been the year of the *Fifth* and *Sixth Symphonies*, of the *Cello Sonata, op. 69*, and the two *Piano Trios, op. 70*. Over the past five years had come such landmark works as *Fidelio*, the *"Eroica,"* the *Violin Concerto in D*, the three *"Razumovsky" Quartets* (just premiered this year), the *"Waldstein"* and *"Appassionata" Sonatas*, four settings of Goethe's *Sehnsucht*, and the *Mass in C Major*, amid a long list of shorter and/or less successful compositions. In short, at 38 Beethoven was a mature and sure-handed composer whose catalog would already guarantee him a place amid any pantheon of the greatest composers (even should he not survive to create the *Missa solemnis,* the *Seventh* and *Ninth Symphonies,* the late piano sonatas and quartets, and the rest).

He had examined Haydn and Mozart scores voraciously, as one grasps quickly when one studies the early Beethoven quartets and sonatas. By the time of his *Symphony No. 1 in C Minor* in 1801, his absorption of the Viennese Classical structures was absolute. Clear also had become the features of his evolving personal style. Many of the forms of this middle period in which the *"Choral" Fantasia* was being written owe much to the sophisticated and innovative sonata allegro designs of Haydn.[1] Now each new Beethoven creation reflected his increasing tendency to let each form evolve on its own, rather than to lace it into an abstract structural corset. In Mozart one almost always finds an underlying prototype; in Haydn one sees always something of a search for a perfect template, one which would serve for multiple works in a given genre; but in the Beethoven of the 1810s and '20s one unearths uniqueness in virtually every architectonic plan.[2]

The Genesis of the Fantasia, op. 80

The tradition of presenting an annual benefit concert by each professional musician, as a primary source of that individual's livelihood for the next year, was still very much in practice in Vienna, London, and elsewhere at the turn of the nineteenth century. Often other musicians—including the famous ones—would perform *gratis,* letting the evening's central figure garner all the ticket receipts.

Short of money, to benefit himself Beethoven scheduled just such a concert at the Theatre an der Wien, where *Fidelio* had been premiered, for the evening of December 22, 1808. The program he designed was incredibly demanding for himself, for his musicians, *and* for the audience. It included, no less, the premier performances of the *Symphony No. 5 in C Minor* and the *Symphony No. 6 (the "Pastoral") in F Major,* the Vienna premieres of the *Piano Concerto No. 4 in G Major,* the *"Ah, perfido"* scene and aria, and excerpts from the *Mass in C Major;* he also improvised at the keyboard for one concert segment, and—finally— introduced his brand-new *Fantasia in C Minor, op. 80.* He created this *Fantasia* expressly as a climax for this extravagant evening, and did so at the last minute; the work was barely finished, and barely rehearsed, we are told. He apparently meant it to summarize a program which had included himself as a soloist and conductor of chorus and orchestra, or—at least—to provide a flashy finale.

---

1. See the first movement of the *"Waldstein" Sonata, Op. 53,* with its double development-and-recapitulation structure as an example of Beethoven's having studied Haydn's experiments with such structures.

2. To your consideration of the evolutionary sonata allegro design of the *"Waldstein,"* add for contrast the first movements of the *"Pathetique," Op. 13,* and the *Sonata in E Major, Op. 109.* By the *Op. 109* one can still discern (barely) the long-established sonata allegro key structure, but no conventional, rigid element of an *"Ars antiqua"* inhibits the unfolding of Beethoven's music.

Choosing Performance Forces

Beethoven scored his new *Fantasia* for piano, brief vocal solos, chorus, and an orchestra of woodwinds in pairs, two horns, two trumpets, strings, and timpani. We know that he had to pay a freelance orchestra that December evening (for there was another important concert in Vienna that night);[3] his forces probably were not large because of that conflict, and because he was short of funds. It is reasonable to assume that he would have wanted a string body of perhaps 6-6-2-4-2, and probably not larger than 8-8-4-4-2, plus the 12 winds and timpani. Singers totaling 18 to 24, plus (or including) the soloists for the *Mass in C Major* excerpts (the soprano almost certainly the same woman who sang the *Ah, perfido* scene) would have completed the ensemble; some of these people probably had been cast in his recent *Fidelio* performances.

Performing Editions

The 1998 score edited by Armin Raab for G. Henle stands as the best source available to you today, and has the practical advantage of using modern clefs.[4] The Breitkopf & Härtel edition, elderly as it is, remains reasonably accurate, if somewhat heavy-handed with respect to punctuation and other details.[5] (There is evidence that Beethoven—alive, demanding by nature, and working regularly with his publisher—supervised the printing of his music more carefully than could the at first unknown, and later deceased Franz Schubert. He was learning to be a good businessman by this stage of his life. He knew well the value of money, and he recognized the importance of the dissemination of his works through publishers who would pay well and were [for the era] relatively honest. Only in the previous generation had publication become a major issue for composers; one thinks of Haydn's dealings with Artaria in Vienna, and of the pirating of his works by unscrupulous printers, especially in Western Europe. Haydn had become very careful about sharing his manuscripts, and Beethoven had learned that same lesson.)[6] The Kalmus orchestral score and parts have been readily available for many years, and are less expensive than other editions. This version is generally true to the Breitkopf & Härtel publication.[7]

---

3. Steven M. Whiting, *Hört ihr wohl*, p. 1.
4. Armin Raab, editor of *(Choral) Fantasia, Op. 80*.
5. Unknown editor, Breitkopf & Härtel edition, *(Choral) Fantasia, Op. 80*, ser. 9 of *Ludwig van Beethovens Werke.* . . . See, for example, the Breitkopf & Härtel editing of the Italian tempo markings at bar 398, where the parentheses and other punctuations could be said to change Beethoven's intention somewhat. There is a Dover Publications reprint from this Breitkopf edition of the *Choral Fantasia*, paired with Beethoven's *"Triple Concerto."*
6. The late Julius Herford, in conversations with one of the authors, consistently described the *Mass in C Major* (after its Eisenstadt premiere) as "the first religious piece ever for which churches had to pay for parts in order to use it for service music." Beethoven and his Leipzig publisher set a significant precedent by charging a small but important fee for the performances of that mass.
7. *Choral Fantasy, Op. 80*, Edwin F. Kalmus, New York.

When you find disagreement about details between these editions you will have to decide which markings to use. By now you have learned a great deal about Viennese Classical style. Employ your own best judgment in choosing an edition, as well as in evaluating the specifics of any version you use.

ANALYSIS OF THE WORK

Since the benefit concert was meant to feature him, he wrote the *Fantasia* as a vehicle for "Beethoven the Pianist." It appears that he improvised the beginning passage on that occasion, as we are told he had done at premieres of one or more of his concertos, and only later wrote out what we see in the score today. Today we know he originally had planned an orchestral introduction (which seems logical);[8] his deletion of that section left the unusual solo opening one finds now. At the start, the *Fantasia* probably struck the audience as something of a continuation of the improvising Beethoven had done earlier in the evening, and likely pleased them; this was the sort of thing for which he had been most famous in Vienna, and his audiences hoped he would improvise, as modern-day crowds hope to persuade a star to do an encore.

The planned orchestral introduction having been discarded, the work divides itself into three large sections:

- This is an idiosyncratic concerto-like work in which a *"cadenza"* comes first! The opening is itself a kind of *bravura* prelude, marked *Adagio,* but without consistent metric continuity.
- The entrance of the 'cellos and basses at the *Allegro* in measure 27[9] commences another series of fragments which still avoid establishing a metric flow. One gets an impression almost of incoherence, and it continues through the repeated horn-and-oboe perfect fifths, with their *fermatas,* in bars 53–57; then at last begins the cohesive material which will predominate through the rest of the work.
- Finally, after a reprise of the 'cellos' and basses' original material at the bar 389 *Allegro,* the choir is joined to the texture at measure 398 for what will prove to be the concluding section of the *Fantasia.*

Through all this, the pianist—Beethoven at the premiere—is a connecting link. It seems clear *he planned to be himself the focal point of this culminating work of the evening's performance in two senses: as the soloist, and as the creator.* It is likely, moreover, that he meant the *Fantasia* as a kind of summary of this giant concert.[10] Into its design he incorporated the orchestra which had played the two symphonies, the vocal soloists and chorus who had sung the concert aria and the mass excerpts, and the pianist who had both played the concerto and improvised for the crowd. Every work from earlier in the evening and every

---

8. Steven M. Whiting, cited earlier, p. 3.
9. The number of measures is somewhat complicated in this movement by the complexity of that opening *cadenza. The authors "count" those first 26 bars throughout the analysis that follows here.*
10. Steven M. Whiting, cited earlier, p. 4.

performer from those works reappeared symbolically in this finale. It became, in short, an apotheosis.

Look at the specifics of the form. Beethoven commences the *Fantasia* with such freedom of design (the improvisational character of the keyboard opening, followed by the various, separated orchestral-and-piano phrases) that right on through the six consecutive *fermatas* in measures 53–57 the effect on the listener is one of structural chaos![11] (Probably Beethoven's bewildered, aggravated musicians felt much the same: the orchestra, playing its scattered fragments, must have wondered how this *recitativo*-like incompleteness would ever shape itself into some sort of cohesive continuity.)

At bars 60–61 Beethoven assigned to himself the clarification of the confusion. The pianist introduces a cheerful, simple song, now in C major, squarely constructed of four phrases, each four measures long, and interrupted only by a *cadenza* in measure 72. This hymn to beauty, peace, joy, art, and power (*"Schönheit, Fried', Freude, Kunst, und Kraft"*) proves to be the theme for a set of variations.[12] Each variation features different instruments: flute with piano, oboes with piano, clarinets with bassoon, a quartet of solo strings, and finally the whole orchestra. Having reserved the pianist for almost fifty measures then, he introduces a coda-like section which modulates, instead, to the dominant in a developmental way, and eventually ends in another piano *cadenza* (at bar 184).

What follows is a sixth variation, now at *Allegro molto* and back in the original C minor, followed by a modulatory Development section one would not expect to find in a standard theme-and-variations structure. By bar 220 Beethoven is in B major! A series of brief tonal cells (generally in a circle-of-fifths) settle on A, the relative minor of the principal key, commencing at measure 251, and an extended dominant pedal, starting at 266, leads to another *cadenza* at bar 290.

The 6/8 *Adagio ma non troppo* in A major that begins at this point is Beethoven's seventh variation of his "hymn" tune; it mixes piano and orchestra, and there appear several opportunities for showy *rubatos* (especially at the end of each of the original four-bar phrases of the theme). After an abrupt shift to F major, the eighth variation (bar 322) is a *Marcia assai vivace* cast in dotted rhythms. It leads to a transitional passage (starting in measure 365), which concludes with another *cadenza* at 388. Two brief reprises of the 'cello/bass fragment originally seen in bar 27—interrupted by yet another *cadenza* at 392—introduce a ten-bar flourish of arpeggios on the dominant of C major, and then the first, tentative entrances of the choir.

The three-part women's entrance at measure 411 is a ninth variation—this one with words. (There is an element here, too, of Recapitulation.) The men give us another at measure 428; this is a "trill variation" for the pianist, as you see.

Notice the double *fermatas* in bars 439 and 440. These permit a small *cadenza*

---

11. This spot (as well as passages in the choral section) is excellent practice for your own technique of *fermata*-cutoff-preparatory beat.
12. The first five variations begin, respectively (after the pickups in the previous bar, in each case), at measures 77, 93, 109, 125, and 141.

for the soloist. The big *tutti* at 444 is the eleventh variation, and leads into a return at 466 of the bar 156 material (again on the plagal side), modulating to the dominant at bar 474. A *solo-tutti* alternation in the chorus brings us to the *Presto* at bar 490 for one last variation, in which Beethoven turns the energy and intensity even higher, driving to the finish. Here the choir's phrases are at first punctuated by scalar outbursts from the piano. Then comes the text *Wenn sich Lieb und Kraft vermählen* ("If Love and Strength are brought together . . ."). Beethoven emphasizes the phrase *"und Kraft"* by repeating the words three times, separated, while moving up stepwise to an unexpected E-flat major chord held for five measures, before a quick resolution back to the tonic C major.[13] The soloists re-enter at 531, singing the *Presto* choral line in an augmented form, and the passage which had begun at bar 490 essentially repeats, including the ascent to the E-flat major chord. A final flurry from the pianist and orchestra at measure 596 brings the work to a ringing C major terminus.

Do you begin to sense something familiar about this? What is becoming apparent in this succession of musical relationships? *The architecture and its elaboration in the* Fantasia *sculpt an overall design which resembles very substantially the choral finale of the* Symphony No. 9 in D Minor, op. 125, *the famous* Ninth *itself,* which Beethoven will not write until some fifteen years have passed.

Review the features our synopsis has just identified: (1) the incoherence of the work's opening, (2) the *"recitative"* passages in the 'cellos and basses, (3) the "hymn to joy, beauty, peace, etc.," (4) the spirited set of variations built upon that theme, (5) the superimposition of a developmental form on top of this variations structure, (6) the employment of chorus to bring to a climax a work which began as instrumental music, (7) the parallel *und Kraft/vor Gott* pinnacles, both set upon rhythmically similar chord patterns ending a minor-third above the tonic, and (8) the final tempos (*Presto* in the *Fantasia,* and *Prestissimo* at the end of the *Ninth*).

What is more, there is a vital parallel having to do with the overall significance Beethoven intended for these two masterworks. The *Fantasia* was written that December to act as a summary of the whole concert. Certainly Beethoven meant the last movement of the *Ninth* as an apotheosis, too: in the early measures of the finale, he reprised and set aside the music of each of the first three movements, in turn, before having the bass soloist sing the famous *O Freunde, nicht diese Töne . . .* as the introduction of that latter-day "Hymn to Joy."

We are speaking about what is, after all, a Beethovian conceit: this sort of summarizing; for the *Fifth Symphony,* premiered that same evening, he fashioned three movements of a "Symphony in C Minor," and then pivoted to the parallel major for the last movement (at the famous trombone entrance), as if to say "O Friends, not these C minor tones; rather let us have these more joyful ones in C major!"[14]

---

13. One scholar writes that "Anyone familiar with the *Ninth Symphony* experiences a jolt of recognition" at this point. Steven M. Whiting, cited earlier, p. 13.

14. Charles Ives in his *Psalm 90* creates a similar apotheosis. After stringing together a lengthy suc-

Almost fifteen years passed between Beethoven's 1808 concert and the completion of the *Ninth Symphony*. That is too long a time to make it seem the *Fantasia* was intended by him as a kind of draft version of the finale of the *Ninth*. Most likely when he wrote the symphony in the early 1820s he remembered that he had always liked the unfolding choral peroration in his 1808 *Fantasia*, and he "plagiarized himself," lifting exactly that *und Kraft/vor Gott* harmonic shift, the instrumental "*recitative*," and the rest for relocation to the *Ninth*.

A composer has certain fingerprints that he leaves on poetry he is setting or on a musical fabric, and those can reappear when he again approaches that context. One can see this in Haydn's settings of the *Gloria* and the *Dona nobis pacem*, and one also can see it in Beethoven's two "Hymns to Joy."

The Opening Fantasia

The celebrated pianist who began his own *Opus 80* that December evening was not given to elegant playing—that is, to the manner we would call "Mozartian" now. We know a great deal about Beethoven's own performance style; it was dramatic, even bombastic at times, with sudden changes of pace and dynamics. It was not chic, but it was arresting, and increasingly popular. One need only look at the piano sonatas he wrote in this period to estimate what sort of theatrics he employed for the opening section of the *Fantasia*.

Your own pianist almost certainly will know all this, too, and should be able to bring to your rehearsal(s) a clear sense of how to interpret this work.[15] Meet with her or him well before your first orchestra session to agree on tempos, articulation, transitions, *cadenzas*, and details.

Most of your rehearsals will take place without the pianist, and you probably will begin at measure 27.[16] At the performance, however, with everyone else onstage, and with the orchestra tuned (to the piano, of course), you and the pianist will take your places. While you wait on the podium, then, the first twenty-six measures belong to the soloist. The pianist will choose this tempo, but it probably will not be far from $\flat = 68$, which will prove to be our "guiding pulse" for the remainder of the work.

Remember that this opening was an echo of the improvisational playing Beethoven had done earlier in the evening, so the spirit of that improvisational

---

cession of disparate fragments (which become increasingly frustrating for the listeners, who may grow disoriented by the lack of continuity), he turns to his straightforward C major conclusion as if he were Beethoven saying: "*nicht* this craggy landscape, but rather these pleasant, reassuring meadows let us have."

15. This is a good moment to remind you that the pianist you choose (and each of your vocal soloists) is a "guest artist." There is an etiquette here, and you probably are familiar with it already; if you are not, we recommend you consult Robert W. Demaree, Jr., and Don V Moses, *The Complete Conductor*, especially pp. 448–449.

16. If your orchestra parts have been used before, the rehearsal numbers *may or may not* count the 26 bars of the piano solo; that is, the orchestra's "measure 1" may be your (and the pianist's) "measure 27." *Check the parts and—if necessary—include both sets of rehearsal numbers in your score.* You can waste a great deal of very valuable rehearsal time with this sort of problem.

style should be reflected here. Encourage your pianist to make this opening section sound as extemporaneous as possible—which seems a rather unusual approach, at first, until one remembers that this passage is *cadenza*-like; and *cadenzas* are improvisatory by nature. Some specific suggestions your pianist might consider:

- Avoid making the metric pulses obvious. (Note Beethoven's marking of the first bar; if the 4th beat is given a metric accent, then the *diminuendo* loses its shape. Think in four—almost in two—even at this slow tempo.)
- Try to keep the phrase shapes flowing, evolving. *Notice, by the way, that measures 4 and 9 have only three beats each, an indication that Beethoven himself was not concerned with an emphatic meter in this passage. Such freedom is in the "fantasia" tradition, of course.*[17]
- Taking a little extra time between the various motifs can create the impression that the music really *is* being improvised on the spot, as it was at that premiere. Tiny hesitations (perhaps before the second chord—the complete E major triad— in measure 10, for example) can create the impression that the pianist is "making it up" as it unfolds.
- The varied rhythmic values (the contrasted quadruplets, quintuplets, and sextuplets in measures 12–16, for example) can become too mannered if they are kept rhythmically rigid.
- Pedaling becomes an important issue here. The *sostenuto* effect probably should be understated, using shallow changes tailored to the instrument itself, and to the acoustics of the hall. (This means some "blurring," but nothing approaching the level of clouding one would find, for instance, in an Impressionistic piece.)
- The pianist can help keep all this fresh by not letting Beethoven's markings seem mannered, and by staying honestly intuitive as the opening section evolves. The more musical your pianist, the more convincing this apparent "improvisation section" will sound.

At the "seam" (the transition to the orchestral *Allegro*), again pause briefly. Let the reverberation of the pianist's arpeggiated octaves virtually die away— but never quite—before proceeding with the 'cello-bass entrance.

The Piano and the Orchestra

The fragmentary nature of the next thirty bars could cause some problems with the orchestra.[18] When you begin your orchestra rehearsals, the players will first find two-measure gaps for the piano, then short motifs which seem not to be arriving anywhere, and eventually (at bar 53) *six consecutive measures in which the strings see only rests and fermatas in each bar—no notes!* The strings do not really enter, in fact, until after the first three variations. At that point things begin to make sense to the players.

---

17. In early sources Armin Raab found ¾ meter signatures in both bars 4 and 9, canceled in each case by C markings in bars 5 and 10. See Armin Raab, cited earlier, pp. 205–206.
18. That may not be the case, however; a choral conductor should realize that an orchestra of any substantial experience will have played this work before.

Orchestras are accustomed to concerto accompaniments. Explain to them that this is essentially the same thing. Sing the piano parts in the rehearsals as much as possible, and they will begin to understand.

And this is indeed a "concerto accompaniment." Recognize the import of the marked tempo changes, as well as the *fermatas*. You should defer to the pianist as far as that is possible for you, giving her or him time to linger, for example, over measures 40 and 46, and other soloistic spots throughout the work.[19] If the pianists' tempo for the opening was about ♪ = 68, it will be very convenient to treat the *Allegro* at bar 27 as ♪ = ♩, so that the entrance of the lower strings is taken in two. Their next attack at measure 34 can come with less delay than at measure 27.

This passage is a dialogue between the pianist and the orchestra: two different entities converse, each "in its own tempo." One is reminded of the "Tamino and the Priest" dialogue in Act I of *The Magic Flute,* or—notably for our study here—of the second movement (the *Andante con moto*) of Beethoven's *Piano Concerto No. 4 in G Major, op. 58,* which was heard earlier on the program that 1808 evening.[20]

The first orchestral phrase—the 'cellos and basses at bar 27—establishes the style of playing to bar 58: the length of the *staccati* in the low strings at measure 27 should match what the winds do at 41 and thereafter. We suggest that the dotted pairs in bars 27–28 be hooked (as upbows). Note, then, the important slurs in bars 29–30: see what emphasis Beethoven gives to these pairs (the only notes in the phrase that are *not staccati*) by slurring them! Have your players take the two pairs of *unslurred* eighths in 29–30 on *consecutive* upbows, maintaining the *staccato* separation. The phrase ends, then, on an upbow. Use this same bowing pattern for each of the string entrances to measure 53.

At the important bar 53 cadence, where the horns enter, each of the *fermatas* can be treated as two beats (in tempo) in duration, with the cutoff as a third-beat preparatory beat. Don't rush this preparation of the crucial theme that will begin in measure 60! All this delay, this fragmentation, this apparent hesitancy stems from Beethoven's intention to raise in the listener a sense of anticipation. The anticipation he builds makes the "Hymn" theme seem all the more significant, once it commences.

Beethoven asks for a slightly slower pace at bar 53; the *fermatas* make this largely theoretical, however. (Even bars 59 and 60 remain introductory, and could be treated somewhat freely, should one choose not to settle fully into the tempo until the downbeat of measure 61.) That does not mean that every beat should remain rigidly metronomic all the way to bar 184, however; *one important concern as you guide the listener through this set of variations is to make the structure audible.* The vital thing, generally speaking, is to focus proportionate

---

19. Again, if this type of conducting (much like what you must do for singers' recitatives) is rather new to you, consult chapter 23 of Robert W. Demaree, Jr., and Don V Moses, cited earlier, for guidance on accompanying technique.

20. See especially, for example, measures 1–26 of the movement. Many pianists speak of this *Adagio* as a "conversation."

attention on the cadences at the end of individual phrases and whole variations. Here are some suggestions about linking style and structure in Beethoven:

- The conductor has to be fully aware of the possibilities of *unmarked ritards.*
- Give solid emphasis to *shaping* the phrases. Beethoven from time to time (here, as in his symphonies) writes a *decrescendo* or *diminuendo* that can sound like a *ritard,* even though he has no wish for you to slow the motion. A *diminuendo* releases some of the energy in the phrase, much like a *ritard* would. (Look, for example, at measures 218–219: Beethoven marks a *diminuendo* to lessen the energy here, before the *dolce,* rather than inserting a *ritard.*)
- Another frequently used device of this sort is his rapid *crescendo.* Beethoven was one of the first to ask for a rapid increase from *p* to *f* or even *ff* within a single measure (no matter what the tempo).
- The *cadenzas* (both the written ones and the *cadenza* possibilities at the *fermatas*) can be newly created (whether improvised or planned in advance), so long as you and the pianist agree on coordination between the two of you. Beethoven certainly improvised his own *cadenzas,* and there is a freshness in doing so, if you as artists are confident and comfortable with it. The better the pianist, the more likely you can risk this.

In the first two variations there is a little problem of primacy: first the flute, and then the two oboes play "solos," which means the guest artist becomes an "accompanist" for measures 77–108. You need to take responsibility here, conducting the ensemble (rather than accompanying the pianist).

Ask the four string soloists to begin *upbow* at bar 124, taking the rest of the phrase "as it comes." The next phrase (bar 128) is bowed the same way, except that the third and fourth notes in bar 130 should be consecutive upbows. Then in measures 132-133-134 the viola and 'cello begin the sixteenth-note groups upbow, while the two violins begin bars 133 and 134 downbow; that brings all four of them to the *fermata* (bar 136) downbow; then everyone can begin the final phrase upbow again.

Bowings are routine now. (After the *fermata* in measure 152, start downbow of course.) The interjected pairs of eighths that commence in 163 can be taken off the string until 172. The motif at the slurs there recurs through 179: mark the first three of the eighths on a downbow, and the next four on an upbow; then continue these patterns.

Bowings for the *Allegro molto* also are routine. Keep good separation between the lower strings' quarter-notes. Measures 220 to 226 should be played at the tip (of the bow), returning to the frog for the pickup to 227. The violin parts through 238, then, show phrase marks, not slurs. At 251, the upper strings should play the repeated eighths off the string, while the 'cellos bow their quarter notes in groups of four. Ask the players to use a brush stroke beginning at 267.

At the *Adagio ma non troppo* (measure 291), after the *cadenza* in the previous bar, you could return—in six—to "your guiding pulse" of 76, like the "guiding pulse of 120" used in chapter 10 for the Haydn *Nelsonmesse.*[21] For bowing pur-

---

21. Pages 151 and 158.

poses ignore the phrase marks starting at bar 295; at 300 mark two notes per bow for the violas, and ask them to shorten the eighth in each pair. At 308 the lower strings should take these sixteenths off the string, carefully matching themselves to the winds.

The *Marcia assai vivace* (an unusual tempo indication, by the way) could shift up to ♩= 84 at measure 322. The reprise at bar 389, then, can again be taken in two, back at ♩= 68, setting up the grand finale. (The authors prefer that the grace notes in the Oboe I part in measures 323 ff. come before the beat, in spite of the shortness of the thirty-second note pickup.) The strings can begin upbow in 322. At 340, play the *sforzando* downbow, and then take two upbows to begin 341; repeat this pattern at 344. Be careful about the quality of *pizzicato* tone after bars 352 and 366.

At measure 389, and at 393, use the original bowing choices from bars 27 ff. (Start the 'cellos upbow in 397.)

The Choir Enters

That the chorus began to sing at this point, in what palpably had been an instrumental work, can hardly have been a surprise to the audience; the crowd would have seen the singers stand and raise their music, preparing to begin. This is not so much a matter of "surprise" as of *uniqueness*, and that is often the case in Beethoven.

The tempo can return here to the "higher side" pace of the *Marcia assai vivace*, ♩= about 84. See how Beethoven struggled with this marking, at last spelling it out word by word: *Allegretto ma non troppo quasi Andante con moto.*

Be careful, too, with the periodic *fermatas*. Do not let them seem mannered, and make certain they enhance the forward energy by anticipation, rather than inhibiting the flow of the music. Commencing at measure 444, and again at 482, we prefer that the upper strings play the triplets on the string. (They start downbow, of course, after the *fermata* in measure 456.) Keep the repeated eighth notes on the string, again, at 490 and at 546. Clean articulation is especially important with these repeated eighths at 562.

As you studied the Baroque works in this text, most of your attention had to be directed toward types of bowstrokes, and the specific bowings needed. By the time you approached the Viennese Classical masterpieces in the last three chapters, however, the authors could begin to explain in more detail the relationships between period style and the handling of your orchestra. Remember, as you mark your own parts, that you can review the basic principles of bowing in chapter 2, in the Omnes generationes section of chapter 8,[22] and in the glossary entries.

We recommend your taking the *Presto* at measure 490 in one, thus again doubling the tempo you set for bar 398. At this point you no longer are accompanying the pianist! The tempo is set, and the entire ensemble—chorus, orchestra,

---

22. Page 127.

and the guest artist—must take the pulse from you, or rather from Beethoven, who has created a metric and rhythmic energy which can drive all the way to the final cadence. The interlocking of the choral/orchestral phrases with the piano's "punctuation"—as we characterized it above—commences each of the two parallel subsections that push through the stentorian *"und Kraft"* repetitions to the peaks. Teach your forces to be cool and precise in this circumstance, and let the emotions rise in the audience, rather than onstage.

Finally, take a glance back. Bach, Handel, Vivaldi, Haydn, Schubert, and Beethoven: an impressive roster of composers, and an impressive repertoire of choral-orchestral masterpieces you now are prepared to conduct. Consider all the other works to which you can turn next, with your new knowledge and skills. You are entitled, henceforth, to begin to think of yourself not only as a choral director (or, for that matter, not only as an orchestra director), but rather as a conductor who can with assurance come face to face with an orchestra and chorus.

Glossary

Articulatory silences: the spaces between the notes, made longer or shorter by the durations the notes themselves are held; in Baroque music, more limited use of *legato* tends to increase these silences.

Basso continuo: linkage of a keyboard instrument with one or more string and/or wind instruments; this unit provides a harmonic and rhythmic foundation under the melodic lines in the upper levels of a Baroque texture. In the historic sources, all the notes to be played by these instruments were implied only by a given bass part, supplemented by numerical chord symbols. *See also* Realization.

Brush stroke: a bowing in which the players lighten the release of each note; in this procedure, they ease pressure on the string just at the end of each stroke. This process of "lifting" (*almost off the string*) is a variant of detaché especially useful for accompanimental passages and for bass lines which demand lightness and finesse. In some passages, this sort of separation is indicated by dashes marked above or below the notes. The conductor may ask for a "brush stroke," or may ask the players to "lift."

C clefs: the system of moveable clefs, each configured to designate a particular staff line as C. For modern-day orchestral work, the alto and tenor clefs (used especially by the violas, violoncellos, trombones, and bassoons) still are commonly employed; one may encounter soprano (and even mezzo-soprano) clefs in older editions of Baroque works, however.

Col legno: the (rare) use of the wooden part of the bow against the string.

Concertino: a small group of soloists operating with and within a larger ensemble. Throughout Baroque music, composers call for alternations of a full ensemble with one or more soloists; in the concerto grosso, the former is called the "ripieno" or "tutti," while the latter is the "concertino." (Both these elements are supported, of course, by the basso continuo unit.)

Concertist: a member of the "concertino," a soloist.

Concertmaster: the first player, or "principal," of the first violin section. By convention, his colleague at the first desk is called the "assistant concertmaster." The concertmaster has some responsibility for the unity and discipline of the first violin section, and is—in a sense—the "chief player" of the orchestra; it is he who is in charge of tuning the orchestra.

Detaché: the most common bowstroke, it is used for passages which require only one note per bow. Properly played, it can be very even in dynamic level from frog to tip, in both directions. Detaché implies some separation between notes; if one asks for "more space," the players will tend to change direction in the middle of the bow; if one prefers briefer separations, they will probably change in the upper third, nearer the tip.

Divisi: on those occasions when two notes are written in a single string part, half the section (the outside players on each stand, for example) may produce one note and the other half play the other.

Double stops: *see* multiple stops.

Frog: (of the bow) the end held in the player's fingers; the opposite end is called the "tip." A (full) downbow stroke thus is begun with the hand of the player over or near the string.

Full bows: these are basic to good technique for string instruments, just as the "legato line" is the central concept of vocal production. When string players produce even, full-length bows, they find it easy to give attention to producing richness and consistency of tone, and to making smooth, efficient direction-changes.

Guiding pulse: a tempo which appears to be interrelated centrally and proportionally to other tempos within the same movement, or to tempos in other movements of the work. It is considered to be a convenience for the conductor in gauging and recalling internal temporal relationships, as well as constituting a reinforcing element of continuity for the musicians and the audience.

Hand positions: generic hand placements which allow string players to reach certain points on the strings with particular fingers. Strong players may accomplish certain melodic skips either (a) by moving up or down a single string, stopping that string with the left hand at the proper acoustical points, or (b) by taking the two notes on separate strings, which can minimize the amount of left hand movement needed. (The former is called "shifting positions.") Normally this choice of fingering in a particular passage is the responsibility of the individual player, and colleagues on the same desk may simultaneously and properly use differing fingerings; on occasion, the concertmaster (in order to have shifts of position occur in unison) may stipulate fingerings.

Harmonics: clearly audible overtones produced when only a segment (mathematically half, a third, a quarter, etc.) of the string is permitted to vibrate. This phenomenon is produced by one's touching the string at the desired dividing point, without pressing it down against the fingerboard; the result is generally a very high pitch with a clear quality. Notation of harmonics is complicated: there is the point (a pitch) at which the string is to be touched, there is the "fundamental" of the overtone series involved, and there is the actual pitch desired. (Some contemporary composers—because of this potential confusion—superimpose all three on the music page, one on top of the other.)

Hooked bowing: the procedure in which two notes are played on the same bow stroke, without being slurred; the forward progress of the bow is interrupted briefly between the two notes, and then resumes. If a separate stroke must be used for a single, very short note, the player may have insufficient bow length for a longer note on the return stroke.

Legato: this bowing implies up- and down-strokes with smooth, virtually inaudible connections between them. When one asks the players for *legato,* or a "singing quality," they seek to minimize the turnaround time at the end of each stroke. *Slurs* are played within what essentially is a *legato* bow, and this stroke is useful also for hiding string crossings.

Madrigalisms: those musical figures which picture the text (melodic lines which descend, as portrayals of Christ's interment in the tomb, ascending arpeggios which picture His resurrection, and the like). Madrigalisms are legitimately part of the style of the Baroque period, and are a special responsibility of the continuo player, among others; to create them, the musician must know something of the text, of course.

Martelé: (derived from the French word for "hammered") a fast, angular, dramatic stroke, usually played in the upper half of the bow. The stroke begins with the bow more firmly planted into the string than is the case with detaché, and continues with a quick, energetic motion either up- or downbow. (The player must be careful at the end of the stroke; if he is careless, he will produce a rough, ugly release.) Martelé bowings accent each attack, of course; they also provide space—a sharply defined separation—between notes.

Multiple stops: if the composer has planned carefully, it is rather easy for string players to produce two notes simultaneously ("double stops"); this is feasible whenever two notes can be played on adjacent strings (within the reach of the fingers of the left hand). Even triple- and quadruple-stops are possible and are frequently used, but—since the bow cannot actually bend enough to contact all four strings at the same moment—these chords must be produced by a quick, rolling, arpeggiated effect. Only the last one or two notes of the arpeggio will be sustainable. (Much of the time in orchestral playing, written double stops are actually played divisi by the section, since the sound and intonation are more secure.)

Nonvibrato: string playing without the (otherwise) customary use of vibrato; for certain passages—for dramatic effect, or an especially subdued *pianissimo*—one may wish to ask the musicians to play nonvibrato. (Composers specify this effect at times.)

Off-the-string bowings: a stroke which approaches the string from above. Generally speaking, off-the-string bowings are more difficult than on-the-string strokes, and are riskier in orchestral work.

On-the-string bowings: a stroke which begins with the bow-hair physically touching the string. Most orchestral playing is done on-the-string.

Open strings: the tuned, unstopped strings of the violin (that is, G, D, A, and E, in ascending order) or any other member of the string family. Violinists tend to avoid playing them "open" (unfingered) because they prefer to produce the warmer, richer sound associated with vibrato (which can only be managed by fingering the string, of course).

Pizzicato: producing sound from a string by plucking, instead of bowing it. The quality of sound generated by pizzicato playing can vary; there is an exact acoustical point—for each pitch—at which one gets the best response from a plucked string. (And vibrato is appropriate for "pizz" notes, as well as bowed ones.)

Portative organ: a small organ, so called because of its portability, which can be particularly useful for Baroque performances, because of the legitimacy of its timbres, and since it can be placed where one wants it—inside one's ensemble, for example—so that one need not deal with the distance factor implicit in the use of most large church organs.

Portato: a bowing in which more than one note occurs within each stroke; the player eases pressure between notes, so that new weight makes the beginning of the next note audible. This technique is particularly useful in repeated-note passages, especially those in the 'cellos and contrabasses. There always is a danger, however, that the gaps between notes will grow too long.

Principal: the first player in each of the orchestral sections; his partner on the first "desk" (or stand) is called the "assistant principal." By a further convention, the principal first violinist is called the "concertmaster" and his cohort the "assistant concertmaster." All the principals have some responsibility for the unity and discipline of their sections.

Realization: the filling out of a figured-bass part by a keyboard player; by analogy, the elaboration of any line by a musician (within the limits of the musical style at hand). In the historic sources, all the notes to be played by the basso continuo were implied only by a given bass part, supplemented by numerical chord symbols. The process of shaping this shorthand into interesting and effective musical lines is called "realization," and it means that the keyboard player, particularly, is responsible for improvising solutions appropriate to the signals given him in the rather limited notation.

Ripieno: the main body of a Baroque ensemble, also called the "tutti." Throughout Baroque music, composers call for alternations of a full ensemble with one or more soloists. In the concerto grosso, the former is called the "ripieno" or "tutti," while the latter is the "concertino." (Both these elements are supported, of course, by the basso continuo unit.)

Rule of the downbow: since in every downbeat there is an implied metric accent, it is traditional that the downbow occur on the downbeat and the upbow on the upbeat. (Of course, there are many appropriate exceptions.) Adjustments in the alternation of bows are made within the measure, or across two or more bars, so that downbows and downbeats coincide at logical places.

Scordatura: the (rare) intentional tuning of one or more open strings to a pitch other than the standard (for the violin, that is, tuning to pitches other than G, D, A, or E).

Spiccato: an off-the-string bowing played with a motion which "drops" the middle of the bow onto the string; one note occurs per stroke. This bowing can be very useful for light accompanimental passages, for it produces quite a short, "dry" (as players sometimes say) sound. One can ask for it by name, or by saying "middle of the bow, and off-the-string, please."

Staccato: for string players, the word does not imply a note with a dot under it; it refers, instead, to a specific type of bowstroke—one in which several short notes are played per bow. This is a very difficult bowing, and is used almost exclusively for solo playing. (If a conductor, seeking short, dry notes, directs the word "staccato" to a string section, he risks confusing them and wasting valuable time.)

Staggered bowing: a procedure which has string players deliberately change bow directions at different times; they will "stagger" their bow-changes, that is to say, just as choir members "stagger breaths" in long phrases. One can ask the players to use this same technique on *very* long notes, of course—the final chord of a movement, for example. Thus they can sustain a *fermata* for as long as one wishes.

Stopped notes: the production, on the French horn, of certain tones by closing a specific amount of the bell opening with the left hand, a technique formerly used (in the era of the valveless horn) to elicit pitches not obtainable from the natural overtone series. In modern usage, "stopping" (notated by a + sign) is used only for timbral effect.

Sul G (or C, or E, etc.): the instruction to string players to produce all of the pitches of a particular passage on a given string; the stipulation is made when one wants the unique tone quality characteristic of that string. Otherwise, fingering—unlike bowing—customarily is a matter of individual preference for string players, as it is for the winds.

Sul ponticello: the technique of producing, on a stringed instrument, a rather more transparent sound by bowing on or near the bridge; a procedure employed for timbral effect.

Sul tasto: the technique of producing, on a stringed instrument, a relatively hollow sound by bowing near the fingerboard (using, perhaps, a somewhat faster bow), a procedure employed for timbral effect.

Tip (of the bow): the end of the bow farthest from the hand of the player; the end one holds is called the "frog." A (full) upbow stroke is begun with the tip of the bow relatively near the string.

Tutti: *see* ripieno.

Vibrato: the technique, on a stringed instrument, of deliberately producing slight variations in pitch by a rapid back-and-forth motion of the finger stopping the string that is in use at that moment. Violinists tend to avoid playing the strings "open" (that is, unfingered or "unstopped") because they prefer the warmer, richer sound created by vibrato.

Wedge: an articulatory marking, denoting shorter duration. There is much controversy among scholars about the precise intentions of those composers who used the wedge sign; for the purposes of this volume, the wedge signals that the note in question should be played approximately as short as a *staccato* dot, but more forcefully (that is, slightly accented).

Bibliography

Austin, William W. *Music in the 20th Century,* W. W. Norton and Co., New York, 1966, 708 pp.

Babitz, Sol. "Concerning the Length of Time that Every Note Must be Held," *Music Review* 28:21–37 (February 1967).

Bach, Carl Philipp Emanuel. *Versuch über die wahre Art das Clavier zu spielen,* Berlin, 1753; facsimile of Parts I and II, ed. by Hoffman Erbrecht, Leipzig, 1957, 2nd ed. 1969. *See* translation by Mitchell, W. J.

Bach, Johann Sebastian. *Magnificat in D Major, Werke,* Bach-Gesellschaft, Leipzig, 1855–1899 and 1926, vol. 11/1, 3, pp. 3–66.

———. *Magnificat in D Major, BWV 243, Neue Ausgabe sämtlicher Werke,* ed. Alfred Dürr for the Johann Sebastian Bach Institut, Göttingen, and Bach-Archiv, Leipzig, Bärenreiter Verlag, Kassel and Leipzig, 1954–, ser. 2, vol. 3, pp. 1–58.

———. *The St. John Passion,* ed. Arthur Mendel, G. Schirmer, New York, 1951, 148 pp.

Barnett, Dene. "Non-uniform Slurring in 18th Century Music—Accident or Design?" *Haydn Jahrbuch* 10:179–199 (1978).

Barrow, Lee. "Editions of Antonio Vivaldi's *Gloria,*" *The Choral Journal* 21/3:22–23 (November 1980).

Beethoven, Ludwig van. *(Choral) Fantasia. Op. 80,* ed. Armin Raab, in *Beethoven Werke,* Joseph Schmidt-Görg, gen. dir., G. Henle Verlag with the Beethoven-Archivs Bonn, 1998, abt. X, band 2, pp. 1–99.

———. *(Choral) Fantasia. Op. 80, Ludwig van Beethovens Werke: Vollständige kritisch durchsegehene überall berichtige Ausgabe,* Breitkopf & Härtel, Leipzig, 1864–1890, ser. 9.

———. *Choral Fantasy, Op. 80,* Edwin F. Kalmus, New York, date uncertain.

———. *Fantasia in C Minor (Choral Fantasy), Op. 80,* Dover Publications, Mineola, N.Y., 1998 (paired with the *Concerto in C Major, Op. 56 [Triple Concerto]*), pp. 105–164.

Brahms, Johannes. *Ein deutsches Requiem, Op. 45,* ed. Eusebius Mandyczewski, vol. 17 of *Johannes Brahms Sämtliche Werke,* Breitkopf & Härtel, Leipzig, 1949, 192 pp.

Brossard, Sebastien de. *Dictionnaire de Musique [etc.],* 2nd ed., Chez Christophe Ballard, Paris, 1703 and 1705, 112 pp.

Brown, Maurice J. E. *Schubert. A Critical Biography,* Macmillan, London, 1958, 414 pp.

———. "Schubert, Franz (Peter)," in *The New Grove Dictionary of Music and Musicians,* vol. 16, pp. 752 ff., ed. Stanley Sadie, Macmillan Publishers, London, 1980.

Bukofzer, Manfred F. *Music in the Baroque Era,* W. W. Norton and Co., New York, 1947, 489 pp.

Burney, Charles, *A General History of Music from the Earliest Ages to the Present Period,* in 4 volumes, London, 1739; later version ed. by F. Mercer in 2 volumes, London, 1935; this edition reprinted in New York, 1957.

Daniels, David. *Orchestral Music. A Handbook,* 2nd edition, Scarecrow Press, Metuchen, N.J., and London, 1982, 413 pp.

Demaree, Robert W., Jr., and Moses, Don V. *The Complete Conductor. A Comprehensive Resource for the Professional Conductor of the Twenty-first Century,* Prentice-Hall, Englewood Cliffs, N.J., 1995, 491 pp.

Donington, Robert. *A Performer's Guide to Baroque Music,* Charles Scribner's Sons, New York, 1973, 320 pp.

———. "Ornaments," in *The New Grove Dictionary of Music and Musicians,* 6th ed., in 20 volumes, ed. Stanley Sadie, Macmillan Publishers, New York, 1980, vol. 13, pp. 827–867.

Dürr, Alfred. "Performance Practice of Bach's Cantatas," *American Choral Review* 16/2:1–33 (April 1974).

Ehmann, Wilhelm. "Concertisten und Ripienisten in Bach's H-Moll Messe," *Musik und Kirche* 30:2–6.

———. "Performance Practice of Bach's Motets," *American Choral Review* 15/2:1–25 (April 1973).

Farkas, Philip. *The Art of Musicianship,* Musical Publications, Bloomington, Ind., 1976, 51 pp.

Galamian, Ivan. *The Principles of Violin Playing and Teaching,* Prentice-Hall, Englewood Cliffs, N.J., 1964, 116 pp.

Geiringer, Karl. *Haydn. A Creative Life in Music,* 2nd ed., University of California Press, Berkeley and Los Angeles, 1968, 399 pp.

Geminiani, Francesco. *The Art of Playing on the Violin, Containing All the Rules Necessary to Attain to a Perfection [etc.],* London, 1751, 9 pp.

Green, Elizabeth A. H. *Orchestral Bowings and Routines,* Ann Arbor Publishers, Ann Arbor, Mich., 1957, 107 pp.

Griesinger, G. A. *Biographische Notizen über Joseph Haydn,* trans. Vernon Gotwals, as *Biographical Notes Concerning Joseph Haydn,* and paired with the A. C. Dies *Biographische Nachrichten von Joseph Haydn,* University of Wisconsin Press, Madison, 1968, 275 pp.

Handel, George Frideric. *Messiah, An Oratorio,* ed. Alfred Mann, in three volumes (score only), with performance notes, ABI/Alexander Broude, and Rutgers University Press, N.Y., 1983. Vol. 1, 91 pp., Vol. 2, 88 pp., Vol. 3, 57 pp.

———. *Messiah, a Sacred Oratorio,* ed. Watkins Shaw, with full score, supplementary volume on performance practice, and two alternative sets of parts, Novello and Co., London, 1965, 283 pp.

———. *G. F. Händel Werke,* ed. F. W. Chrysander, Ausgabe der Deutschen Händelgesellschaft, in 110 vols., Leipzig, 1858–1894.

Harriss, Ernest C. Translation of Johann Mattheson, *Der vollkommene Capellmeister;* original version Hamburg, 1739; translated and edited by Ernest C. Harriss, University Microfilms, Ann Arbor, Mich., 1981, 920 pp.

Haydn, Franz Joseph. *Nelsonmesse,* ed. Günter Thomas, in *Werke,* dir. by Georg Feder, Joseph Haydn-Institut, Köln, G. Henle Verlag, Munich-Duisburg, 1965, Ser. 23, vol. 3, pp. 1–139.

———. *Mass in D Minor (Missa in Angustiis, Nelson Mass),* vocal score ed. H. C. Robbins Landon, Schott & Co., London, for B. Schott's Söhne, Mainz, 1963.

———. *Missa in Angustiis (Nelsonmesse, Missa Nr. 11 in D), Hob. XXII:11,* miniature score ed. Wolfgang Hochstein, Carus-Verlag, Stuttgart, 1999.

Knocker, Editha. *A Treatise on the Fundamental Principles of Violin Playing,* 2nd ed.; translation of Mozart, Leopold, *Versuch einer gründlichen Violinschule,* 1756; translated version from Oxford University Press, London, 1951, 231 pp.

Landon, H[oward] C[handler] Robbins. *The Collected Correspondence and London Note-books of Franz Joseph Haydn*, Barrie and Rockliff, London, 1959, 312 pp.

———. *Haydn: Chronicle and Works*, in 5 vols., Indiana University Press, Bloomington, especially vol. II, *Haydn at Esterhaza 1766–1790*, 1978, 799 pp., and vol. IV, *Haydn: The Years of 'The Creation' 1796–1800*, 1977, 656 pp.

———. *The Symphonies of Joseph Haydn*, Universal Edition and Rockliff Publishing Corp., London, 1955, 823 pp. *See also* his *Supplement to the Symphonies of Joseph Haydn*, Barrie and Rockliff, London, 1961, 48 pp.

Marpurg, Friedrich Wilhelm. *Kritische Briefe über die Tonkunst, mit Kleinen Clavier Stücken* . . . , F. W. Birnstiel, Berlin, 1760–64, 246 pp.

———. *Die Kunst das Clavier zu Spielen*, Haude & Spencer, Berlin, 1750.

Mattheson, Johann. *Der vollkommene Capellmeister;* original version Hamburg, 1739. *See* translation by Harriss, Ernest C.

Mitchell, W. J. *Essay on the True Art of Playing Keyboard Instruments;* translation of Carl Philipp Emanuel Bach, *Versuch über die wahre Art das Clavier zu spielen*, Berlin, 1753; translated version from W. W. Norton and Co., N.Y., 1949, 445 pp.

Monosoff, Sonya. "The Role of Early Music in Modern Violin Teaching," *American String Teacher* 33/4:33–39 (Autumn 1983).

Mozart, Leopold. *Versuch einer gründlichen Violinschule*, J. J. Lotter, Augsburg, 1756. *See* translation by Knocker, Editha.

Neumann, Frederick. *Ornamentation in Baroque and Post-Baroque Music With Special Emphasis on J. S. Bach*, Princeton University Press, Princeton, N.J., 1978, 630 pp.

Newbould, Brian. *Schubert. The Music and the Man*, Victor Gollancz, London, 1997, 465 pp.

Pincherle, Marc. *Vivaldi, Genius of the Baroque;* orig. version *Vivaldi*, Editions Le Bon Plaisir, Paris, 1955; trans. Christopher Hatch, Victor Gollancz Ltd., London, 1958, 277 pp.

Piston, Walter. *Orchestration*, W. W. Norton and Co., New York, 1955, 477 pp.

Quantz, Johann Joachim. *Versuch einer Anweisung die Flöte traversiere zu spielen*, Johann Friedrich Voss, Berlin, 1752, 334 pp. *See* translation by Reilly, Edward R.

Ratner, Leonard. "Harmonic Aspects of Classical Form" in the *Journal of the American Musicological Society*, 2:159–168 (Fall 1949).

Reilly, Edward R., *On Playing the Flute;* translation of Johann Joachim Quantz, *Versuch einer Anweisung die Flöte traversiere zu spielen*, orig. version Berlin, 1752; transl. version from Faber and Faber, London, 1966, 365 pp.

Rothschild, Fritz. *The Lost Tradition in Music: Rhythm and Tempo in J. S. Bach's Time*, Oxford University Press, New York, 1953, 325 pp.

Roy, Klaus George. Liner notes for Robert Shaw's recording of Handel's *Messiah*, RCA Victor album LSC 6175, New York, 20 pp.

Sachs, Curt. *Rhythm and Tempo: A Study in Music History*, W. W. Norton and Co., New York, 1953, 380 pp.

Scheibe, J. A. *See* Marpurg, Friedrich Wilhelm, *Kritische Briefe über die Tonkunst (etc.).*

Schenbeck, Lawrence. *Joseph Haydn and the Classical Choral Tradition*, Hinshaw Music, Chapel Hill, N.C., 1996, 514 pp.

Schubert, Franz. *Mass in G Major, D.167, for Soloists, Chorus, Orchestra, and Organ*, ed. Franz Beyer, Breitkopf & Härtel, Leipzig, 1995. This is the first edition based on Schubert's autograph parts, long thought lost, but recently rediscovered in Klosterneuburg Monastery.

———. *Mass in G (Major)*, ed. Alice Parker and Robert Shaw, G. Schirmer, New York,

1954. This edition is for voices with piano accompaniment, and includes no orchestra parts.

——. *Mass in G Major No. 2 for Four Voices, Orchestra, and Organ,* miniature score reprinted from the Mandyczewski edition, Kalmus K00451, New York, date uncertain.

——. *Messe (in G) für vier Singstimmen, Orchester, und Orgel,* ed. Eusebius Mandyczewski, *Franz Schuberts Werke: Kritisch durchgesehene Gesamtausgabe,* Breitkopf & Härtel, Leipzig, 1884–1897, ser. 13, vol. 1, pp. 121–156; reprinted as *Mass in G Major, D.167,* Dover Publications, New York, 1965, vol. 6, pp. 121–156.

——. *Neue ausbage sämtlicher Werke,* Bärenreiter Verlag, Kassel, with the Internationalen Schubert-Gesellschaft, 1964–. In serie I this edition-in-progress contains most of the Schubert masses, including his first complete one, the *Mass in F Major, D.107* in band 1, but has not yet offered the *Mass in G Major, D.167.*

Shaw, George Bernard. *Music in London 1890–1894,* in 3 volumes, Wm. H. Wise and Co., New York, 1931; vol. I, 317 pp., vol. II, 342 pp., vol. III, 332 pp.

Shaw, Robert. Liner notes on Handel's *Messiah. See* Roy, Klaus George.

Spitta, Philipp. *Johann Sebastian Bach,* in 3 volumes; orig. version Breitkopf & Härtel, Leipzig (1878–1880); trans. Clara Bell and J. S. Fuller-Maitland, Dover Publications, New York, 1951, vol. I, 656 pp., vol. II, 721 pp., vol. III, 419 pp.

Taylor, Sedley. *The Indebtedness of Handel to Works by Other Composers;* original from Cambridge University Press, London, 1906; reprinted by Johnson Reprint Corp., New York, 1971, 196 pp.

Veilhan, Jean-Claude. *The Rules of Musical Interpretation in the Baroque Era,* trans. John Lambert, Alphonse Leduc, Paris, 1979, 100 pp.

Vivaldi, Antonio. *Chamber Mass,* ed. Vahe Aslanian, Lawson-Gould Music Publ., New York, 1964, 85 pp.

——. *Gloria [in D],* ed. Clayton Westermann, Edwin F. Kalmus, New York, 1967, 87 pp.

——. *Gloria [in D],* ed. Mason Martens, Walton Music Corp, New York, 1961, 63 pp.

——. *Gloria [in D],* "elaborated" by Alfredo Casella, Ricordi and Franco Colombo, Milan and New York, 1941 and 1958, 64 pp.

——. *Gloria [in D],* ed. Gian Francesco Malipiero for his edition *Le opere di Antonio Vivaldi,* Instituto Italiano Antonio Vivaldi, G. Ricordi & Co. S. p. A., Milano, 1977, 130 pp.

Westrup, Jack, with Neal Zaslaw. "Orchestra," in *The New Grove Dictionary of Music and Musicians,* 6th ed., in 20 volumes, ed. Stanley Sadie, Macmillan Publishers, New York, 1980, vol. 13, pp. 679–691.

Whiting, Steven M. *Hört ihr wohl,* unpublished paper for the American Musicological Society, November 1986, 22 pp.

Index

DON V MOSES is former Director of the School of Music, University of Illinois (now retired).

ROBERT W. DEMAREE, JR., is former Dean of the Ernestine M. Raclin School of the Arts, Indiana University South Bend (now retired).

ALLEN F. OHMES is currently Professor of Violin at the University of Iowa.